PLANNING·ENVIRONMENT·CITIES

Series Editors: Yvonne Rydin and Andrew Thornley

The context in which planning operates has changed dramatically in recent years. Economic processes have become increasingly globalised and new spatial patterns of economic activity have emerged. There have been major changes in political ideology with the rise of the New Right and the collapse of communism. New debates have arisen over the relationship between the market and state intervention. A new environmental agenda following on from the Brundtland Report and the Rio Earth Summit has prioritised the goal of sustainable development and control of pollution, air and water quality.

Cities are today faced with new pressures for economic competitiveness, greater accountability and participation, improved quality of life for citizens and global environmental responsibility. These pressures are often contradictory and create difficult dilemmas for policy-makers, especially in the context of fiscal austerity. New relationships are developing between the levels of state activity and between public and private sectors as different interests respond to the new conditions.

In these changing circumstances, planners, from many backgrounds, in many different organisations, have come to re-evaluate their work. They have had to engage with actors in government, the private sector and non-governmental organisations in discussions over the role of planning in relation to the environment and cities. The intention of the *Planning, Environment, Cities* series is to explore the changing nature of planning and contribute to the debate about its future.

The series is primarily aimed at students and practitioners of planning and such related professions as estate management, housing and architecture, as well as in politics, public and social administration, geography and urban studies. It will comprise both general texts and books designed to make a more particular contribution, in both cases characterised by an international approach, extensive use of case studies, and emphasis on contemporary relevance and the application of theory to advance planning practice.

D0240953

PLANNING·ENVIRONMENT·CITIES

Series Editors: Yvonne Rydin and Andrew Thornley

Published

Patsy Healey
Collaborative Planning

Yvonne Rydin
Urban and Environment Planning in the UK

Geoff Vigar, Patsy Healey, Angela Hull and Simin Davoudi
Planning, Governance and Spatial Strategy in Britain

Forthcoming

Bob Evans and Sue Percy
Environment Policy and Planning in Britain

Ted Kitchen
Skills for Planning Practice

Peter Newman and Andrew Thornley
Planning World Cities

Huw Thomas
Planning for Diversity

Other titles planned include

Introduction to Planning
Planning Theory
Urban Design

Planning, Environment, Cities
Series Standing Order
ISBN 0–333–71703–1 hardcover
ISBN 0–333–69346–9 paperback
(outside North America only)

You can receive future titles in this series as they are published by placing a standing order. Please contact your bookseller or, in the case of difficulty, write to us at the address below with your name and address, the title of the series and one of the ISBNs quoted above.

Customer Services Department, Macmillan Distribution Ltd, Houndmills, Basingstoke, Hampshire RG21 6XS, England

Planning, Governance and Spatial Strategy in Britain

An Institutionalist Analysis

Geoff Vigar, Patsy Healey, Angela Hull and Simin Davoudi

First published 2000 by
MACMILLAN PRESS LTD
Houndmills, Basingstoke, Hampshire RG21 6XS
and London
Companies and representatives
throughout the world

ISBN 0–333-77316–0 hardcover
ISBN 0–333-77317–9 paperback

A catalogue record for this book is available
from the British Library.

This book is printed on paper suitable for recycling and
made from fully managed and sustained forest sources.

10   9   8   7   6   5   4   3   2   1
09 08 07 06 05 04 03 02 01 00

Printed in Hong Kong

Published in the United States of America by
ST. MARTIN'S PRESS, INC.,
Scholarly and Reference Division,
175 Fifth Avenue, New York, N.Y. 10010

ISBN 0–312–23125–3 (cloth)

Contents

v

List of Figures and Tables

Figures

Tables

Acknowledgements

Much of the empirical material in this book derives from an Economic and Social Research Council (ESRC) project, *Development Plans and the Regulatory Form of the Planning System*, grant number R000235745. We are grateful to the ESRC for providing the funds without which this book would not have been possible and to almost 80 interviewees in Kent, Lancashire and the West Midlands who helped us with our case study work. We would particularly like to thank the 12 practitioners who attended a seminar in Newcastle to discuss our findings and others who have discussed the material with us at various stages in the book's production, notably, Alain Motte, Ted Kitchen, Michael Purdue and Alan Wenban Smith.

Our thanks must also go to colleagues who contributed directly or indirectly to the production of this text. First our thanks to Tim Shaw at the University of Newcastle who provided valuable input into the ESRC project mentioned above. Second, to Anton Lang, who conducted some of the primary research work as part of the ESRC project. Third, our grateful thanks extend to Ann Rooke in the Department of Geography at the University of Newcastle, who generated most of the maps and illustrations in this book. Finally, we would like to thank Yvonne Rydin, editor of the *Planning, Environment, Cities* series, for her very helpful comments on earlier drafts, and our publisher Steven Kennedy for his help and encouragement through the course of this project.

The author and publishers also wish to acknowledge the Ordnance Survey for permission to reproduce copyright material in Figures 3.2, 3.3, 3.4 and 3.5, licence number MC 0100029172.

Geoff also wishes to thank Jen Stepney for her support through this book's production and for providing a constant reminder of the greater significance of things beyond it.

GEOFF VIGAR
PATSY HEALEY
ANGELA HULL
SIMIN DAVOUDI

Part I

RESEARCHING PLANNING PRACTICE AND THEORY

.

1 Planning Systems and Territorial Governance

Territory, place and planning

Across Europe, towards the end of the twentieth century, there was a rediscovery of the significance of locality, place and territory as foci for policy attention (Le Gales, 1998). This new emphasis could be found in discussions of regional economic development and its preoccupation with regional competitive assets and institutional qualities. It also emerged strongly in the discussion of the concept of environmental sustainability, which linked concern for respecting environmental capacities with local action to monitor change and instigate less environmentally damaging practices. In a more muted way, there was a developing awareness that quality of life is intertwined with the qualities of places. This rediscovery of place and territory, many argue, is linked to the evolution of the global economy and the diminished role of the welfare state as a model for service delivery. The first undermines the role of the nation state as a focus of business attention and economic policy development, replacing it with an emphasis on the quality of locales as sites for economic activity. The second reduces the significance of nationally organised public services, focusing attention on individual and localised forms of provision. At one level, these changes emphasise supranational governance and, in Europe, the role of the European Commission. At the subnational level, the policy spotlight turns to regional and local governance, and their capacity to mould diverse governance elements, scattered among state, economy and civil society institutions, into strategic directions which can foster economic health, environmental quality and quality of life, in sustainable ways, in places and territories.

This territorial rediscovery and its implications for the emergence of place-based strategic governance alliances and networks presents a major challenge for the organisation of government in Britain. Britain's

3

government has traditionally been highly centralised (Rhodes, 1988), with a strongly developed welfare state, organised into policy sectors for the delivery of specific functions. In this model, state officials were providers of services, while citizens and firms were receivers of benefits. Since 1979, this structure has been remoulded through neoliberal strategies of deregulation and privatisation. These have reduced the powers and finances of local government and spread governance activities among a wide variety of different agency forms involving business and the voluntary sector, while at the same time strengthening the role of national government (Gamble, 1988; Thornley, 1991). The result by the end of the century was a fragmented governance landscape, with power over public investment and over regulatory actions dispersed among diverse agencies with often overlapping and conflicting remits, oriented to nationally specified funding and performance criteria. For citizens, memories of being cast into a dependency relationship with the welfare state combined with new realisations of the confused and sometimes self-serving nature of government agencies to produce a profound disaffection with the state (Hutton, 1995; Mulgan, 1994). In this context, many players in the dispersed-power world of subnational governance searched for ways to make horizontal linkages with other players with a stake in territorial development. The objective was to replace vertical and sectoral relationships with territorial ones and to build up a capacity to build strategic policy frameworks to guide and co-ordinate the actions of the multiplicity of stakeholders in territorial development. A new regionalising and localising momentum thus developed in the 1990s to challenge the power of the nation state in shaping the future of places and territories (Bradbury and Mawson, 1997). This momentum was accelerated by the New Labour administration which came to power in 1997, with proposals for regional devolution in Scotland and Wales, and regional development agencies in England. But, as these proposals were emerging into concrete organisational changes and specific practices, it was becoming clear by the end of the century that there are many forms which a more localised governance can take. Formal regional organisations do not necessarily guarantee a strategic approach to the economic, environmental and social dimensions of territorial development. Nor do they inherently encourage a broader base of democratic participation in governance or help to reduce the so-called 'democratic deficit'.

In this book we examine these evolutions in British governance from the perspective of attempts at articulating spatial strategy in England in the 1990s. Specifically, we focus on the relationship between strategic policy initiatives for territorial development and the formal procedures and associated practices of the land use or spatial planning system. In theory, spatial planning systems provide governance processes which explicitly focus on territorial development and the qualities of places. They should force consideration of the way different government policies affect the qualities of life and the business environment in different places. With its requirements for consultation and public objection, unusual for government policy processes which more commonly rely on politicians and pressure group politics to articulate public concern, the planning system in Britain also has mechanisms with the potential to encourage wider citizen involvement in policy development, and hence reduce the democratic deficit. Yet, rather than being at the forefront of the regionalising momentum in the late 1990s, planning practices and the planning community were being referred to as part of the problem, and as in need of transformation (Kitchen, 1998; CPRE, 1998a; Roberts, 1998). This suggests that, while potentially the planning system has a significant role in a governance landscape which emphasises qualities of place, integrated trans-sectoral policy approaches and broadly-based processes of stakeholder involvement in policy development, this potential may be constrained in two ways. Firstly, it may be limited by the weakness of the pressures outlined above for more decentralised, place-focused, collaborative governance. Secondly, its capacity to respond to such pressures may be undermined by the internal institutional inheritance which shapes its current practices.

This book uses the 'window' of strategic spatial strategy development and its relation to the practices of the planning system to assess the challenge for the regionalising and localising momentum in the context of the evolution of subnational governance in England into the twenty-first century. The book's approach derives from our perception that governance processes are not changed merely by the acts of law makers or the pressures of broad contextual forces, but evolve through complex interactions between localised practices, 'ways of thinking and ways of acting' which build up over the years, and broader forces which introduce new players, new ideas and new forces to be recognised, interpreted, mediated and struggled over. We illustrate this through accounts of the evolution of policy discourses and the institutional context of their production which reveal transformative struggles in practice. These provide a picture of the world of strategic spatial planning practice in 1990s England and show both the potential for movement in new directions and the ways in which this potential is being limited.

Any assessment of how a planning system and its practices could evolve requires some way of describing what such a policy system consists of, and consequently, where transformations may be found or could be encouraged. In this chapter, we introduce our approach to such a description, before returning to the discussion of the various arguments about the way the land use planning system is changing. Our description also serves to introduce some of the key actors and professional and administrative 'technologies' which appear in our accounts.

The elements of the English planning system

Spatial, territorial and land use planning systems are examples of the formalised arrangements and associated practices which collectively form a specific field of public policy. Their focus is the spatial organisation of cities and territories, and the allocation of rights to use and develop land. A key function of such systems is to resolve the inherent conflicts which arise over the qualities of places and territories. Most countries with significant levels of urban living have a planning system in some form, and all societies have ways of addressing land use rights and local place-related conflicts. Because the evolution of spatial planning in the twentieth century was closely associated with the development of the nation state and welfare state policies, archetypal manifestations of the 'modernity' which is said to characterise the passing century, planning as an activity is often described as a tool of this modernity. Some have suggested that such systems become redundant in 'post-modern' times (for example, Dear, 1995). However, changed ways of thinking about society and social process do not remove the reality of problems regarding who gets the right to develop what land and whose vision of the quality of place prevails when actions are taken to defend or change these qualities. As in the case of education or health policy, it is the form of the policy system and its practices which change, not the focus of policy attention.

If our concern is to assess how far the system and its practices have been changing in the 1990s, and where that evolution may lead in the next century, some way of describing a planning system is needed. However, there is no agreed way of doing this in the academic literature, partly because all systems are deeply embedded in nationally specific constitutional and legal arrangements, and in a historical politics of the power relations over land and property. Most comparative accounts of planning systems focus on the tools of the system (plans and regulatory powers) and on competencies (which level does what) (CEU, 1997; Newman and Thornley, 1996). Such accounts emphasise the formal procedures and institutional responsibilities of a system (Cullingworth and Nadin, 1994). Our account focuses instead on the practices and relationships through which the system becomes alive. This leads us to identify the actors and networks involved in bringing the system to life, the policy communities they belong to, the policy arenas where strategies are articulated and developed, and the policy discourses which shape specific agendas. We introduce this approach in Chapter 2. Our assumption is that, if there are significant changes in policy communities, policy arenas and policy discourses, the tools and competencies of the policy system will be used differently too. However, these formal elements also carry power built into them through their original design and the accretion of practices built up over time. These are also the principal elements which governments can change when they seek to shift the direction of a policy system. The formal elements of a system thus have significant structuring power, acting as a form of 'hard infrastructure' of the system (Healey, 1997). Here we describe these elements in order both to identify their significant characteristics, as compared with planning systems developed elsewhere, and to assess the extent to which the system and its practices have been transformed in recent years. We focus on three such elements: the tools of the system, the allocation of responsibilities and the purposes of the system. We start with this last element.

Purposes

There is inherent ambiguity about the purposes of spatial planning systems. Whereas the purpose of a medical policy system is to promote health and a social welfare system to promote social welfare, the objective of planning systems is typically intermediate to some other policy goal. Thus promoting the proper use of land is of value, not in itself, but because it achieves some purpose of environmental management, social welfare, cultural conservation or economic development. A major purpose of the British planning system in mid-century was to provide space for economic growth and housing demand, within the constraints of environmental conservation strategies. But if matters of land use and development are left as adjuncts to other policy systems, there are likely to be conflicts between different objectives and different interests over access to a particular piece of land or environmental quality. The purposes of spatial planning systems can be set in this context.

They are brought into being and subsequently continue in existence to sort out potential conflicts over the use and development of land and the spatial arrangement of activities which arise because qualities of land, of spaces and places are not evenly spread around. Every piece of land is unique in location and attributes. Every development on it has multiple impacts on other people nearby and in other places. The more society is urbanised and the more people have to live within already developed areas, the more complex the conflicts over access to space and development opportunity are likely to be.

There are two broad divisions in thinking about managing such conflicts. They interrelate, often uncomfortably, with each other and emphasise a different mixture of tools and allocation of responsibilities. On the one hand, the purpose can be conceived as the regulation of conflicts between neighbours, that is, between those who seek to develop and those who will be affected by the development. This focuses on the regulation of development impacts. On the other hand, the purpose may be to promote the particular qualities of specific places, to achieve some quality of life purpose, to promote economic objectives or reinforce particular environmental qualities. This second approach requires some articulation of these wider purposes. In most planning systems these days, there is an expectation that the two approaches are related. Strategic public interest purposes define the objectives which act as criteria for detailed regulation. This regulation thus becomes more than merely a sorting out of conflicts among neighbours: it acts as a mechanism to secure the wider public interest in the use and development of land.

The British town and country planning system as it has evolved this century has placed as much emphasis on the achievement of public interest objectives as on the regulation of development impacts. Every British planning student is taught that the system came into being to address urban problems to do with public health and housing (Cullingworth and Nadin, 1994, p.1) and that the form of the system introduced in 1947 was innovative in its attempt to manage development comprehensively in town and country. In 1947, with a depressed development sector and a strong political ideology in support of the production and delivery by the public sector of many goods and services, the regulatory function was considered a minor strand of a major state-led development effort in urban development and redevelopment. Improving living environments was seen at that time as having a key role in improving the quality of life (Ward, 1994). Many commentators have subsequently considered that the role of the planning system was to promote good housing conditions for all, and hence redistribute resources to benefit poorer groups. It has been much criticised subsequently for its failure in this redistributional objective (Hall *et al.*, 1973; Ambrose, 1986). A parallel objective was growth management, to protect the countryside from sprawl. This derived from a deep-seated cultural attachment to the English rural landscape, which supported strong policies of rural conservation. These policies have been much more enduring and effectively implemented (Hall *et al.*, 1973; Elson, 1986; Healey and Shaw, 1994).

However, the system as specified in legislation concentrates not on the substantive specification of purposes but on the procedures to be followed in establishing planning principles and policies. The way in which the principles and policies are specified (government advice and development plans) is through administrative mechanisms rather than legal instruments. This has allowed a continual reinterpretation of the purposes of the system, reflecting the evolution of pressures for development, public concerns about environmental qualities and political philosophies about the role of the state. Where the emphasis in the 1940s and 1950s was on providing better town centres and improving the provision and quality of housing and infrastructure, that of the 1960s was on accommodating growth within the constraints of landscape protection policies. In the 1970s, there was more concern with urban regeneration and countryside management, which focused on managing change in the urban and rural fabric at the finegrain. The major changes that have occurred in the 1980s and 1990s have been the rise of a more ecological approach to environmental quality and the prioritisation of economic considerations (see Table 1.1). The incoming New Labour administration indicated a shift to a more positive role for the planning system (DETR, 1998a), with a rhetoric about strategy and policy integration.

In parallel to this evolution of policy purposes, there have also been shifts in the broad focus of the system. While the role of the system in sorting out the 'bad neighbour' or adverse impacts of development was, throughout the 50 years from 1947, combined with broader public

Table 1.1   Purposes of the planning system

1988   Planning Policy Guidance 1: General Policy and Principles
Essentially, the system is designed to regulate the development and
use of land in the public interest... It is an important instrument for
the protection and enhancement of the environment in town and
country, for the preservation of historic buildings and the rural
landscape and for the maintenance of Green Belts. (DoE, 1988a,
para.2)

1997   Planning Policy Guidance 1 (revised)
A key role of the planning system is to enable the provision of
homes and buildings, investment and jobs in a way which is
consistent with the principles of sustainable development. It needs to
be positive in promoting competitiveness while being protective
towards the environment and amenity. (DoE, 1997, para. 1)

1998   Modernising the Planning System
The planning system exists to reconcile the benefits of development
with the costs it can impose. It has a key role not just in controlling
land use, but in positively promoting sustainable development.
(DETR, 1998a, para. 1, p. 5)

---

interest objectives (such as promoting economic competitiveness and
environmental sustainability), the system has become increasingly
detached from a lead role in promoting development and redevelopment. From the 1970s, national government regularly asserted that
planners should focus on land use matters only, emphasising the
system's independent regulatory role, rather than a strategic policy
approach concerned with economic, environmental, social and infrastructure policy as it affects spatial arrangement and the qualities of
places (Bruton and Nicholson, 1987). In this way the system has been
pulled away from a role in strategic territorial integration. It has
become a 'sectoralised' regulatory system, co-existing and sometimes
coming into conflict with other regulatory systems, most notably that
concerned with environmental quality led in the UK by the
Environment Agency.

The tools of the system

Planning systems develop their tools for intervention from a toolbox
with four compartments (Lichfield and Darin-Drabkin, 1980, Healey

et al., 1988). One deals with mechanisms to regulate what private interests can do with their land. These are grounded in legal mechanisms which limit individual rights. The form of these regulatory constraints is significantly affected by the legal system of a specific country (Newman and Thornley, 1996; Booth, 1996). The second deals with financial measures, such as tax penalties and incentives, or subsidy payments designed to promote particular forms of development or environmental management. These measures will be affected by the fiscal policy of a specific country and by the power over the definition of fiscal measures held by different levels and agencies of government. The third deals with the power of the state to undertake development itself, as purchaser of land for development, or as provider of serviced sites or buildings, or infrastructure. These measures will be affected by the financial resources available to the public sector, the rules governing the limits of the power of each agency, and political ideology as to the appropriate relation between public and private sector involvement in the development process. The fourth compartment deals with measures to shape the thinking of the various parties concerned with land use change and environmental qualities. This may include different forms of plans, as well as a whole range of information documents of various kinds. These information tools operate by reducing uncertainty for the various parties (Healey, 1992; Keogh, 1981) and by 'shaping attention' (Forester, 1989). Their form and content is significantly affected by the professional communities involved in their production, by the practices of their use and by national and local political ideologies about spatial policy development in general and about specific policy issues. Table 1.2 summarises these tools. Below we discuss the evolution of each.

Tools: the regulatory machinery   While the toolbox of the English planning system has been continually adjusted over the years, and the balance between the tools has shifted over time, its contents remain substantially as established in 1947. Individual rights to develop land are regulated through the development control system. This is a politico-administrative system, in which judgements are made on individual cases, according to both planning principles and the individual circumstances of the case. Local authority elected councillors make planning decisions, advised by their professional officers. The decision is seen as a judgement, in the light of formally articulated planning principles, but also bearing in mind other 'material considerations'.

Table 1.2   The tools of the English planning system

Tools	Characteristics
Regulatory	The nationalisation of development rights
	The political–administrative regulation of development
Financial	Limited use, primarily by national government
	Planning obligations provide primary local mechanisms
Direct development	Strong enabling power available to undertake development
	Well-established, but procedurally complex, powers of compulsory purchase
	Scale of use depends on resources available
Information and policy guidance	Development plans, regional guidance; supplementary planning guidance
	Production of information reports

(DoE, 1997). This approach, which emphasises discretionary judgement rather than bureaucratic rules, reflects the distinctive legal traditions which have evolved in Britain, in which disputes are resolved in terms of what a 'reasonable person' would think and do, with public law as a context, not a formal rule (Perrins, 1995). The state, through the machinery of the planning system, can limit private rights to develop so long as the procedures of the system are followed correctly. Those developers who feel that they have been wrongly treated can appeal to national government to have local decisions reviewed. This semi-judicial arbitration system (the appeal system) has expanded into a robust mechanism for conflict resolution, although only applicants for development can use it. Thus, in the English planning system, developers have no rights in law to develop their land. However, there is a policy presumption in favour of granting planning permission, unless there are strong public interest reasons against this. Development plans and national planning policy guidance became, in the 1990s, the key vehicles for articulating this public interest (DoE, 1997). The system also provides freedom to develop within certain categories (defined in the Use Classes Order) and below certain thresholds (defined in the General Development Order).

Since 1947, this regulatory power has grown in importance within the system, as resources for direct development have been cut back. From the 1970s, it has been the dominant mode of action available to the system. The discretionary form has proved a very flexible mechanism for adjusting to changing political and economic conditions, as it encourages continual reinterpretation of principles. The major changes in the late twentieth century were the increasing sophistication of the specification of policy criteria in development plans and in government guidance to local planning authorities. This evolution can be linked in part to the demands upon the state for greater openness, clarity and consistency in its decisions. It also reflects the increasing political interest at national level in the planning system, both as a guardian of environmental qualities and as a regulatory regime which could, unless carefully monitored, undermine national policy objectives of overall economic competitiveness. The system was also subject to pressure from EU environmental legislation. This tended to encourage greater specification of policy and procedure, more in line with continental legal traditions (CEU, 1997; Newman and Thornley, 1996).

Tools: direct development and financial incentives In 1947, it was expected that the state would undertake most development. It was therefore given powers to acquire land from unwilling owners for clearly specified planning purposes, to organise and manage the development process and to own and rent land and buildings. These powers have been used to undertake comprehensive town centre redevelopment, slum clearance and housing construction and build new towns. They are still available to local planning authorities and the Commission for New Towns and were modified to provide authorisation for the work of urban development corporations. However, although the tools still exist, the resources and ideology for using them rarely do. Although some local authorities in the 1970s sought to increase their role in the development process, the 1979–97 Tory administrations were strongly opposed to local authorities undertaking such a role and more generally to the notion of the 'provider state'. Local authorities were encouraged instead to sell their land and property assets and to encourage private investment to replace public investment. Even ideologically reluctant local authorities were forced into promoting private investment, owing to the lack of resources available to them and constraints on their freedom to use what they had. However, it soon became obvious that private investment would not happen by itself except in locations and on sites where market demand was very strong. With a continuing policy concern with urban regeneration, the national government introduced financial incentives to promote private investment in urban redevelopment and renewal. These measures included urban development grants, enterprise zone designation, urban development corporations, the City Challenge initiative and the Single Regeneration Budget (Atkinson and Moon, 1994; Oatley, 1998). There were also increasing links between these financial measures and sources of finance available to local authorities through European Commission funding programmes, the various lottery funds, and the funding provided by agencies such as English Heritage and the Sports Council. A proliferation of partnership arrangements of various kinds evolved to capture funding for particular schemes (Edwards, 1997; Shaw and Robinson, 1998; Oatley, 1998). However, these were seen as initiatives separate from the planning frameworks and the regulatory powers of the planning system.

The evolution of these financial measures has been constrained by the preference in British fiscal policy for nationally based systems. The Treasury resisted giving local authorities powers to provide tax-related incentives selectively in relation to particular sites and policies, preferring national measures rather than local ones for this purpose. It also severely constrained local authority tax-raising powers and, until the late 1990s, resisted 'hypothecating' (or ring-fencing) funds raised from taxes on one activity (for example, the motor vehicle tax) for reinvestment in that activity (that is, improved transport provision). A form of hypothecation has now been introduced in relation to congestion charging in the transport field (DETR, 1998c) and also in relation to the landfill tax. The financial toolbox available to British local authorities was thus severely constrained compared to the experience of their counterparts in Europe and elsewhere, where local taxes and payments linked to land and property development processes are much more prevalent (CEU, 1997; Cullingworth, 1993). In this context, local authorities tried to use the powers they have for negotiating private agreements with developers to help deal with some of the adverse impacts of development while still allowing development to proceed. The Tory administrations consistently sought to limit and rationalise this practice of negotiating 'planning gain', currently called 'planning obligations', but did little to change the context which encouraged the practice (Healey, Purdue and Ennis, 1995). An improvement in development conditions in the mid-1990s and the more interventionist stance of the New Labour administration led to a resurgence of such negotiations. By 1998, the discussion of planning obligations had been incorporated into wider discussion of the use of 'economic instruments' in the context of the planning system (DETR, 1998a).

Tools: plans and policy guidance Because its designers recognised that the planning system was expected to pursue public interest objectives as well as to regulate the impacts of development activity on neighbours (Cullingworth, 1975), the system is well-equipped with mechanisms to express these objectives. The primary tool is the development plan. Its content is framed by national government policy guidance and regional policy statements. None of these documents has the standing of legal documents which express rules which must be followed or which give rights to developers. Instead, they provide developers and other interested parties with information on the considerations which the state will bear in mind when making planning decisions, and they constrain the state to act within its own expression of planning principles and policies. However, the content of this advisory material is continually reinterpreted, in relation to specific projects and in conflicts which reach the media, the appeal system and, in a few cases, the courts. Similarly, the status of this policy information has to be continually interpreted, as the weight being given to the different sources of policy changes over time. A government circular in 1985 demoted the status of the development plan to one consideration among many (DoE, 1985). This was reversed by Section 54a of the Planning and Compensation Act 1991, which required planning regulatory decisions to be made 'in accordance' with the development plan. This change was often referred to by national government politicians, civil servants and others in the planning policy community in the 1990s as a decisive shift to a 'plan-led system'. However, it is the backing given to it by national government (DoE, 1997) as much as the legal change itself which has produced the greater emphasis on the plan framework in the 1990s (Purdue, 1994; Gatenby and Williams, 1996). It was certainly the case that, during the 1990s, the attention given by stakeholders to involvement in development plan preparation increased substantially and there was some increase in legal challenges to plans. The substantial flexibility to shift the weighting given to national policy, development plans and other considerations nevertheless still remains in the system, with the power to wield it largely controlled by national government (Tewdwr-Jones, 1997).

Of greater significance in the later twentieth century was the change in the form of the plan and the growth of national policy guidance. Because the form and content of development plans are not specified with any precision in legislation and because plans do not have formal legal work to do, their form evolved easily from 'command and control' master plans or blueprint plans to policy plans. Since 1947, it was recognised that two levels of plan might be needed: broad strategic frameworks and detailed land allocation maps. In the 1950s, these two tended to co-exist in a single plan, which took the form either of a master plan design for a new or reorganised town or, less ambitiously, a land use map with new road alignments and development areas indicated. Both types of plan proved overly restrictive and were quickly outdated. In 1968, legislation split the development plan into two, the structure plan and the local plan. In the 1970s, structure plans for the whole of England were produced, focused on developing a broad overview of the spatial development trajectory for each county and the main policies which should guide development. They sought, if with rather cumbersome technical methodology (Drake *et al.*, 1975; Cross and Bristow, 1983), to produce territorial development strategies. Local plans were then to be produced for those areas where specific development actions or regulatory pressures were expected. However, the whole system became complicated by changes in the local government context, which divided structure and local plan preparation between levels of government. It also became bogged down in a morass of conflicts over policies in both structure and local plans, which consequently took a long time to approve (Healey, 1983).

The organisational context for development plan production was further complicated in the 1980s. The metropolitan counties were abolished in 1986, and with them the structure plan for metropolitan areas. The metropolitan districts were required to produce unitary development plans (UDPs) with two parts. Part I contained the strategy and Part II was supposed to provide the detail, combining the functions of the structure and local plan in one document. This was supposed to produce greater efficiency in preparation, consultation and conflict resolution. In practice, the plans continued to take a long time to produce, with extensive and strongly contested public inquiries (DoE, 1996b; DETR, 1998a). Nor was it easy for individual districts to develop strategies in isolation from each other. In the 1990s, government again sought to simplify local government and create more single tier authorities. The outcome by 1998 was a patchwork of different arrangements, with UDPs replacing structure plans in areas organised on a single tier basis, or arrangements for voluntary joint strategic plan preparation.

In the 1980s, national government, influenced by its neoliberal ideology, was ambiguous about the role of development plans. Civil servants criticised structure plans for their cumbersome methodology and failure to focus on key strategic issues. The new ministers of the Tory administration objected to the interventionist stance the plans seemed to represent, challenged the potential for structure plans and local plans to develop policy directions of their own and, with little understanding of the problems of uncertainty in the development process, preferred to focus attention at the level of the project. The level of regional guidance was reduced to a minimum and, after a struggle in which the structure plan came near to abolition (DoE, 1986), it was proposed that development plans should focus primarily on detailing national planning policy as it affected localities. At the end of the 1980s, the local plan was given greater emphasis as all county and metropolitan districts were required to produce a plan for their whole area, rather than just those areas of particular significance for development change. This resulted in the district-wide development plan, or, in single-tier authorities, the unitary development plan.

National government itself came under fire because its own policies were articulated in an ad hoc fashion through the medium of administrative circulars and ministerial statements. This practice was seen to lack openness, coherence and consistency (Nuffield Foundation, 1986; Tewdwr-Jones, 1997). This led in 1988 to the introduction of Planning Policy Guidance Notes, known colloquially as the 'PPGs'. These do not represent a national plan. They are instead a set of periodically updated statements of policy on specific topics (see Table 1.3).

The topics covered by these notes in the 1990s were the product of particular ministerial preoccupations and practical problems rather than a systematic review of the issues likely to need attention in considering land and property development management in the public interest. The 'PPGs', however, provided a more coherent policy background for debates and negotiations between planning authorities and developers over development plan policy and over the limitations on individual projects. They also provided the vehicle for the increasing emphasis on environmental policy constraints on development activity, a policy stance which was finally taken up by central government in the late

Table 1.3   National Planning Policy Guidance Notes
(correct at end of 1999)

Guidance note	Title	First produced	Revisions
PPG 1	General Policy and Principles	1988	1992, 1997
PPG 2	Green Belts	1988	1995
PPG 3	Housing	1988	1992, 1999 (draft)
PPG 4	Industrial and Commercial Development and Small Firms	1988	1992
PPG 5	Simplified Planning Zones	1988	1992
PPG 6	Town Centres and Retail Development	1988 (as 'Major Retail Development')	1993, 1996
PPG 7	The Countryside and the Rural Economy	1988 ('Rural Enterprise and Development')	1992, 1997
PPG 8	Telecommunications	1988	1992
PPG 9	Nature Conservation	1994	
PPG 10	Planning and Waste Management	1999	
PPG 11	Regional Planning Guidance	1999 (draft)	
PPG 12	Development Plans	1988 ('Local Plans'), (also: former PPG15 on Regional Strategic Guidance, Structure Plans and the Content of Development Plans); also included guidance on Regional Planning Guidance prior to 1999	1992, 1999 (draft)
PPG 13	Transport	1988 ('Highway Considerations in Development Control')	1994, 1999 (draft)
PPG 14	Development on Unstable Land	1990	1996 (additional annex)
PPG 15	Planning and the Historic Environment	1994	
PPG 16	Archaeology and Planning	1990	
PPG 17	Sport and Recreation	1991	
PPG 18	Enforcing Planning Control	1991	
PPG 19	Outdoor Advertisement Control	1992	
PPG 20	Coastal Planning	1992	
PPG 21	Tourism	1992	
PPG 22	Renewable Energy	1993	
PPG 23	Planning and Pollution Control	1994	
PPG 24	Planning and Noise	1994	

Note: The most recent title is indicated in each case.

1980s. The PPG topics largely paralleled the sectoral division of responsibilities in national and local government, focusing on particular types of development, such as housing (PPG3), industrial and commercial development (PPG4), telecommunications (PPG8), sport and recreation (PPG17) and tourism (PPG21). There was also some attempt to take a place-based focus, for example in relation to town centres (PPG6) and coastal areas (PPG20) (Quinn, 1996).

There has also been increasing emphasis on providing policy guidance at the regional level. Initially, such guidance was treated as a PPG, but a special series of Regional Policy Guidance Notes was introduced later (see Table 1.4). (Boundaries were changed between earlier and later RPGs so that, by the end of the 1990s, RPGs were either prepared or in preparation which no longer separated metropolitan areas from their hinterlands, and which were prepared commensurate with government offices for the regions (GOR) boundaries.)

National PPGs are prepared by the Whitehall office of the Department of Environment, Transport and the Regions (DETR). RPGs are prepared by regional groups of local authorities acting in concert and adjusted by the GORs. GORs have, since 1994, been part of a central government effort to integrate its own activities in a more coherent way at regional level (Mawson and Spencer, 1997).

The New Labour administration strengthened the vehicle of Regional Planning Guidance to provide a loose spatial framework for the work of both the new regional development agencies, which were given responsibility for urban policy funds, and the regulatory work of the planning system (DETR, 1998b). Some signs of a more territorial emphasis in planning policy articulation were thus emerging in the 1990s. However, this potential was limited by an opposing tendency, in local planning authority practice and in government thinking, to treat the RPG and the levels of development plan as little more than a translation of national planning policy in local arenas. This perpetuated the treatment of the planning system as a separate regulatory 'sector', entrenching a hierarchical and issue-based way of articulating the public interest, rather than a strategic, territorially integrated one. Members of the policy communities involved acknowledged this in references to the contemporary 'regime of the PPGs'. By 1998, there was increasing criticism of this approach, with demands for a more strategic, locally focused and territorially integrated approach (Kitchen, 1998).

The result by the end of the century was a confused picture. On the one hand, there was increasing emphasis on the principles articulated in formal policy documents, that is, the development plan and the PPGs,

Table 1.4 Extant Regional Planning Policy Guidance Notes (correct at end of 1999)

Guidance note	Title	First produced	Revisions
RPG 1	Tyne and Wear	1989	To be superseded by revised RPG 7
RPG 2	West Yorkshire	1989	Superseded by RPG 12
RPG 3	London	1989	1996
RPG 3A	London (strategic views)	1991	
RPG 3B	London (River Thames)	1997	
RPG 4	Greater Manchester	1989	Superseded by RPG 13
RPG 5	South Yorkshire	1989	Superseded by RPG 12
RPG 6	East Anglia/Eastern	1991	Expected early 2000
RPG 7	Northern Region/North-East Region	1993	Expected Autumn 2000
RPG 8	East Midlands	1994	Draft published November 1999
RPG 9	South East	1988 (as PPG 9)	1994 (revision expected early 2000)
RPG 9a	Thames Gateway	1995	
RPG 10	South West	1994	Draft published August 1999
RPG 11	West Midlands	1988 (as PPG 10, for the metropolitan area only)	1995 (changes were made in 1997 with regard to housing); (further review commences in year 2000)
RPG 12	Yorkshire and Humberside	1988	1996 (draft published August 1999)
RPG 13	North West	1988 (as PPG 11 for Merseyside only)	1996 (revision expected Spring 2001)

as guides to the exercise of the planning functions of local authorities. On the other hand, there were tendencies which emphasised the development of territorially focused planning policy frameworks. Among these, EU requirements to set demands for funding in the context of a strategic development framework were particularly important. This issue was emphasised in New Labour proposals for the role of Regional Planning Guidance (DETR, 1998b). But the tendencies towards a more territorially integrated strategic approach were evolving in a situation where the role of the largely topic-based PPGs had been strengthened, in the form of topic-based and largely aspatial principles or policy criteria. These inhibited integrated consideration of topics as they interrelate in localities. This internal constraint on a territorial focus throughout the 1990s was compounded by the separation of funding for urban and rural regeneration from the planning regulatory process arising from within the organisation of the DETR. This separation looked set to continue into the twenty-first century, with the regional development agencies and their investment budgets only loosely coupled with the government offices and the RPGs (DETR, 1998d). In addition, the organisational changes produced by local government restructuring, privatisation of the utilities and the creation of new partnerships and special agencies fragmented many of the ties which encouraged local authorities to work together to produce common strategies for urban regions. The result was a formally plan-led and policy-driven planning system, but focused narrowly on an ad hoc agenda of issues strongly shaped by national policy preoccupations. We show in Part II how, in practice, the different main players in specific localities managed to operate in this confused and hierarchical situation, and how they related their planning system work to their other activities, particularly the need to develop strategic frameworks to capture funding for projects.

The distribution of responsibilities in the planning system

Development happens on sites in places. Any policy system aimed at promoting and regulating development needs to have a strong local focus. Local responsibility is a feature of most planning systems. But even minor developments may raise issues of concern to stakeholders elsewhere or questions of policy at regional, national and international levels. The distribution of formal responsibilities within planning systems has an important structuring effect on planning practices, specifying in legal terms who has the power to use the different tools, to change the tools and to oversee others in their use. The patterns of responsibilities usually involve more than one level of government, and sometimes other public and private agencies. There are very significant variations between countries and over time in the pattern of distribution of responsibility (CEU, 1997; Cullingworth, 1993). At one extreme, the national level merely provides enabling legislation or adjudication, allowing municipal or regional level governments to develop their own approaches (in the USA, and Australia for example). At the other extreme, a national government could keep tight control over the development of the system and its practices (as in England in recent years). Most European planning systems achieve a balance somewhere in between (CEU, 1997). These patterns serve to generate the formal arenas where strategies are legitimated, decisions about the use of rules and the allocation of responsibilities are confirmed and conflicts are adjudicated upon.

The problems which the institutional context creates for the operation of the planning system in England are evident from the above discussion of the tools of the system. As Table 1.5 shows, roles in the system are distributed between the national government and its regional offices, local authorities and special agencies, with the EU playing an increasingly important role in shaping the form and content of policy principles.

The primary actor in the system is the local planning authority, which may be a unitary district, a county and a district in a two-tier situation, or a special urban development agency, which has planning powers. Compared to other European countries and the USA, English local planning authorities, at district and county level, tend to cover large areas (the largest authority being Birmingham City Council, with a population of 990 000) and to have a group of staff with professional qualifications in planning. This arises because of the workload created by the judgemental nature of the regulatory process. In the past, local planning authorities also typically had their own in-house expertise and rarely used consultants. This had changed by the 1990s, as a result of national government pressure to reduce local authority budgets and to 'privatise' local authority functions, resulting in more contracting out of planning work.

However, despite this strong position of the local planning authority, it is surrounded by constraints which allow the national government to exert a powerful influence in shaping the detail of planning practices. Central to this influence is a circular system of checks and balances.

Table 1.5 Formal responsibilities in the English planning system in the 1990s

Level/agency	Tools: regulatory	Tools: financial	Tools: direct development	Tools: information and policy
European Union	Requirements arising from environmental legislation			European Spatial Development Perspective
National: Department of the Environment, Transport and the Regions	Adjust legislation Overview of appeal system Powers to 'call in' plans and applications for decision	Vary tax regimes to provide incentives (e.g. enterprise zones) Provide subsidy Fund highways	Define enabling legislation	Produce Planning Policy Guidance Produce national waste strategy
Regional: government offices for the regions	Advise on exercise of 'call in' powers	Recommend grant allocations and locations for tax regime variations		Modify and approve Regional Planning Guidance Comment on development plans
County:	Review major planning decisions Waste planning Negotiate obligations	Limited funds for projects Bio for transport funding	Environmental management projects Build transport infrastructure	Prepare structure plans Prepare minerals and waste local plans Promote public transport Prepare local transport plans

Table 1.5 Continued

Level/agency	Tools: regulatory	Tools: financial	Tools: direct development	Tools: information and policy
District authorities	Make planning decisions Negotiate obligations	Limited funds for projects	Wide-ranging potential role	Prepare unitary development plans or district-wide development plans Prepare simplified planning zone/enterprise zone regimes Prepare waste recycling plans
Special agencies:				
Planning inspectorate	Conduct appeals			
Urban Development Corporations/Housing Action Trusts, etc.	(Some) make planning decisions Negotiate obligations	Provide funding for projects	Assemble sites Provide infrastructure Market sites and buildings	Provide informal development and design briefs Propose simplified planning zones

The national government articulates its policies and demands that local planning authorities follow them in development plans and regulatory practice. Dissatisfied developers can then appeal against an adverse decision, first through appeal to a semi-judicial inquiry organised by the planning inspectorate and then to the courts. The appeal via the inspectorate can ask for the decision to be reviewed. In this review, the inspector is required to establish whether due consideration has been given to national policy, that is, to the PPGs. The inspectorate is answerable to national government, in the person of the Secretary of State for the Environment, Transport and the Regions. A local authority that seeks to follow a line different from national policy will be challenged at appeal and may have to pay for the costs of the appeal and damages to the successful appellant.

Thus national government holds the balance of power in defining the parameters of the regulatory system, and used it with a tight grip during the 1979–97 administrations, although increasingly challenged (see, for example, Jones, 1996). It also holds the balance of power with respect to resources for local government, during the 1980s and 1990s enforcing progressive budget reductions and the channelling of funds through special programmes for which authorities had to make bids. As a result, in the 1990s, local planning authorities had to live within the constraints of a limited conception of the purposes of a planning system, and a set of idiosyncratic national policy preoccupations expressed through planning policy guidance. One result of this national structuring of the work of a local planning authority was that the tendencies to integration with the work of other local authority departments, particularly economic development and housing functions, actively pursued in the 1970s, were replaced by tendencies towards a narrower regulatory perspective, grounded in the authority of national policy. This further encouraged the separation of planning as a regulatory activity from other areas of local authority work concerned with the development of a local authority's territory.

These tensions were compounded by other pressures on local planning authorities. One was a long-standing problem of conflicting priorities between adjacent authorities and between counties and districts. The dependence on the national level encouraged those concerned to leave conflicts unresolved, in effect passing the buck to a higher tier, rather than developing horizontal relationships to resolve disputes. Another was the proliferation of special agencies and partnerships which emerged in the 1980s and 1990s. Some of these, such as the urban development corporations and housing action trusts, were allowed to take on planning regulation powers if they wished. In addition, there were the partnerships referred to earlier, which complicated the agency landscape. A third pressure was the challenge to the democratic model of simple representative democracy. Parish councils, pressure groups, neighbour lobbies and amenity societies as well as the lobby groups of business organisations and individual developers all increasingly demanded influence over planning policies and planning decisions. This reflected the general rise of pressure-group politics and the distrust of politicians and 'expert' officials (Evans, 1995), and an increasing popular concern with the environment and qualities of place. Although some of this pressure landed at the door of national government, either in the work of particular departments or as challenges to the electoral base of the majority party, it was the local planning authority which was routinely at the centre of these pressures. It was a major contradiction of the 1990s that local planning authorities were forced into this central position in relation to environmental conflicts, but were heavily constrained in the way they could respond (Grove-White, 1991; Owens, 1997).

In this context, the policy arenas of the European Union began in the 1990s to have an impact on British planning practice. Initially, the effect was felt through the regulatory tool, through requirements to incorporate European environmental appraisal legislation into the system. But a more pervasive impact was emerging through the requirements for spatial strategies when bidding for EU structural funds, and then through the publicity for the European Spatial Development Perspective (CSD, 1998). Inspired by the commitment in parts of Europe to local and regional spatial strategies in guiding investment, this European policy discourse was eagerly embraced by the New Labour administration (DETR, 1998a, 1998b).

Thus the institutional relations of the planning system in the Tory years were characterised by a kind of hierarchical sectoralism, increasingly isolated from other policy systems and, within its own practices, adopting a topic-organised rather than a place-focused approach to defining policy agendas. This encouraged local authorities to decouple their regulatory work from their other activities. But, at the same time, they were under pressure for more horizontal linkages with a multiplicity of agencies. This pressure was substantially driven by dynamics arising in other areas of national policy, notably the rules for gaining access to special funding sources. Local authorities also had to meet demands from many pressure groups and those concerned with particular projects and the qualities of specific places for a wider involvement in policy making and regulatory practice. This generated an acute tension between the planning system understood as a functional sector of government in its own right, an autonomous regulator of development activity of any kind, and the system as a vehicle for promoting particular public interest policies as regards the qualities of places, territory and local environments, whether those of national government, of local authorities or of concerned citizens.

The English planning system in transition

As with any policy field, planning systems are sites of struggles over the form and content of governance. During two decades of Tory administrations (1979–97), the structures and practices of the system were increasingly drawn into wider forces for change, as the institutions of the postwar welfare state were transformed. There were conflicting views as to the extent to which the English planning system had been redesigned as a result of both this wider agenda of governance transformation and the challenges to respond to new policy agendas of economic competitiveness and environmental sustainability. For many commentators, the system exhibited extraordinary continuity, in contrast to other areas of public policy which were vigorously reshaped in the previous 20 years (Brindley *et al.,* 1989; Healey *et al.,* 1988; Healey, 1988; Tewdwr-Jones, 1997; Quinn, 1996; Cullingworth and Nadin, 1994). This continuity showed, some argued, the robustness of the original system design, and the continuing societal need for the management of land use change and development in the public interest: 'The planning system's survival, in much the same form as that in which it was created in the 1940s, owes much to its inherent flexibility and the wide respect that it commands' (Quinn, 1996, p.29).

There are others, however, who argued that the system was a leftover from the era of the mid-century welfare state and in need of radical change (Roberts, 1998; Cullingworth, 1997). Calls for such change in the system increased in the months after the election of the New Labour administration in 1997 (Kitchen, 1998; Hall, 1998). Meanwhile, there were some who claimed that such a change had already happened, through the major reshaping that was experienced in the 1980s and on into the 1990s (Thornley, 1991; Tewdwr-Jones, 1996).

Table 1.6 Significant changes in the English planning system

Planning system elements	1980s	1990s	2000s
Purposes	Negotiating development impacts/conflict resolution Dominance of economic considerations	Negotiation role continues Increasing environmental emphasis Concern with qualities of city centres	Strategic framework for economic development; social, economic, environmental integration?
Tools: regulatory	Major emphasis	Regulatory emphasis continues, separate from financial and direct development role	Regulatory emphasis continues?
Tools: financial	Tax incentives via enterprise zones Expansion of negotiation of developer contributions	Enterprise zone incentives reduced Separation of investment and regulatory power Developer contributions accepted as necessary	Expansion of developer contributions? Use of tax incentives for various purposes?
Tools: direct development	Reduction of local authority role in development New agencies/budgets for urban regeneration activity Fragmented budgets	Reduction of local authority role continues Promotion of partnerships	Link to urban regeneration budgets? 'Joined up thinking and working'

29

Table 1.6 Continued

Planning system elements	1980s	1990s	2000s
Tools: information and policy guidance	Reduction of the development plan role	Increased emphasis on the development plan	Development plan's importance as a land allocation mechanism and strategic framework maintained, but other local and regional strategies reduce its wider role? Role of Regional Planning Guidance expanded?
Responsibilities	National government power strengthened Introduction of new agencies	Slight shift towards decentralisation Reduced role for agencies, but increase in partnerships	Shift away from national government to regional level?

How the relative balance of continuity and change is perceived depends on which dimension of the system and its practices is emphasised. Table 1.6 attempts a summary of the changes in purposes, tools and responsibilities which have taken place, as outlined in the previous section. Table 1.6 suggests a substantial continuity in the formal regulatory form of the English planning system. It still operates through discretionary judgements, made by local councillors advised by professional planning officers, in the light of what is in development plans as well as other relevant considerations. The content of the plans is developed through procedures which include provision for public comment and some form of inquiry. This content, as well as what is considered relevant (or 'material'), evolves through processes of continual interpretation, in national and local policy revisions, in specific regulatory decisions, in inquiry arenas and in the courts. The regulatory decision focuses on establishing, through these discretionary judgements and evolving interpretations, what is the public interest in a development or land use change proposal, and whether there is any reason, as a result of this interest, to modify or refuse a proposal.

However, this stable form allows enormous flexibility in developing the purposes of the system, in the way the elements of the 'toolbox' are combined, and in the location of power in the judgemental and interpretive process. It is this flexibility which has been used over the years since 1947 to shift the trajectory of the system. Viewed as a 'policy system', there have been two major shifts in trajectory in the past 40 years. The first, which began to occur in the 1950s, was from a public sector-led development process, guided by development plans which provided the blueprints for a 'command and control' approach to managing development, an approach which still survives in some parts of the European Union. This was steadily displaced by what became a guidance framework for the regulation of private development, in which the development plan acted as a basis for negotiation (Healey, 1983). The second shift, evolving from the late 1960s, was towards a regulatory process guided by clear policy criteria, which were intended to provide a transparent framework within which regulatory negotiation can take place. This policy-led regulatory process became increasingly elaborate in the 1980s and 1990s, evolving into the 'regime of the PPGs'. But as this trajectory developed, two major terrains of struggle emerged over the regulatory form of the planning system. One was over who controls the policy criteria. The other was over the appropriate relation between the policy criteria pursued through the regulatory power, and the policy objectives of other areas of national and local government policy as they affect the qualities of localities.

This book focuses primarily on this second terrain of struggle. Our approach is to look underneath broad generalities about the planning system, to examine the way the practices of spatial strategy development were evolving in the 1990s, and the evidence this provides for the opportunities to move in this second direction. We examine how such practices are being realised in particular places, given the varying issue agendas and specific governance dynamics that arise in locales. We seek to assess how far they are being transformed, in what ways and as a result of what driving forces. We examine how far such changes were affecting or being affected by the continual reinterpretation and reconstitution of the planning system-in-practice. Policy rhetorics may change, and examples of new practices may capture headlines, in public debate and in academic discourses. But the social practices of policy systems flow on, embedded in specific relations and shaped by past practices and specific challenges. New rhetorics need to penetrate these embedded practices to achieve transformative effects in regulatory and investment actions. Did an inheritance of a strategic past live on in the practices of the planning system during the 1980s and 1990s, to provide a foundation for a new strategic impetus in the next century? Or was it lost in the onslaught of regulatory sectoralism and fragmentation of project initiatives? If the latter, is there any sign of its reinvention, and, if so, in what form? To address such questions, some conceptual means are needed with which to focus an account of policy practices. In the next chapter we develop our approach to the analysis of such practices.

2 Constructing Accounts of Planning Practices: Theories and Concepts

Describing policy practices

Just as there are conflicting views on what planning systems are for and how useful they are, so there are different ways in which accounts of strategic planning practices could be made. One way would be to focus on the accounts of the key people involved (for example, the key planning officers and councillors). Another would be to look at a chronology of formal events (for example, plan inquiries) and the documents related to them (for example, development plans). A third might be to look at some key decisions or projects, to see how far strategic ideas and policy principles affected specific actions. It might be possible to undertake such work through a national survey across the country, or a case study focus could be taken. The choices which authors make in writing their accounts reflect their interests, their knowledge and their conceptual approach to making sense of complex evolving realities.

In this book our knowledge base derives from an empirical study of strategic spatial planning practices, as they evolved from the late 1980s into the late 1990s. Our empirical work drew on discussions with many of those involved, as well as document review and analysis of key decisions. In focusing our work and writing our accounts, we have been guided by the questions raised in the previous chapter. The overall purpose of our analysis is to explore the nature and extent of transition and transformation in the planning system. What forces are driving these dynamics, and along which trajectories? More specifically, we are interested in three dimensions of these trajectories. Firstly, we ask to what extent there is evidence that pressures are being experienced for a more territorial basis for policy development. Are these manifest in the formation of regional and local alliances and mobilisation efforts to promote qualities of territory and place? Are they successfully challenging the functional/sectoral organisation of policy communities and policy action which has characterised English public policy development and delivery since the postwar welfare state settlement? Are they evident in and around the relationships of the planning system? Does this mean that the policy arenas and practices of the planning system are becoming of greater significance in wider governance contexts?

Secondly, such a shift towards more territorially focused governance relations might create pressures for integrating policy systems developed for the delivery of particular functional/sectoral programmes. The tension between economic development and environmental policy agendas in the 1990s in Britain has already been mentioned in Chapter 1. A new emphasis on providing more integrated and holistic policy agendas was surfacing in many policy arenas by the late 1990s. We ask how far the policy agendas in localities are being driven by attempts to integrate the economic, environmental and social dimensions of issues and what kind of integration is involved.

Thirdly, while there has been much rhetoric in recent years in England about the need to forge new relationships of local governance, with the formation of special purpose agencies and encouragement for partnership arrangements of various kinds, what are the qualities of these new relationships? Are they merely a reconfiguration of elites, a new form of local corporatism? Or do they open up a potential for a more broadly based form of governance, in which a much wider range of stakeholders are able to have a voice, as demanded by advocates of more participatory forms of governance?

These are complex questions which relate to the way policy agendas are formed, how policies are translated into actions, who gets involved in policy, how they work together and the social networks through which they work. They involve consideration, not just of what the formal agencies of government do, but about the dynamics of the relations between levels of government, and the linkages that develop over governance activity between the state, business and citizens. They raise issues about the way in which broad economic, environmental, sociocultural and political forces work out in particular places at specific times, and about the dynamics of power relations, both with respect to the way one group gets to play a dominant role and to the way people get to mobilise to change things. They lead to consideration of the patterning of governance relationships in different contexts, and whether particular sorts of governance patterns or regimes emerge at particular times.

Social theory about urban and regional change and urban politics has debated such issues for many years and offers helpful conceptual resources with which to organise our accounts. Specifically, we draw inspiration from the 'institutionalist' turn in urban and regional analysis and in urban planning. This emphasises the significance of the various relationships which those involved in governance bring to policy processes, both within and beyond the formal agencies where they work. In this chapter, we locate the institutionalist approach within recent social theory with respect to urban and regional analysis and urban politics and planning. We then introduce three organising concepts, policy communities, policy arenas and policy discourses, before journeying to the social worlds of spatial strategy-making practices in our three localities.

Analysing local politics and planning practices

In the 1960s, the dominant emphasis in the study of planning systems and local government in Britain was on formal descriptions of structures and procedures. These accounts tended to assume that structures were created to perform specific functions and had the powers to follow them through. Early postwar accounts of the British planning system described the powers given by government and focused on the development plans produced for existing settlements and new towns, on the assumption that that these would control the way spatial futures developed (Cullingworth, 1964; Keeble, 1952). In these accounts, in line with the frame of thinking of the welfare state, the public sector was presented as the dominant player. The private sector worked within the rules set by the public sector, while citizens, it was assumed, could rely on government to provide for them.

This kind of account was challenged by case studies of local politics and urban development which emphasised that what actually happened in city government was the result of individuals in key positions using their powers to pursue particular agendas (Saunders, 1979; Elkin, 1974; Meyerson and Banfield, 1955; Ambrose and Colenutt, 1973). These studies of 'community power' highlighted the informal processes which lay behind formal structures and showed the ways in which people outside government, such as businessmen, property developers and landowners, could get influence over local government activity. Such a perception was pursued in the analysis of local politics in the USA, where the interrelation between business and local politics was very obvious, leading to debates over the way power was distributed in localities (Judge *et al.*, 1995; Dunleavy and O'Leary, 1987). Some argued that local politics was 'corporatist', in that a few major players from local politics and the business community ran local government. In this context, the practices of planning systems could be used by local elites to pursue their specific land and development policy agendas. Others argued that, while local politics was driven by the power and interest of elite groups, it was not merely business and labour groups who got involved in local governance. Instead, there was a plurality of sources of power in a locality, all competing with each other (Judge, 1995). How spatial strategies evolved depended on interaction and negotiation among competing groups, with planning regulation having an important role in mediating conflicts among different interests in the quality of local environments (Healey *et al.*, 1988; Brindley *et al.*, 1989). Nevertheless, case studies showed that power was typically concentrated, with local power elites dominating local affairs, though their composition could be varied (Harding, 1995). 'Power' here was understood in terms of having power over the actions of others (Dyrberg, 1997).

These accounts of local politics and planning practices and the conceptual debates they generated, emphasised two dimensions of governance neglected in the formal accounts of government structures and formal policies and plans. Firstly, they gave attention to 'agency', to the active work of key players in developing and carrying through policy ideas. Secondly, they highlighted the interactions through which key players related to each other, through negotiation and bargaining, through the relationships they built up to get things done and the alliances they made to mobilise support for strategies. From this viewpoint, planning practice came out of the drawing office and the rule books, to become a social process.

This agency emphasis was also felt in the field of planning theory, which in the 1950s and 1960s had been dominated by models of ideal urban forms or ideal policy processes intended to guide the production of comprehensive urban development plans (Healey *et al.*, 1982; Friedmann, 1987). It soon emerged from practitioner accounts and from case studies of decision making that such models rarely worked out as expected (Meyerson and Banfield, 1955; Altshuler, 1965; Cross and Bristow, 1983; Wannop, 1985; Black, 1990). Many commentators began to notice the conflict between planners' ideal models of rational, technical management of urban change and a reality of complex political struggles over access to resources and over patterns of domination and oppression in localities. In this conflict, planners are often cast as the champions of a rationalising order and the technical servants of dominant groups and interests (Ambrose and Colenutt, 1973; Boyer, 1983; Castells, 1977; Flyvberg, 1998).

Policy analysts and planning theorists developed the 'agency' perspective in a different direction in the 1970s and 1980s, focusing less on the more obvious power games. Instead, they began to look at the nature of the interactive social processes through which formal policy systems were translated into practices. It was soon recognised in this work that the translation from 'policy' to 'action' involved many stages, in each of which initial ideas were given specific meanings and modes of behaviour (Barrett and Fudge, 1981). Those involved in these interpretive processes, government officers and consultants for example, were not just cogs in an administrative machine, or even merely tools of the powerful. They exercised discretion as active 'agents' (Crozier, 1964). In giving meanings to policies and devising working practices, they transformed formal policy systems into living practices. It was through these reinterpreted practices that policy could affect action, not merely through the direct power of command of a law or government statement.

As a result, policies did not neatly flow into 'action'. Thus, rather than policy development being conceived in a 'top-down' way, policy-as-practised evolved in an interactive, non-linear way, giving voice to 'bottom-up' viewpoints (Barrett and Fudge, 1981). In Britain this led to an interest in the late 1970s in the appropriate relationship between central and local government (Goldsmith, 1986). Such views led policy analysts to map the policy 'networks' through which the translation from system and strategy to action actually took place (Friend *et al.,*1974; Marsh and Rhodes, 1992). These studies identified both the strength of the vertical linkages between central and local government and the sectoral divisions in the organisation of government in Britain. Friend *et al*'s analysis (1974), also emphasised the horizontal linkages between actors involved in tasks such as major urban development projects.

In the more localist environment of the USA, analysts also emphasised horizontal linkages, through exploration of the evolution of strategic alliances in cities and regions (Cox and Johnston, 1982; Fainstein and Fainstein, 1986; Feagin, 1988). Informed by these insights, attention in planning theory began to move away from the development of urban analysis models and rational ways of designing policy processes, to focus on the way planners as active agents could and should conduct themselves in complex interactive contexts, within which knowledge and expertise flowed in non-linear ways through social communicative processes (Forester, 1989; Innes, 1990, 1995). By the 1990s, the focus on policy development as a communicative process was being developed in work on consensus building, particularly as regards ways to deal with politically difficult environmental dilemmas (Susskind and Cruikshank, 1987; Innes *et al.*, 1994), as well as in community development work (Schneecloth and Sibley, 1995; Bishop, 1998). Meanwhile, to complement these ideas about the 'how' of communicative planning processes, the concept of 'stakeholder' was translated from the business management field. This focused attention on who got involved in policy development and how, and why some with a 'stake' got excluded (Bryson and Crosby, 1992; Huxham, 1996).

These ideas greatly enriched the contribution made by those studying local power elites. They moved the focus of analysis beyond the world of local governance as one of power games between individuals and factions seeking to capture control of government and of policy development opportunities. They showed that policy was made as much in its practices as in its design, and that power was evident in the way people make things work, as well as in power games with regard to capturing control. For these authors, power lay in the ability to 'make a difference', the 'power to' as much as the 'power over' (Dyrberg, 1997). This power lay as much in the everyday interactions of communicative practice as in the 'grand strategies' of political manifestos and technically designed analysis. These analysts located individual actors in their wider networks, and explored how the relations of one network and the 'community' of people bound together within it related to other networks people had access to. This helped to show how knowledge and social connections developed in one arena could be carried forward into another. Thus they put the spotlight on 'agency' across the spectrum of governance relationships in a locality. This is the approach we take in our accounts.

The focus on agency, and the fine grain of the social processes of policy development and delivery, was a valuable corrective to the previous emphases on the power of the formal dimensions of policy systems and of rational technical analysis. However, it ran the risk of neglecting the way the wider context in which agents practised might shape the content of their agendas and practices. Individuals might not be cogs or tools in government structures, but neither were they and their relationships autonomous of wider forces which shaped the opportunities available to them. Just as pluralist accounts of local politics were challenged (Healey *et al.*, 1982; Judge, 1995), so the developments in communicative planning theory were challenged in the 1990s for their apparent neglect of these broader structuring forces (Richardson, 1996; Tewdwr-Jones and Allmendinger, 1998; Lauria and Whelan, 1995). In this context, 'structure' was used to mean, not the formal structures of government, but the powerful patterning of social relations produced by the organisation of economic production processes, or the overall manner of governance in a society. The dominant voice in this critique in the 1970s came from those working within a Marxist perspective, who understood social ordering as structured by a struggle between the capitalist class and the working class over control of the means of production; that is, over economic activity. There was much debate over the role of the state in the context of this struggle, with some arguing that government, and hence local government, was an instrument of the capitalist class, and hence driven by an economic dynamic (Cockburn, 1977; Castells, 1977). This seemed to confirm and extend the 'corporatist' analysis outlined above.

As the state of the British economy was called into question in the 1970s, the power of international economic forces to shape local economies, affect people's life opportunities and change local political agendas became very obvious. In this context, more than in the USA for example, the recognition of the power of structural forces in shaping local trajectories was difficult to avoid. However, there has been increasing resistance among analysts to restricting this structuring power to 'the logic of capitalist economic development'. It is now widely appreciated that the dynamics of the way the relations of governance work may have an 'autonomous' role as a driving force, affected by what is happening in the economy, but not totally driven by it. Similarly, changes in civil society generate new ways of responding to economic and political conditions. These forces create material needs and cultural innovations which in turn shape economic activity and governance processes (Giddens, 1990; Bauman, 1992). Despite the difficulty of sorting out the balance of power between these various forces, such analyses all emphasised that the sources of change in local governance dynamics lie outside a territory. They suggested that strategic plan-making practices do not just transform themselves. They are pushed and pulled by outside forces. In our accounts, we too have sought to take account of these broader driving forces.

During the 1980s, many of these broader attempts to interpret the 'logic' of transformation in the face of changes in economic, political and social–cultural organisation were challenged by a wave of 'post-modern' analysis. This denied the value of such 'grand narratives' and rejected the idea of the fettering of agency by wider structuring forces or even by governance activity of any kind (Seidman, 1998). This has been of great value in emphasising the contingent and essentially unpredictable nature of human action, and celebrating the diversity of human experience (Sandercock, 1998). But it provides little guide to the analysis and design of emerging governance processes. More valu-able for this purpose are emerging strands of analysis which see 'struc-ture' and 'agency' not as alternatives, but as interlinked and which seek to situate specific relations, whether those of firms, households or gov-ernment agencies, within the context of the range of social relations which sustain them. Here we discuss in particular recent contributions in regulation theory, the analysis of urban regimes and the 'new institu-tionalism' in urban and regional studies and planning theory. We then summarise our own approach, which is a development of a strand of the 'new institutionalism'.

Regulation theory and urban regime theory

Our interest in this book is in the extent of the transformation in subna-tional governance in the late twentieth century in Britain and the quali-ties of such governance forms. Regulation theory focuses on the dynamics of the transitions from one social formation to another, emphasising the broad structural forces which shape processes of change. Urban regime theory emphasises the patterns which emerge in governance forms, placing the emphasis more on the world of agency and the sphere of local action. Both strands of analysis seek to identify the patterning processes in the dynamics of governance relations and the way these may lead to clearly evident and enduring sets of relation-ships through which governance is accomplished. These are referred to as 'regimes', 'modes of regulation' or, in the language of David Harvey, 'structured coherences' or 'permanences' (Harvey, 1985, 1996).

The starting point of regulation theory is the challenge of explaining macroeconomic and political change which leads to the transformation of societal relations from one 'form' to another. The term 'regulation' derives from the French usage, meaning the systematic patterning of practices through which the state shapes processes of capitalist accumulation. It does not mean the specific legal power to regulate, as in British 'development control'. Nor is it even as specific as the notion of the 'regulatory form' of a policy system. Its meaning is much broader, and linked to attempts to relate shifts in patterns of capitalist production processes, the 'mode of accumulation', to shifts in the way governance works (the 'mode of regulation') (Boyer, 1990; Painter, 1995; Le Gales, 1998). The 'mode of regulation' refers to the ensemble of institutions involved in governance, while the term 'governance' is used to embrace both what government does and the wider relations of activities which relate to the collective co-ordination of matters of mutual concern to many parties. The mode of regulation is

the set of social, cultural and political supports which promote the compatibility between production and consumption in the regime of accumulation. These supports operate through particular norms, networks and institutions which are the outcomes of social and political conflicts. (Painter, 1995, pp.278–9)

The regulationist argument has focused in particular on a shift from 'Fordism' to 'post-Fordism' (Amin, 1994). Fordism is understood as a distinctive type of labour process, a stable mode of macroeconomic growth, a social mode of economic regulation and a general pattern of social organisation (Jessop, 1994). Thus the notion of regulation does not mean merely the rules and regulations which the state deploys but the wide array of formal and informal ways in which relations in and between the economy, civil society and the state are mediated. Regulation theorists focus on transformation processes in the structure of the economy, society and governance (Boyer, 1990; Lipietz, 1992; Jessop, 1991). This parallels Harvey's argument that a shift has occurred from the 'managerialist' state to the 'entrepreneurial' state (Harvey, 1989). If such shifts are happening generally, should not the English planning system show evidence of such changes in its regulatory form and its practices? Until recently, regulation theorists gave little attention to such detailed practices, or to local governance (Moulaert, 1996). However, a key theme in debates about modes of regulation is that, in a 'post-Fordist' world, the nation state and its machinery for welfare state delivery are less important as a locus of governance activity (Jessop, 1991; Esping-Anderson, 1990). This

encouraged some regulation theorists to explore subnational governance processes to examine whether 'local' modes of regulation exist
and whether these could evolve in a direction different from that at the
national level (Jessop, 1994; Goodwin *et al.,* 1993; Peck and
Emmerich, 1994; Mayer, 1995).

The development of ideas and research within the regulation theory
framework evolved rapidly in the 1990s (Amin, 1994; Painter, 1995;
Lauria, 1997a; Goodwin *et al.,* 1993; Jones 1997). Its value is that it
has a clear theorisation of the dynamics of the processes of transition
from one societal period to another, a 'grand narrative' with an underlying emphasis on the structuring driving force of changes in global
economic organisation. It also stresses that public policy practices
should not be seen as confined within the organisations of the state,
but involve relations between those in government, the economy and
civil society. In the context of our analysis, it encourages an emphasis
on the way the processes of transition and transformation in the planning system's purposes, tools, responsibilities and discourses relate to
wider changes in governance processes. But the approach remains at a
high level of generality, with a strong emphasis on structuring dynamics. This becomes a weakness when it is used to analyse local governance practices (Peck, 1993; Moulaert, 1996; Goodwin and Painter,
1997; Gandy, 1997).

Firstly, it overemphasises structural driving forces and particularly
economic dynamics, at the expense of the active work of people in
localities seeking solutions to the situations they find themselves in
(Lauria, 1997; Painter, 1995, 1997). It has little to say about the
detailed practices of accomplishing transformations. Secondly, it privileges global economic forces over local histories and geographies, and
gives limited attention to the power and durability of ways of thinking
and acting, that is, local governance cultures, which build up in particular areas over time (Le Gales, 1998). Thirdly, it encourages researchers
to search for patterns, for discernible 'modes' of regulation. This dis-
tracts analytical attention from the complexity of the governance relations to be found in a locality and the way changes are accomplished or
resisted in the fine grain of policy practices. The more interesting question, especially for the analysis of governance relations in localities and
for practical mobilisation for change, is how and in what circumstances
sufficient stability in governance arrangements arises to produce an
enduring pattern of local power relations and what are the effects of
such arrangements. How are such patterns maintained over time and

what leads to changes in relational patterns? How do such changes occur? Such inquiry has been the focus of urban regime theory (Stoker, 1995; Lauria, 1997). Drawing on a rich body of city case studies, principally in the USA, this too emphasises the importance of governance relations, rather than merely the internal relations of levels of government. In a development of the power elite approach, Logan and Molotch (1987) argued that US city politics was driven by coalitions of local politicians and 'rentier' interests (developers and landowners) seeking to extract profits from maintaining the growth dynamic of their cities. Fainstein and Fainstein (1986) provided a more differentiated approach, explicitly using the term 'urban regime'. They recognised that who the participants in a regime were and how it operated varied from city to city, depending on local geographies and histories. Meanwhile, Stone's analysis of Atlanta provided more precise tools for describing urban regimes (Stone, 1989). Although these various contributions have different emphases, the approach is advocated by many present-day analysts of urban governance because it seems to address the complexity of the social relations within which governance activity takes place and the variety of forms such governance could take. It emphasises that identifiable regimes can arise and endure to create governance coherence. It highlights the competence to act, not just to maintain the power of governing coalitions, but to mobilise local resources and develop the qualities of localities.

> In a complex, fragmented urban world the paradigmatic form of power is that which enables certain interests to blend their capacities to achieve common purposes. Regime analysis directs attention to the conditions under which such effective long-term coalitions emerge in order to accomplish public purposes. (Stoker, 1995, p.55)

It also provides hypotheses about what the analyst should look for when studying an urban regime. For example, Stone suggests that the content and outcomes of urban public policies can be assumed to be the product of the 'composition of the governing coalition', the 'nature of the relationships among members of that coalition' and the 'resources that members bring to the coalition' (Stoker, 1995). This parallels the notion of public policy as the outcome of power dependencies developed by Rhodes (1986). The approach focuses analytical attention on key actors and their networks, and on their mobilisation capacity, emphasising the dimension of agency missing in regulation theory. Yet urban regime theory may be criticised for its assumption that 'regimes' exist and that 'permanences' are a likely occurrence. As with regulation theory, it sets the analysts off in a search for patterns, rather than exploring the multiple processes which produce the governance relations in a locality at a particular moment. Others have argued that there may be several relations, potentially each with their own 'regimes', layered across the political space of a city or that there may be too much instability or too little political and economic power for any coherent regime to arise (Leo, 1997). The focus on the nature of a regime thus tends to distract analytical attention from the micro-processes of contestation and change in urban governance processes. It concentrates too much attention on the obvious 'power elite' and too little on other arenas where governance processes may be emerging. It thus sits uncomfortably between the analysis of structuring dynamics and the practices through which governance action is achieved.

There is considerable interest these days in forging some kind of merger between regulation theory and urban regime theory (Lauria, 1997). The structural emphasis of the one can usefully complement the agency emphasis of the other. However, as Painter (1997) points out, there are some conceptual problems in such an enterprise. He highlights in particular the restricted assumptions about the way regime members operate. In ways which parallel our own thinking, he turns to socio-anthropological inspiration, and Bourdieu's concept of 'habitus', to emphasise that regime members may come from different 'actor groups'. As a result, they may inhabit different 'thought worlds' and policy communities, with different ways of thinking (discourses) and acting (practices). This focuses attention on the different relational webs or networks through which governance activity is accomplished in a locality, and the qualities of their linkages as these evolve over time (Healey *et al.,* 1995; Le Gales, 1998). Such analysis has become a major focus of attention in the regional economic development literature, which has been concerned with the qualities of the institutional context for economic activity and why some contexts seem to be more fruitful for economic innovation than others.

The institutionalist turn in urban and regional analysis

In the context of the economic transformations being witnessed across Europe resulting from changes in production processes and the increas-

ing opening of economic activity to global competition, the analysis of
urban and regional economies became a major focus of academic attention in the late twentieth century, paralleling an equivalent focus in
public policy in Europe. This drew on various inspirations, including
the regulationist analysis of the transition from Fordism to post-
Fordism. Analysts were interested in why firms behaved the way they
did and how they related to their localities. Increasingly, the analytical
emphasis moved away from an analysis of factors within the firm to an
understanding of the chains of production, or *filières*, in which a particular firm was located. A focus on *filières* emphasises the qualities which
specific localities or local milieux provide to support firms, cultivate
new firm formation and attract inward investment. As analysts looked
at the fine grain of the way in which these relations were accomplished
and what firms drew from their localities, it became evident that economic relations were intertwined with the other relations that actors were
involved in, and were shaped by cultural assumptions about appropriate
ways of thinking and ways of acting. Thus, despite the power of
extralocal economic driving forces to shape local circumstances, these
analysts argued that economic activities were embedded in wider social
relations, many of them strongly tied to locality (Granovetter, 1985;
Storper and Scott, 1992; Amin and Thrift, 1994; Belussi, 1996;
Moulaert, 1996; Camagni, 1991; Storper, 1997). They argued that what
made a difference to regional performance was not merely the specific
variations in factors of production (raw materials, sites, labour quality,
technology and specific production knowledge, and so on), or even the
agglomeration economies associated with the qualities of successful
'industrial districts', but the general social and cultural qualities of a
place. Some localities seemed able to draw on qualities of the relationships in a locality, along with reserves of, and attitudes to, knowledge
resources which encouraged adaption, both in firms and in the governance context to support firms. Other localities had difficulty in achieving these changes.

   This turned the spotlight of regional economic development analysis
on local institutional relations and governance capacities. Much of this
work has centred upon the idea of the 'learning region', and the ways in
which innovations – in technology in particular – are dispersed (or not)
within a locality (Camagni, 1991; Asheim, 1996; Hassink, 1997). As
with the more fine-grain work emerging out of regulation theory and
urban regime theory, it focuses on the networks which develop around
innovatory activity and the way learning takes place. The resultant

interpretation of the institutional milieux of local economic activity stresses the significance of the historical 'store' of relational and knowledge resources available to those involved and the significance of the interactive, communicative processes through which trust is built up, relational links are developed and learning is promoted (Storper, 1997; Amin and Thrift, 1995; Asheim, 1996; Moulaert, 1996). This has parallels with three other intellectual developments which reinforce the focus on institutional capacities understood in relational terms. The first is the development of institutional analysis in the discipline of economics itself. This has various strands, not all of which focus on the institutional embedding of the firm. The most interesting of these in terms of the understanding of the governance dynamics of localities is North's analysis of local development 'pathways' (North, 1990; Lambooy and Moulaert, 1996). This emphasises that the way an economy evolves depends on its previous trajectory and the qualities of the various sociocultural resources that have developed in a place over time. In a very similar vein, the second development arises from both the analysis of the social embedding of economic activity and the study of the adaptions of governance relations to new innovations. This focuses on the idea of the 'social capital' which builds up in a locality over time, creating cultural resources which shape contemporary behaviours and make some sorts of adaptions easier than others (Coleman, 1988; Putnam, 1993; Fukuyama, 1995; Lang and Hornburg, 1998). Both these strands of work are rather broad in their analytical sweep, and produce generalisations about qualities and trajectories which are readily contestable through detailed analysis of the qualities of local governance. But they encourage a valuable emphasis on the strength of historical continuity, to offset the regulationist emphasis on transformations and the positive hopes of policy makers trying to turn their local economies around. These ideas also focus attention on the qualities of the broader social relationships and cultural assumptions within which both economic activity and governance efforts are conducted.

The third development which is infusing the 'new institutionalist' interpretation comes from the work of 'communicative' planning theory already referred to. Such theory emphasises how planning work is actually done, set within an intellectual framework which drew ideas from American pragmatists (Harper and Stein, 1995) and Habermasian critical theory (Forester, 1989, 1993; Innes, 1995). This work emphasised how people learn through practising (Schon, 1983) and how, for planners, their activity is inherently a communicative one, through which participants in policy development processes learn about each other and about the problems they face, and develop shared meanings and understandings through which policy co-ordination in a shared-power world could take place (Bryson and Crosby, 1992; Innes, 1992). These ideas feed into the work on conflict mediation and consensus building already referred to.

Much of the focus in communicative planning theory has been on the intricate world of the everyday life of planning practice, that is, at the level of agency. However, there has been an increasing development of this work, to examine how disparate actors in dispersed governance contexts come together to build consensus around difficult local environmental and development issues (Innes, 1992; Innes *et al.,* 1994). This work emphasises the processes of active mobilisation to make changes happen, and the social learning and relation building which occurs through these processes. It directs attention not merely to what institutional capacities there may be in a locality but to the processes through which this capacity gets built and transformed. In this context, Innes and colleagues used notions of three forms of 'capital' to describe the capacities they saw developed: intellectual capital, or knowledge resources; social capital, or relational resources; and political capital, or mobilisation capacity.

By the end of the 1990s, these various strands of analysis were beginning to infuse each other (Healey *et al.,* 1997a; Gualini, 1998; Suh, 1998; Healey, 1997; Muller and Surel, 1998). The analysis of the relational dynamics and trajectories of local milieux in the context of broader forces of structural change provided the basis for contextualising and situating the analyses of what policy actors do, while communicative planning theory had the potential to enrich the understanding of the interactive processes through which relational resources are built, knowledge is developed and diffused, and mobilisation for change is achieved (Healey, 1998b). This encourages analysis which brings structuring dynamics and the worlds of agency together, in the exploration of the way different players mobilise to maintain and change their situations, the constraints they face, the local resources they draw upon and the wider forces which continually push and pull them in different directions. The result is a significant contribution to the development of the rapidly developing 'institutionalist' and interpretive approach to policy analysis generally (Muller and Surel, 1998). In the next section we summarise the main concepts within the 'new institutionalism' and how it links to an analysis of planning practice.

An institutionalist approach to policy analysis and planning practices

By the end of the 1990s, an 'institutionalist' focus was spreading across the social sciences, both conceptually and in empirical research (Powell and Dimagio, 1991; Hall and Taylor, 1996; Amin and Thrift, 1994; Muller and Surel, 1998). The planning field was no exception (Healey, 1997; Healey and Barrett, 1990; Rydin, 1993; von Krabben and Lambooy, 1993; Adams, 1994). In our own work we have sought explicitly to make the links between institutionalist developments in urban and regional analysis and communicative planning theory (Healey, 1997), drawing in particular on sociological theory and cultural anthropology. From the first, we have made use of Giddens' structuration theory (Giddens, 1984). This emphasises the continual interaction between the microsocial practices of daily life and the power relations which are consolidated in the 'abstract systems', or macrosocial dynamics, which shape our lives. Thus planners in practice dealing with a planning application both apply their judgement and sensitivity to the particularity of a case and at the same time draw on their professional training, the ways of thinking which have become normalised in their department, their awareness of what their councillors may do and their appreciation of the rules of the regulatory game. In this way, planners bring these various sources of power to life as active forces and interpret them in particular ways, while themselves being simultaneously channelled by the thought patterns which these 'thinking resources' provide.

Structure is thus not something which is merely an external constraint. It is actively present in the flow of action. This emphasis in structuration theory parallels Foucault's perception that power lies in the micropolitics of daily routines (Rabinow, 1984). Foucault focuses on the task of the critical observer, who aims to uncover the dimensions of this routinised power (its 'archaeology') in the discourses and practices which evolve in different situations. Giddens focuses on the dynamics of the processes through which social life is actively constructed, through the way people interpret the world and their relations with others. In these processes, people draw upon and reinterpret the formal and informal rules governing social relations and situations and deploy material resources of various kinds. Decisions are not taken in a linear fashion from intent to choice, but in a complex, socially structured interaction between acting, perceiving problems which need action and justifying action when taken (Muller and Surel, 1998; Barrett and Fudge, 1981). Giddens argues that the power of structuring driving forces, and the power of agency to reshape these, may be found in the analysis of the manifestation of the rules and resources in play, and the interpretive ideas in contestation in any empirical situation.

This focus links to the work of cultural anthropologists who show how daily practices and specific ceremonies and rituals express and maintain the continuity of cultural assumptions about how the world works and how people should behave (Geertz, 1983; Douglass, 1987). There are also strong parallels in French sociology, particularly the work of Bourdieu on the 'cultural capital' which develops in people's living contexts, their 'habitus' (Bourdieu, 1977; Seidman, 1998), and that of actor-network theorists on the way ideas and technologies developed in one social arena get extended and diffused as they are 'translated' into others. (Callon, 1986; Latour, 1987).

This 'sociological' institutionalism thus focuses on the dynamics of social relations and how these get to be patterned in particular ways, rather than on organisations understood in terms of their formal structures. Power, in this perspective, is understood not simply as 'power over' the actions of others. It is also embodied in the capacity to do things, the power to 'make a difference' (Dyrberg, 1997). With respect to the analysis of governance processes, the approach both emphasises how the relations through which governance activity is produced are tied into relations with the economy and civil society and explores the way in which those involved in governance build up common discourses which develop as 'cultural communities' of their own, with their own ways of thinking and acting. The more links are developed within one grouping, shaping common perceptions and a shared sense of identity, the more differences with other groupings may open up. Thus there are many possible ways in which the 'coherences' and 'permanences' of interest to the regulationist and urban regime theorists may be established.

The concept of 'institution' in this approach has to be distinguished from 'organisation'. In the context of structuration theory, Giddens argues:

> The most important aspects of structure are rules and resources, recursively involved in institutions. Institutions by definition are the more enduring features of social life. In speaking of the structural properties of social systems, I mean their institutionalised features, giving 'solidity' across time and space. (Giddens, 1984, p.24)

Giddens' interest, in developing his structuration theory, is in the relational processes through which institutional forms are produced, rather than the resultant patterns in themselves. He emphasises that these processes of the social making of reality do not occur on an even surface of opportunity. They are structured by the history and geography of what has gone before. As a result, they produce and reproduce uneven patterns of both economic and cultural resources, and of discourses in time and space. Much of the time, people treat the structuring dynamics within which they live as taken for granted, as part of the normal flow of discourse and practice to which they are accustomed. However, Giddens also recognises that people are continually inventive, reinterpreting their inheritance of rules, resources and ideas in new ways, discarding those which are less relevant to them and creating new ones. Thus the power embodied in structuring dynamics is always subject to challenge in the flow of events. The dynamics of power relations cannot simply be 'read off' from an analysis of what a particular constellation of actors and interactions are doing, nor can it be inferred from assumptions about the power which a formal governance position apparently gives to an actor.

Giddens' structuration theory has been subject to considerable criticism, not surprisingly given its ambition to provide a major new perspective on society. Some have objected to the attempt to create a 'grand narrative' about social organisation. Others argue over whether and how the link between 'macro' and 'micro' social processes can be made (Seidman, 1998). Analysts trying to use the theory puzzle over whether it is empirically 'testable' (Layder, 1987) and some social commentators seek greater commitment to social change (Hajer, 1995). However, from the point of view of policy analysis and the study of governance processes, where the explicit concern is to assess how the tools and organisation of responsibility of a policy field 'structure' the flow of action in policy processes, the insights of structuration theory are very helpful. Empirically, they suggest that the nature and scale of change in policy practices may be found in the way rules are established and used, material resources deployed and policy ideas and ways of thinking developed.

These broad ideas from the 'new institutionalism' may thus be recast to provide an approach to the analysis of policy practices. We encapsulate their contribution in the following five points. Firstly, they are founded on a dynamic and relational view of the world, which focuses on the processes through which living and acting are accomplished and how patterns or continuities are established, maintained and changed, rather than seeking to analyse the particular patterns which arise per se. It is assumed that what happens in specific instances is shaped by the particularities of local circumstances as well as broader forces and cannot easily be predicted or generalised about.

Secondly, the approach gives people, as active agents, a key role in shaping and inventing processes of change. It recognises the power of agency along with the power of driving forces. It emphasises that all actors carry with them their networks of relations with others. Every actor network and every interaction between such networks has its own contingencies and generates its own particularities. These actor networks are understood not just as a source of support and a means of getting access to specific resources for network members. They are relations of power, obligation and understandings which structure how actors think and act. Complex policy problems typically touch the lives of many people and echo through multiple networks, each with their particular social worlds and mores. The activity of developing and changing policy may itself create such cultural 'policy communities'. Analytically, this focuses attention on the nodal points in networks, the arenas where ideas are generated, and on mobilisation initiatives aimed at changing discourses or networks.

Thirdly, institutionalist analysis takes for granted that the social worlds of people in formal agencies of government are intertwined with wider social forces, embedding governance processes in the wider relations of economic activity and civil society. This focuses analytical attention on the way people in different policy communities construct their identities in relation to others and what they consider are significant boundaries. These processes of identity construction in turn help to frame how issues are perceived and repertoires of action are called upon. They also shape the kinds of relationships which governance actors build upon and how they go about developing and maintaining their relational resources.

Fourthly, the approach puts a major emphasis on the analysis of policy ideas and the often taken for granted frames of reference used by members of particular 'cultural communities'. Such frames of reference are critical in understanding how policy discourses carry authority through being structured and institutionalised (Hajer, 1995). This does not mean that discursive practices displace a consideration of regulatory and resource allocation practices. Instead, it means that the relation between meanings and ways of thinking must be seen as integral to the way policy communities consider rules and resources. Policy innovation is thus not just about the formal design of regulatory legislation and resource allocation systems: it also involves changing the discourses in all arenas which are significant for that policy to have effect. Thus a policy change which involves a new rhetoric in policy statements but which does not change the discourses and practices of those who carry through a policy will have limited power to 'make a difference'.

Finally, the approach provides an empirical way of seeing how the power of external forces is made manifest in specific instances, and the extent to which these influences are accepted, reinterpreted and struggled over. Analytically, such forces can be identified through the rules, resource allocations and frames of reference which participants draw on, remould and invent in the flow of their thinking and acting.

Policy discourses, policy communities and policy arenas

In what follows we seek to provide accounts of the social worlds of strategic spatial planning practices, in order to assess how far these are changing and in what directions. From our knowledge of the broad conceptual developments in social theory discussed above, we focus our accounts on two dimensions of these practices. The first emphasises the substantive policy content, the issues under discussion, the conflicts and debates between points of view and the way these get expressed in different contexts, including formal plans and policy statements. This dimension emphasises the policy agendas which get developed and the policy discourses through which these agendas are constructed. This helps to identify how the purposes of policy practices are interpreted, maintained and changed. Through the second dimension, we focus on processes, the social relations which underlie the production of these agendas and the use of these discourses. We consider the actors who are involved in policy practices, the networks and policy communities they relate to, and their relation to the wider universe of stakeholders, those with a 'stake' in a policy issue (Bryson and Crosby, 1992). We also identify the nodal points in these networks of relationships in policy practices, the key policy arenas where discourses are developed and how they are disseminated. We are concerned with the extent to which these arenas include or exclude the various stakeholders. This helps to illustrate the significance of the connections between informal arenas and the formal responsibilities and tools of the planning system.

We return to the concepts of policy discourses, policy communities and policy arenas in Part III. We now 'travel' to the worlds of planning practice. How far are planners and planning policy communities involved in spatial alliance formation and strategy development efforts in localities? How significant are the arenas of the planning system in developing and disseminating new agendas? How far are the practices which bring the planning system to life generating new discourses to shape policy agendas? Perhaps these practices are merely arenas for the interpretation of discourse innovations developed elsewhere or are a completely separate institutional nexus which is merely a regulatory constraint on the mobilisation activities of other alliances in localities? Do the practices of the planning system reflect any stable and enduring approach to dealing with the difficult issues of the location of development and the use of land? Can a coherent policy 'regime' be identified?

To investigate these issues, we present empirical material undertaken in three different parts of England: Lancashire in the north west, the West Midlands conurbation centred on Birmingham, and Kent in south east England. The policy agendas and policy communities with a potential stake in strategic spatial planning in these areas are very broad. We have therefore limited our attention to four clearly identifiable subfields of strategic policy. Each represents a focus of sectoral policy attention, following the dominant tendencies in British subnational governance identified in the previous chapter. As developed in the three areas, each has provided a window through which to explore the social relations of spatial strategy-making practice. The first is the allocation of sites for housing development. The second is the allocation of sites for what is variously known as employment-generating development, business development or economic development. The third is the determination of major transport investment policies and projects and the fourth is the location of waste disposal sites.

These windows of inquiry serve as starting points for our accounts. Our objective is to explore the extent to which, in each area, the social relations of planning practice are stretching out to engage in wider relations to other policy communities and policy arenas in which spatial strategy issues may be discussed. At the same time, we look into the arenas specifically associated with the planning system to see how far they are used and valued by the other policy communities involved in strategic spatial planning and how effectively they are related to the arenas where such strategic work takes place. Before moving on to these accounts, the next chapter provides a brief introduction to the three localities of our investigation.

Part II

PLANNING, GOVERNANCE AND SPATIAL STRATEGY

3 Planning and Governance in Three Localities

Three windows into English local governance

Institutional histories, local knowledge resources and the legacies of past policies imply that local planning practice will vary from place to place. In addition, national policies will be interpreted and acted upon in different ways in different places. This chapter sets out background information on the three localities from which most of the empirical material in the book is taken, setting the context for the detailed examination of strategy making that follows. The localities were selected to illustrate different configurations of issues and different governance relations. For each we provide outlines of socioeconomic characteristics, administrative structures and major development projects. This chapter also takes a preliminary look at the range of stakeholders involved in governance, their policy agendas and the arenas in which policy is discussed in each area. Details of the planning framework in the three areas are also sketched and some preliminary conclusions drawn as we move into the more detailed empirical material.

There are many ways in which localities may be identified. Given the purposes of our inquiry, we have used administrative areas. Our localities constitute two areas governed by county councils, Kent and Lancashire, and also the former West Midlands Metropolitan County Council area, now formally administered by unitary authorities (see Figure 3.1). Our discussion of stakeholders and policy agendas focuses primarily on these levels. The county level provides the 'window' into the case studies. Policies at lower tiers of government and the way these interact with higher-level policies are explored in the issue-based chapters later in Part II.

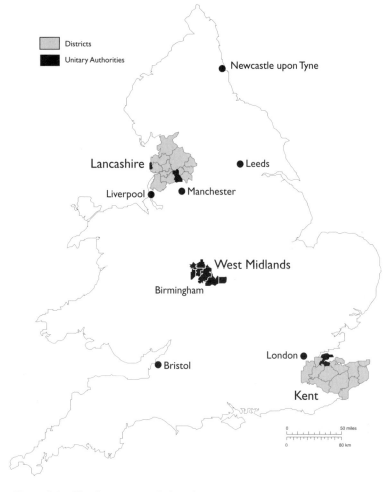

Figure 3.1   The three case study locations

Socioeconomic and administrative contexts

Kent

Kent occupies a position of considerable strategic importance. It acts as the 'land bridge' for much of the UK into Europe. This county of 1.5 million people is experiencing increased development interest as people and companies move to capture the opportunities this brings. As a consequence many felt that the county was shifting as a place from being a 'peninsula to a corridor' (county planner). The proximity of London exacerbates the pressures on this historic shire county with its range of sensitive physical environments. These pressures, coupled with local economic difficulties in certain localities, create some interesting policy dilemmas for the county council, the 12 district councils and the one unitary authority.

Although no single settlement dominates in labour market or commercial terms, Maidstone is the administrative centre of the county and is home to Kent County Council and Maidstone Borough Council. A considerable proportion of the county's labour force is drawn to London, particularly from west Kent, despite a concentration of employment opportunity in and around Maidstone itself. Much of the rest of the county consists of small, relatively self-contained local economies. The current administrative boundaries of the county illustrated in Figure 3.2 are, in common with many others in the UK, thus based on historical factors and bear little relation to labour markets or land markets.

Kent is widely regarded as a prosperous county, but this perception is a partial picture. Table 3.1 illustrates that gross domestic product (GDP) per head was below both the UK national average and the average for the south east of England. The unemployment rate in the county is consistently higher than elsewhere in the region. The County can be divided into three distinct areas in local economic terms: mid- and west Kent, north Kent and east Kent. The three divisions also represent the political divisions in the county. Prosperous mid- and west Kent sustain the conventional image of the county, with an attractive landscape,

Table 3.1   Gross domestic product for Kent
in comparative context

Geographical area	GDP per capita 1996, (£)
UK	8481
Rest of South East	9949
Kent	8278
Mid- and West Kent	9126
North Kent	7696
East Kent	7839

Source: Kent County Council (1996).

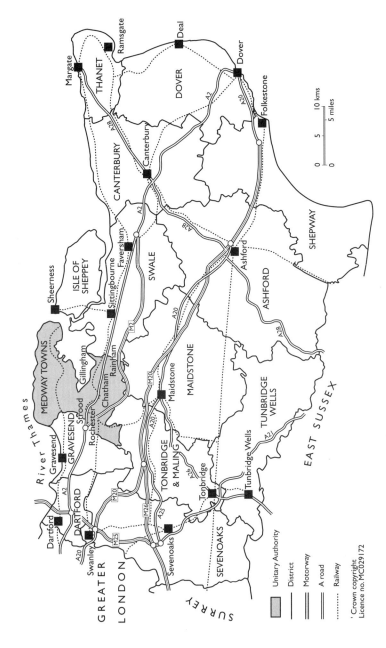

Figure 3.2   Administrative boundaries, communications infrastructure and main towns in Kent

Conservative members of parliament and incomes boosted by a large number of commuters into central London. North and east Kent tend to elect Labour and Liberal Democrat politicians and are economically less buoyant.

This poor economic performance in east and north Kent resulted from a number of factors: the closure of the east Kent coalfield; long-standing agricultural decline in north-east Kent; the demise of maritime and extractive industries in the north of the county; the decline of coastal tourism; a concentration of employment in some under performing manufacturing sectors; and a predominance of small firms who find it difficult to capture new commercial opportunities (KCC, 1996). The resulting unemployment has been a contributory factor to various social problems in these less prosperous areas. Indeed, some wards in the east Kent ports were, throughout the 1990s, amongst the most deprived in the south-east of England, including inner London. Concern existed for the economic future of such areas and the maintenance of social cohesion in these places. These economic conditions led to the designation of four east Kent districts (Dover, Shepway, Swale and Thanet) as an assisted area in UK regional policy in December 1993, and Thanet as an area for assistance under Objective 2 of the European Regional Development Fund.

Kent is unique amongst our case study areas and in the UK as a whole in terms of two major regional developments. First, the Thames Gateway regeneration initiative, an ad hoc project begun in the early 1990s, sought to shift development pressure from west of London to the east. This shift provided a hitherto absent land-use planning focus on the area. It also sought to use brownfield development to take the pressure off greenfield sites in Kent and the rest of the south east of England.

The second major development was the Channel Tunnel Rail Link (CTRL), planned to provide for rapid movement between London and Europe. Many stakeholders in Kent were concerned that it would pass through the county while doing little for its economy, particularly the weak economies of north and east Kent. At the same time, it was feared that it would damage the built and natural environment and contribute to congestion on existing infrastructure. Considerable lobbying efforts on the part of Kent members of parliament, the county council, elements in the private sector and some districts proved vital in securing stations on the CTRL at Ashford and Ebbsfleet, and obtaining investment in complementary road infrastructure, to try and capture some of the potential benefits of the activity flowing through the Channel Tunnel into the UK.

The location of the two CTRL stations was seen locally as vital in capturing possible benefits for north and east Kent, and possibly changed the economic development potential of the two areas considerably. The Ebbsfleet station, in tandem with the Thames Gateway initiative, created the potential to transform north-west Kent, from an area where a poor physical environment was partly responsible for weak development markets, low rents, low land values and low levels of investment by owners and tenants to one with considerable appeal to a range of users attracted by its proximity and connections to opportunities in mainland Europe and the south-east of England. A new initiative, 'Kent Thames-side' (see below), aims to provide a coherent focus for a range of commercial and housing developments in the vicinity of the Ebbsfleet station and beyond.

In east Kent, Ashford has been designated in regional guidance as a growth point for the county and the south-east of England since the mid-1970s. The markets for housing and employment land have, however, been fairly weak despite this status. The CTRL station potentially transforms local land markets, although there is some concern that development in Ashford will do little to solve the economic and social problems of the rest of east Kent.

Lancashire

Lancashire, like Kent, is one of the historic shire counties of England and contributes 1.4 million people to the north-west standard planning region, a region dominated by the two conurbations of Manchester and Liverpool (see Figure 3.3). Postwar population growth in Lancashire has been particularly concentrated around the former Central Lancashire New Town area (comprising the settlements of Preston, Leyland and Chorley).

Preston is the administrative centre of the county, with both Lancashire County Council and Preston Borough Council based there. Lancashire consists of 11 district authorities and two unitary authorities based on the former districts of Blackpool and Blackburn. Lancashire's urban centres have a strong Labourist tradition. Lancashire County Council has been in the control of the Labour Party for many years and the majority of the county constituencies consistently return Labour members of parliament.

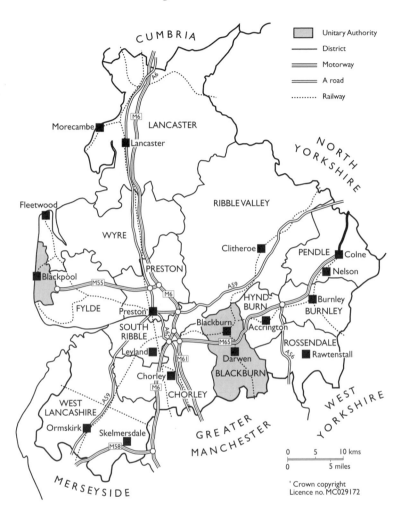

Figure 3.3   Administrative boundaries, communications infrastructure and main towns in Lancashire

In the 1980s and 1990s, the north-west region, in common with many other parts of the UK, suffered extensive loss of employment in manufacturing industry, with consequent social and environmental problems. A greater dependence on defence-related industries than in the north-west as a whole partly cushioned Lancashire from the processes of economic restructuring in the 1970s and 1980s. Since then, however, defence industry restructuring has affected many local economies, and the county is eligible for funds under the European Union's KONVER initiative to aid the restructuring process. Lancashire's GDP in 1995 was 89 per cent of the UK average (Office for National Statistics, 1998).

Lancashire divides into a number of distinct areas. Central Lancashire around Preston has relied traditionally on defence industries and vehicle production. East Lancashire suffers from high unemployment associated with decline in the textile industries and relatively poor access to transport infrastructure, at least until the M65 was completed in 1996. Blackburn had a City Challenge team under national urban regeneration policy funds in the 1990s and, along with other parts of east Lancashire, was eligible for EU Objective 2 structural funds (see

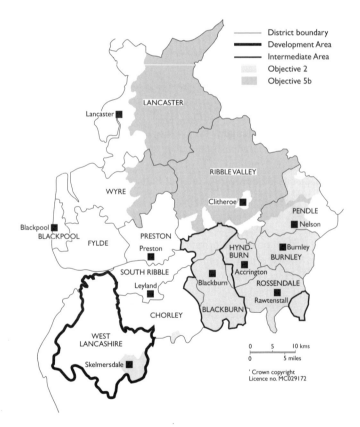

Figure 3.4   Regional policy funding eligibility in Lancashire, 1994-99

Figure 3.4). Blackburn, Burnley and Preston were all eligible for Urban Programme monies throughout the 1990s.

North and west Lancashire have mixed local economies, with a significant agricultural element. In addition, tourism is an important economic activity on the Fylde coast, centred on Blackpool. Parts of southwest Lancashire form a component of the Merseyside travel-to-work area and are eligible for EU Objective 2 funds. The two ports of Fleetwood and Heysham play a significant role in providing links between the UK, Ireland and mainland Europe. Chemical industries, electricity generation, agriculture and forestry are also significant employers. Lancaster is a historic town which suffers, along with Morecambe and the port of Heysham, from being peripheral to the major markets in the region. Partly as a result, the Lancaster travel to work area had the highest unemployment rate in Lancashire in the mid-1990s.

Overall, despite the growth of service industries, around Preston in particular, the Lancashire economy is considered to have many vulnerable large companies and relatively weak growth in new companies (Taylor, 1994). The winding up and sale of former New Town sites in Central Lancashire and Skelmersdale has exacerbated problems over the redevelopment of sites left vacant following defence industry restructuring, whilst demand for employment land in the north of the county remains low. Lancashire is also peripheral to markets in Europe and the south of England. All of these factors influence the policy responses discussed below and later in Part II.

West Midlands

Our focus in this locality is primarily upon the area of the former West Midlands Metropolitan County Council within the wider West Midlands Region (Figure 3.5). This area is predominantly urban in character and administered by seven unitary metropolitan authorities which tend to be Labour Party-controlled. In 1991, the West Midlands metropolitan area had a population of 2.7 million out of a total in the wider West Midlands standard planning region of just over 5 million. From the 1970s to the late 1990s, the conurbation suffered from the decentralisation of population and economic activity to the surrounding region. Stemming this flow of people and activity provided a major focus for policy in the conurbation in the 1990s. In its administrative structure and geographical form the West Midlands provides us with a very different case from our other two areas.

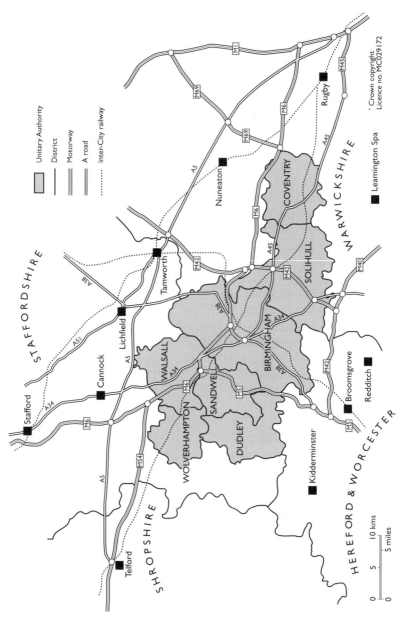

Figure 3.5 The West Midlands conurbation

The perception of the West Midlands as the manufacturing heartland of Britain still has some validity. Motor vehicle industries are a significant employer, although economic restructuring hit this sector hard in the 1980s. The vehicle industry's presence and the conurbation's position at the heart of major rail and road intersections heighten the influence of transport in policy discussions.

As a result of employment decline in manufacturing industry, virtually all of the West Midlands metropolitan area was eligible for EU Objective 2 structural funds and UK Urban Programme monies in the 1990s. GDP per head for the former Metropolitan County Council area stood at 96 per cent of the UK average in 1995 (Office for National Statistics, 1998). Economic and social problems in parts of the conurbation resulted in the designation of two Urban Development Corporations and two City Challenge initiatives in the 1990s.

We might usefully distinguish between three distinct areas of the conurbation. As in Kent, the GDP figure for the whole conurbation masks significant differences in socioeconomic conditions within it. For example, Birmingham and Sandwell districts are considered amongst the 10 most deprived districts in the country according to UK government criteria (ibid.), whilst other areas are very prosperous. Birmingham occupies a pivotal position. The city has reoriented itself, with some success, towards being a major commercial centre in a European context. Whilst this reorientation has 'knock-on' effects in the wider metropolitan area, this sort of diversification has little potential in the second distinct area, the Black Country, a collection of industrial towns occupying the western half of the conurbation which still has a predominantly manufacturing base. The third area of the conurbation, Coventry, is in many ways less integrated into the conurbation than the other metropolitan districts, being separated from the main area of the conurbation by a substantial area of undeveloped, green belt-designated land. Coventry also has a strong manufacturing tradition, however. Coventry and Solihull Borough experienced considerable development pressure in the 1980s and 1990s arising from the concentration of transport links (air, rail and road) in the area.

The governance context: major stakeholders, alliances and arenas

Each locality has its own specific governance landscape and dynamics. This section looks beyond the formal organisation of government towards the participation of other stakeholders. It considers the arenas where policy is discussed and looks briefly at the formal alliances which have developed to shape policy agendas in each area. More detailed institutional history and its consequences for the development of policy are presented where appropriate later in Part II. This section sets the scene for these discussions.

Kent

Beyond local government in Kent a number of agencies played a central role in the discussion of spatial strategy in the county. The regional body of local authorities, in this case the South East Regional Planning Conference (SERPLAN), performed a strategic role, principally through the development of regional planning guidance (see below). Also at the regional level, although working across an area which excludes London, the Government Office for the South East (GOSE) is organised on a matrix system based upon issues and geographic areas and as a consequence had a specific team responsible for Kent. Other regional groupings are important to Kent. The South-East Assembly is a member-led initiative developed in the mid-1990s as a fledgling regional governance body. The coherence of such regional groupings in the south-east was not as strong as those of the north-west and the West Midlands. This resulted in part from the scale of the south-east region and the dominance of London situated at the region's heart. Kent County Council did, however, look to Europe to form alliances, and became part of a 'Euroregion' including Nord–Pas de Calais and the three regions of Belgium.

Kent had significant environmental lobbies which garnered considerable grassroots support, particularly in terms of landscape and amenity protection and the defence of the green belt. This support operated on a fairly ad hoc basis, partly through groups such as the Council for the Protection of Rural England (CPRE) and English Nature, but also through less formal contacts and personal relations with Westminster and Whitehall as well as with local authorities. Examples of this influence are reported later in Part II. The CPRE operated at a county-wide level with salaried staff, and also on a volunteer basis at local levels through area offices. The environmental lobby appeared to be more active in mid- and west Kent than in the north and east of the county. In part related to a strong agricultural lobby based loosely upon Wye College. Such interests were turning up more frequently in land-use planning arenas in the county, in relation both to sites, projects and development plans.

Kent business was involved in governance through a variety of mechanisms, most notably the Kent Chamber of Commerce which provided an umbrella representation for local chambers. Local chambers of commerce were not strongly involved in spatial strategy making compared to our other areas, particularly the West Midlands. Chambers in Kent tended to get more involved in 'one-off' projects. Thus the Shepway Chamber was very active in support of a Rank Oasis leisure development at Lyminge Forest and in developing links to organisations in the Euroregion. Local chambers of commerce and training and enterprise councils often tended to bypass local authorities and liaise directly with central government and its regional office over issues such as training schemes. Property interests and major business players also proved to be active in strategy-making arenas, in part through an Economic Forum comprising business and local government representation which was set up in the mid-1990s, prompted by the county council's economic development department. Perhaps the most important business interest in the 1990s in such forums and discussions was Blue Circle Industries (BCI) which was a significant landowner in north Kent, as well as a major employer.

Social interests were poorly represented in spatial strategy-making arenas. Some examples of strategy making associated with nationally funded regeneration initiatives (the Single Regeneration Budget in particular), Local Agenda 21 and development plans drew in stakeholders with a social agenda. Shepway District Council and Ashford Borough Council were particularly active in attempts to do this, but generally the social agenda was poorly articulated.

Public–private partnership working was represented principally through three examples of regeneration work. First, the East Kent Initiative (EKI) was a partnership charged with securing investment in east Kent in response to some of the economic issues noted above and as a result of the potential impact of the Channel Tunnel on Kent's local economies (Ball, 1995). Besides local government, British Telecom, P&O Ferries, Eurotunnel, Kent Training and Enterprise Council, the Port of Dover and central government through the Employment Service were all involved.

Second, in north Kent a public–private partnership, North Kent Success (NKS), was set up in 1994 to promote the area, and more particularly to capture the opportunities of the Single European Market, the Channel Tunnel and the Thames Gateway initiative (See figure 3.6). It built on, and extended the remit of, the work of the North Kent Joint

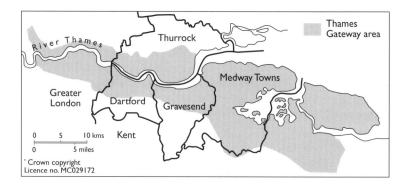

Figure 3.6   The Thames Gateway Area

Consultative Committee, a local authority grouping. NKS involved five district councils, Kent County Council (KCC) and a large number of public, private and voluntary organisations. English Partnerships were extensively involved in this area, especially in the former Chatham Dockyard as part of a major regeneration project within the Thames Gateway initiative.

Third, the major landowner in north Kent, Blue Circle Industries, joined with the two districts of north-west Kent, KCC and the University of Greenwich to create the Kent Thames-side Partnership. The Partnership aimed to capture the possibilities for transforming the area following the construction of the Ebbsfleet international passenger rail station. Many commentators were sceptical about the designation of the Ebbsfleet station in the mid-1990s and the links between business and government. Certainly, the station provides the potential to transform local land markets (see Hull and Vigar, 1998).

The partnership produced a consultation document (KTP, 1995) outlining its vision for the area. In summary the strategy involves the construction of 14 000 homes, 1.5 million square feet of employment uses, new areas of open space and a science park by 2020. A light rapid transit system is also mooted. The strategy involves a complete reorientation of the area as it is intended that the new Bluewater Retail Park will become the central focus for the area rather than the two existing town centres of Dartford and Gravesham. Further aspects of the Partnership's intentions are explored later in Part II.

Thus we see a changed governance system emerging in Kent. New and relatively autonomous partnerships were contributing significantly to improving economic conditions in the north and east of the county and taking on roles typically associated with the public sector alone. Environmental lobbies were strong, with a long history of 'defending the green belt'. There is less capacity-building activity at the regional and indeed county level than in our other two cases, however.

Lancashire

In the 1990s, politicians in Lancashire County Council, after many years of neglecting regional links, sought to position the council as a key regional actor. In the early 1990s, many Labour Party-controlled local authorities in the north-west sought to secure stronger regional coherence, principally in order to benefit more from EU regional funding. In this way they hoped to bypass a perceived hostility in Conservative national governments toward its arguments and ideology, and help secure local economic objectives. Partly as a result of these factors, the North West Regional Association (NWRA) was established in 1992, comprising representatives of the region's three county councils and a number of district councils (see Wannop, 1995).

Business interests in the region also saw the benefits of regional partnership working at this time. The North West Business Leadership Team (NWBLT), a consortium of the top 30 private sector companies in the region, was formed in 1989 to promote the long-term prosperity of the region through pressing central government for improved transport infrastructure, promoting inward investment, lobbying to lever in investment to the region from the UK government, the European Union and private sector sources, and strategic support for a variety of key projects in the region. Together NWBLT and NWRA sponsored the preparation of a *Regional Economic Strategy* (Pieda, 1993) and worked with NWRA to produce a *Regional Transport Strategy for North West England* (NWRA/NWBLT, 1993). This vision was launched in Brussels in 1994 before an audience of European members of parliament and UK government officials.

The public and private sectors came together under the umbrella of the North West Partnership (NWP) which was established in 1995 to provide a common platform and discussion arena for business interests (through the NWBLT) and local government interests (through the NWRA). NWP was also used as a vehicle to bring public, private and voluntary sectors together to co-ordinate and secure investment.

In relation to the promotion of economic competitiveness agendas, two other stakeholders were of significance in debates over spatial strategy. The chambers of commerce were present, but, as in the Kent case, appeared to concern themselves more with issues of business support and ad hoc regeneration activities where appropriate. More significant in debates over spatial strategy was Enterprise plc (formerly Lancashire Enterprises Ltd). Enterprise plc was originally contained within Lancashire County Council (LCC) but became a semi-public agency in 1982. It became a public company in 1989 to gain financial and operational flexibility and avoid increased government regulation in the economic development arena. At this time it adjusted its operational focus to specialise in investment promotion, property management, training and consultancy. The county council put a lot of political and financial resources into Enterprise plc, and its involvement in one particular economic development debate is described in depth in Chapter 5. Enterprise plc's influence in Lancashire, and particularly with the county council, both in economic development and in other policy areas, should not be underestimated. Much of this influence derives from its position as an insider within LCC and in the agenda of economic competitiveness it shares with LCC.

There were no examples of area-focused regeneration partnerships, as in Kent for example, apart from those linked to specific Urban Programme projects. This deficit is perhaps partly explained by the strong position of Enterprise plc, and also by the problems being defined as 'inner-urban', that is associated with towns rather than larger areas, as in the Kent case. This urban focus tended to encompass social issues which were then closely tied into a 'jobs' agenda. Beyond this, social issues were not well articulated in spatial strategy-making debates although the county council was very proactive in relation to such issues in other policy areas.

The environmental lobby in Lancashire had a similar profile to that in Kent. The CPRE was the main organisation involved in land-use issues. Lancashire Wildlife Trust and Friends of the Earth local groups were also active, particularly in relation to transport issues (see Chapter 6). The latter's involvement in spatial strategy making was patchy, depending upon the resources and commitment of one or two active volunteers. Public agencies such as English Nature and the Countryside Commission also featured in spatial strategy-making debates.

Lancashire County Council became increasingly interested in environmental matters in the late 1980s, in part because its then leader was looking for issues around which to contest local elections. From this somewhat opportunist start, LCC became a leading local authority in the UK in addressing environmental issues. A key element in this approach is the Lancashire Environment Forum, which is frequently cited as a model for other areas in attempting to build capacity to tackle environmental issues (Selman, 1996). Set up in 1989, by 1997 it embraced over 100 organisations including utility companies, representatives of transport organisations, local authorities, national and local environmental organisations, and agricultural interests. It attempts to build agreement on the parameters of a sustainable future. The emphasis is on collectively identifying environmental improvements, both those which participants can implement themselves and specific actions to be addressed by higher tiers of government and other key actors. The work of the Forum led to the production of a Green Audit and follow-up study (LCC, 1991; LCC, 1997a) and the *Lancashire Environmental Action Programme* (LEAP), (LEF, 1993). The Forum's agenda was broadening in the late 1990s to include social issues through a quality of life approach. This broadening is discussed in more detail later in this chapter.

Thus Lancashire's governance culture underwent a period of rapid change in the 1990s. The county council moved from being an inward-looking paternalist Labour authority to an active networker in regional arenas, promoting the county and the region in Europe. At the same time it became a leading UK local authority in the translation of an emergent environmental agenda into policy action. Renewed public sector interest in the regional level was mirrored in the business community.

West Midlands

By contrast with the other two areas, the regional context has occupied a strong position in spatial strategy in the West Midlands for some time. The region has a strong identity reinforced through a prominant regional Local Government Association, formerly the West Midlands Regional Forum (WMRF). The Forum had a long history of activity in a number of areas; in relation to the West Midlands presence in an EU context, in the production of policy and spatial strategy, and in a brokerage capacity amongst the local authorities. The Forum was also thought to perform a useful function in balancing the interests of Birmingham City Council with the other metropolitan authorities. Its importance appeared to increase following the abolition of the West

Midlands County Council in 1986. The levels of trust and subsequent capacity to act that have been built up over time were a major benefit to the region in achieving co-ordination: '[as] an outsider you will have difficulty in understanding [the] trust and ways of working at various levels and networking between people. Joint committees, chief officers' groups are all of long standing. That makes us unique' (district planner).

Business in the West Midlands was comparatively well represented in discussions of spatial strategy through a number of agencies and partnerships, perhaps owing to the coherent industrial base of the past. The Chambers of Commerce across the conurbation played significant roles in such debates. The Birmingham Chamber of Commerce and Industry (BCI) performed a regional co-ordination role amongst the local chambers and its director was a key nodal figure in many discussions between business, government and the voluntary sector and in providing a business voice in urban policy initiatives.

The West Midlands Regional Economic Consortium was an important alliance where a number of interests, such as the regional Confederation of British Industry, local government through the WMRF, members of European and national parliaments, unions through the Trades Union Congress and quangos such as the Training and Enterprise Councils, came together to discuss issues and develop strategies. It did a lot of work in relation to lobbying for transport infrastructure such as the West Coast Main Rail Line and the Birmingham Northern Relief Road (see Chapter 6). It has also been the body through which strategic employment sites have been determined (see Chapter 5).

Environmental interests were poorly articulated by comparison. The environmental voice present in Kent was less prevalent in the West Midlands and local authorities were slower to incorporate environmental issues in policy outputs than in Lancashire. However, the West Midlands Regional Forum took on an environmental role in the mid-1990s, and environment forums at regional level and in some districts proved to be important places for environmental groups to meet local authorities and business. Despite initial conflict between environmentalists and business, the forums have proved to be useful exercises in debating issues and sharing understanding: 'I nearly walked away as environmental extremists targeted business representatives. [I] stayed on board and now people are less hostile and more attuned to compromise than they were' (business representative).

In more general terms, however, environmental issues were slow to get leverage in comparison with our two other areas, and the WMRF was reluctant to discuss issues with environmental groups until it had formulated its own ideas as to how environmental issues should be tackled. The green belt was strongly defended, however, and Friends of the Earth were active at local levels in the conurbation, although they were stronger in certain parts than others, reflecting the presence of local activists in particular places.

Social interests were articulated in ad hoc regeneration forums and are present, although largely implicitly, in the long-standing discourse of urban regeneration which pervades much of the conurbation's spatial strategy. Many local government officers were deeply concerned about the articulation of social issues in spatial strategy making. Proactive efforts were made by these officers to involve community representatives in regional guidance preparation, for example.

In summary, the West Midlands governance culture involved a well-developed public sector network, with significant representation of business voice. Through the 1990s, the policy agenda slowly widened to encompass environmental issues.

Policy agendas: the driving forces of territorial strategy making

This section briefly reviews the general policy agendas of the major stakeholders to assess how they address economic, environmental and social issues. The section therefore examines the issues preoccupying the governance cultures described above.

Kent

The driving forces behind spatial strategy making in Kent in the 1990s varied across the county broadly in line with the socioeconomic concerns outlined above. It is clear that in mid- and west Kent there was a long-standing concern for landscape protection, and the green belt was vigorously defended. In addition, the county is overlaid with a number of protected area designations (see Figure 3.7) including a number of sensitive geological environments often associated with the underlying chalk.

Kent County Council (KCC) was one of a number of UK local authorities which recognised the wider environmental and social

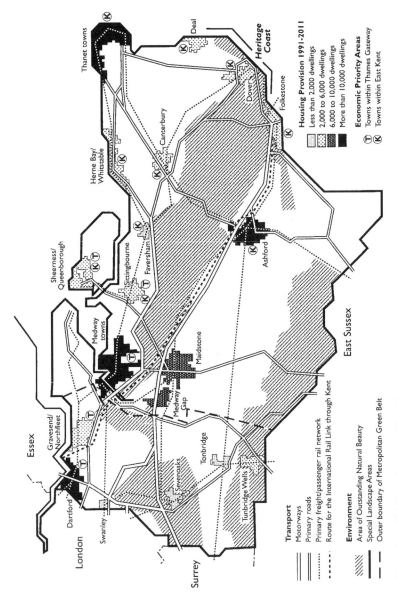

Figure 3.7 The 1994 Kent Structure Plan Strategy

implications associated with sustainable development. Driven by pressure from the public and from some of its officers, KCC attempted to put environmental issues at the heart of policy making. Such environmental concerns were reflected in some of the policy outputs of the districts, although this is variable across the county. District authorities with a history of landscape protectionism were in advance of others in the county in embracing wider environmental concerns and in making environmental concerns the key driving force in the production of development plans.

Economic competitiveness has also long been an important policy driver, particularly in north and east Kent. The 1984 Structure Plan put economic growth as its primary objective in recognition of Kent's poor economic performance relative to the rest of the south-east of England. More recently, KCC recognised that the Channel Tunnel and CTRL presented a set of threats, as well as opportunities, to the Kent economy. Concerns over the structure of local economies, and the decline in certain industries referred to above, also contributed to an emphasis on 'jobs' issues. These emphases tended towards a division of the planning framework, with development directed towards north and east Kent, and a strong regulatory policy of development restraint in mid- and west Kent. This strategy meshed well with local politics in that there was political pressure to create employment opportunities in north and east Kent whilst the local politics of mid- and west Kent favoured development restraint.

The representation of social issues in spatial strategy was weak across all our case studies. National government gave little encouragement to the recognition of such issues in the 1980s and 1990s. However, in north and east Kent, concern for residents in very deprived wards was reflected both in the organisation and in the policy outputs of local authorities such as Shepway District Council. Such issues were, however, often poorly articulated in development plans and in other aspects of spatial strategy making.

The influence of Europe and the EU on the approach of stakeholders to issues and policy is strong and wide-ranging. With money from central government becoming harder to obtain, KCC led the way in the region in looking to the EU for finance. Kent districts, often in partnership with KCC, have acquired monies under a range of EU initiatives: the European Social Fund, INTERREG and the European Regional Development Fund. The proximity of Kent to Europe partly explains this and links were multiple and well-developed: '[it] wouldn't surprise me if we just didn't cut our relations with England completely. I go to Tesco in Boulogne once a month, never been to Manchester [for example] in my life, [I] don't want to' (KCC employee).

Lancashire

A key driving force, unique in the way it was articulated amongst our case studies, was the extent to which Lancashire County Council (LCC) and other local stakeholders saw the county as being 'peripheral', in relation to markets in the south-east of England and continental Europe. This feeling of peripherality was partly responsible for efforts at region building in the 1990s. It was also reflected in spatial strategy which sought to emphasise 'first-class transport links' to Europe and the south-east of England (Pieda, 1993). This emphasis led LCC into extensive lobbying for improvements to the West Coast rail network and for major road building in the county (see Chapter 6). The concern about peripherality was driven by a desire to keep Lancashire economically competitive. The dominance of this agenda in LCC activities led to direct conflicts with emerging environmental agendas (Hull *et al.*, 1996).

Throughout the 1990s, Lancashire County Council was at the forefront of UK planning authorities in its approach to environmental issues. Initial interest in environmental issues came from local politicians looking for issues with significant political leverage with which to fight elections. The issue of bathing water quality and waste water sea outfalls near to its tourist beaches provided this focus. Since then, LCC's environmental agenda has broadened considerably, first with an environmental audit carried out by the county's Environmental Unit (within the Planning Department) in 1989. This audit brought together data on environmental components (geological structure, air, water, waste, noise, energy, land and agriculture, wildlife, landscape and townscape, open space and transport) and assessed their interaction. This information was widely disseminated through a *Green Audit* (LCC, 1991) and through computerised software available in libraries and schools. Second, the Lancashire Environmental Action Programme (LEF, 1993) looked to implement measures to conserve aspects of the county's environment. This work was guided by the Lancashire Environment Forum (see above).

In the mid-1990s, debates in these local environmental arenas led to a further broadening of the agenda of the LEF to include social issues within a 'quality of life' focus. The social agenda had been an issue in spatial strategy making previously, but more in the context of employment issues and bound up in a discourse of urban regeneration. The quality of life/environmental justice agenda became a major force in the outputs and workings of the county council, as evidenced in the update of the *Green Audit*, for example (LCC, 1997a). It led to the closer integration of social issues into spatial strategy making. In this regard Lancashire is ahead of the other two areas in the incorporation of both environmental and social agendas into spatial strategy. The quality of life agenda appeared to be driven largely by officers within the authority as they assessed the implications of a sustainability agenda for citizens. Pressure for the incorporation of social and environmental issues into Lancashire's strategies did not appear to be strong outside local government, although it did arise over certain issues, such as road building (see Chapter 6), and specific housing and employment land allocations (see Chapters 4 and 5).

West Midlands

The West Midlands conurbation has a long-standing history of urban regeneration-focused spatial strategy-making. In the 1990s this focus was driven by a number of economic and social concerns: for reversing the decline in manufacturing industry; for stemming continuing population and employment decentralisation from the urban core into surrounding shire districts; and concern also for the quality of life of residents in the conurbation. The social agenda was well articulated in the region compared with our other two areas. It was centrally concerned with the provision of jobs and as such deeply enmeshed with a concern for the economic competitiveness of the conurbation, the two agendas coming together in a discourse of urban regeneration. As in the Lancashire case, although perhaps not as pronounced, concern over peripherality to markets in Europe was also prevalent in strategy documents. This filtered into policy outputs and in particular an emphasis on maintaining congestion-free interurban transport links.

Environmental issues were something of an 'add-on' to this regeneration focus, backed by a belief that the existing strategy was, to a large extent, 'sustainable'. Improving the environment was seen as being 'closely linked to economic activity levels. By improving the environment the city will be more attractive to investment' (district planner). This attitude reflects a narrow view of the environment. It privileges the physical attractiveness of sites and landscapes over other environmental concerns as it views the 'environment' as a series of assets to mobilise as a lever for investment purposes. This perception was much narrower than the conceptions of the environment employed in our other two case studies.

There were indications that the environmental agenda was gaining in influence and a deeper understanding of what sustainable development might mean for spatial strategy making was emerging. This was observable in regional arenas and those created as part of Local Agenda 21 processes within individual metropolitan districts. Some districts were looking more closely at notions of environmental capacity as the key underlying principle for development plans in future. However, this approach was largely driven by the desire to deflect strong demand for new housing land release. This reflects the poor articulation of environmental agendas across the conurbation and the fact that such agendas are not the major force for change they are in some other areas of the UK.

Planning frameworks in the three localities

This section examines the statutory land-use planning frameworks in the three case study areas. It briefly outlines regional and local-level planning guidance and seeks to assess how the governance cultures previously outlined and the issues driving local policy agendas have shaped plan-making histories.

Kent

The planning framework for south east England is set by Regional Planning Policy Guidance Note 9 (RPG9), (DoE, 1994a), which covers the period 1991–2006. In the north-west of Kent this guidance is supplemented by RPG9a (GOSE, 1996). The emphasis in RPG9 adopts SERPLAN advice which seeks to affect a west-to-east shift in development, by taking development pressure from west of London and facilitating regeneration in the Thames Gateway area.

RPG9a sets the framework for this development in the Thames Gateway, part of which includes north Kent. The objectives of RPG9a are largely concerned with economic and physical regeneration. KCC and the districts in Kent were supportive of the general approach of

RPG9 and RPG9a, although SERPLAN was frustrated in the late 1990s in developing revised guidance by disquiet throughout the south-east over the implications of government household projections and what these meant for individual districts (see Chapter 4).

Structure planning　The Kent Structure Plan (KSP), adopted in 1996, is the third for the county. It replaces the 1990 County Structure Plan and provides the planning framework for the county until 2006. There is a greater emphasis in this plan than previously on connections with Europe. This reflects the growing importance of funding from the EU and the positioning of Kent in a wider pan-European economic space in an effort to capitalise on its unique geographical position in the UK. The Structure Plan (see Figure 3.7 and Table 3.2) represents one response of the county council to these challenges.

Whilst previous Kent structure plans were focused principally upon the creation of employment opportunities within certain landscape constraints, the 1996 plan talks of a greater emphasis on a wider set of environmental and quality of life issues. Thus 'the overall requirement [of the Plan] is to improve the quality of living and standard of environment within Kent' (KCC, 1993a, p.11). The breadth of this new environmental emphasis and the extent to which it goes beyond rhetoric is discussed later in Part II of this book.

As part of this revised approach to environmental issues, the new structure plan was subjected to an environmental assessment. This assessment and the process of undertaking it were seen as a positive exercise by county council officers and others (Merrett, 1994). The plan

Table 3.2　Strategic issues in the Kent Structure Plan

Achieve a sustainable pattern and form of development
Conserve and enhance Kent's environment
Stimulate economic activity
Promote Ashford as having a key role in local economic regeneration
Improve the economy and environment of the East Thames Corridor
Allocate appropriate land for housing
Improve accessibility and transport facilities to enable a better balance between transport and land use
Encourage the vitality and viability of town centres
Have regard to the need for community facilities

Source:　Kent County Council (1996).

changed little as a result of the appraisal, however, apart from a reordering of sections. In essence there remains a continuity of policy from previous structure plans, with strong landscape protection policies in mid- and west Kent, and a focus on brownfield development in north and east Kent. However, the process of structure plan preparation has been part of a process of 'policy learning', or learning though acting (Schon 1983), on the part of KCC and others and a fuller understanding of environmental issues has arisen as a consequence. Partly as a result, the notion of a structure plan led by environmental issues was considered highly likely by KCC when preparing the next plan. In contrast, the narrowing of the remit of development plans over the last two decades has undermined attempts to put social issues to the fore and such issues are poorly articulated in the structure plan. A more recent widening of the environmental agenda to embrace social issues through a quality of life perspective goes some way to addressing this limited articulation.

It is beyond the scope of this chapter to detail progress on all district development plans in Kent. We can, however, highlight local authorities who were innovative in terms of plan preparation. Ashford and Tonbridge and Malling districts took their local plans straight to a deposit version bypassing one stage of the customary preparation process. This 'fast-tracking' process received strong approval from the Government Office for the South East after initial reservations. Other Kent districts are proposing to do this with their next plans. Ashford also employed an innovative consultation process involving discussion groups consisting of over 100 invited organisations, many of which had not participated in planning before, to get a broad range of views and feed them into the early stages of plan preparation. This exercise was felt to have generated a useful dialogue and diffused knowledge about plans, planning and strategic ideas amongst a wider selection of the public than previously.

Lancashire

Lancashire County Council (LCC), particularly through former leader, and now member of parliament, Louise Ellman, and Cheshire County Council took on pivotal roles within the North West Regional Association in producing the advice that was to lead to regional planning guidance in 1996. LCC perceived an opportunity to promote an agenda of regionalism, building a cohesiveness that had previously proved problematic owing to conflicts between the conurbations of Merseyside and Manchester, and the peripherality of Cumbria. LCC also saw region building as a way to get money and support from the EU and avoid what it perceived as a hostile Conservative administration in London. The subsequent advice, in *Greener Growth*, contained a strategic emphasis on promoting new development along two axes: a north–south spine running from Cumbria through to Cheshire and an east–west link running from Merseyside across to Manchester (NWRA, 1995). The development of these axes was partly an attempt at building regional cohesiveness.

Greener Growth also attempted to put an emerging agenda of sustainability into the heart of spatial strategy making in the region (NWRA, 1995). It sought to promote an integrated approach to transport and land-use planning, and attempted to guide development to locations which would minimise the need to travel. The problem has been in carrying these intentions through to implementation (Hull *et al.*, 1996). The Regional Policy Guidance Note which emerged in 1996, covering the period 1991–2011, maintained this approach (DoE, 1996a). The structure plan developed in Lancashire in the mid-1990s (see Table 3.3) supported the principles in the RPG.

Table 3.3   The development of Lancashire structure plans

Date	Structure plan status
1974	North East Lancashire Structure Plan start of preparation
1979	Central and North Lancashire Structure Plan (report of survey)
1979	North East Lancashire Structure Plan approved by central government
1983	Central and North Lancashire Structure Plan approved by central government
1986	Lancashire Structure Plan review submitted to central government
1989	Lancashire Structure Plan approved by central government
1991	Conclusion of high court challenge to the plan (relating to a boundary dispute)
1993	Lancashire Structure Plan consultation draft published
1994	Lancashire Structure Plan deposit draft published
1995	Examination in public
1996	Report from examination in public panel received
1997	Lancashire Structure Plan approved

Table 3.4   Lancashire Structure Plan: strategic issues

Sustainability and growth
   how to conserve resources, reduce waste, pollution and congestion, and
   begin to create a more sustainable pattern of development, while at the same
   time securing further economic growth
The image of the county
   how to improve the image of the county so as to maximise inward
   investment
Accommodating growth
   how successfully to accommodate future population growth, new houses,
   offices, factories and other needs
The west–east divide in the county
   how to correct the past imbalance in development between the west and east
   of the county
Quality in the urban areas
   how to improve the image, appearance and environmental quality of
   Lancashire's towns and the quality of life of the residents
Managing development pressures
   how to manage the economic, social and technological forces that lead to
   dispersal of development, to the benefit of both urban and rural areas
Managing transport
   how to manage the demand for transport effectively, especially in urban
   areas

Source: Hull *et al.* (1996).

The 1997 Lancashire Structure Plan (LCC, 1997b) details a number
of strategic issues (see Table 3.4). In many ways it is the resolution of
the conflict between these strategic issues which is of interest, and this
is discussed throughout in Part II.

The Structure Plan took forward the regional guidance emphasis on
strategic development corridors (see Figure 3.8). It also prioritised the
promotion of job-creating economic development, the restraint of peri-
urban development in order to conserve landscape and agricultural land,
and the redistribution of economic opportunity to benefit older and
poorer industrial areas to the east of the county. However, LCC was also
very aware of the need to capture investment for the county as a whole. It
adopted a new emphasis on positioning the regional economy in a
European context, derived in part from the North West Regional
Economic Strategy (Pieda, 1993). The 1994 Lancashire Structure Plan
also placed a stronger emphasis than past plans on managing the amount,
form and location of development to reduce damage to the environment.

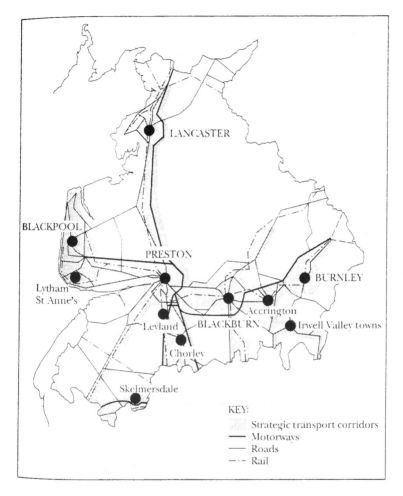

Figure 3.8   Lancashire's corridors strategy
Source: Drawn from Lancashire Structure Plan, 1993.

This shift required a rhetorical reorientation of previously accepted strategies, by both public agencies and private interests involved in development and infrastructure. The plan-making task thus involved both developing new strategic ideas and persuading others of its merits.

There have been technical developments in monitoring and reviewing the Lancashire Structure Plan. A Strategic Environmental Assessment

(SEA) of the 1986 Structure Plan was carried out at the beginning of the review process in the early 1990s so as to feed into the discussion of strategic issues in the new plan. This was a fairly crude impact analysis of the 165 policies against 11 environmental components covered by the Green Audit information database. A rudimentary scoring system produced negative scores for 46 policies, mainly covering minerals, transport and waste disposal. A SEA of the 1994 deposit Structure Plan used a similar assessment procedure, and 18 policies in this plan were considered to have adverse effects, most notably in relation to transport policies.

Again, it is not the purpose of this chapter to detail the progress of local plans in the county. Where necessary such issues are raised in Chapters 4–7.

West Midlands

Regional planning guidance takes on a greater significance in the West Midlands conurbation's spatial strategy, given the absence of a structure plan. We therefore discuss its preparation in some depth as a counterpoint to the analysis of structure plan development in the other two cases.

The first regional guidance policy statement following the dissolution of the West Midlands County Council was Planning Policy Guidance Note 10, adopted in 1991, which covered the conurbation area only. The principal aim of the PPG was to revitalise the sub-regional economy and regenerate inner city areas. The West Midlands Forum began revising this guidance in 1989, to encompass the wider West Midlands region, and presented its advice to government in 1993 (WMRF, 1993).

The early papers (WMRF, 1991, 1992) produced in preparing regional guidance pose a series of questions about the environment, the economy, housing needs, accessibility and physical form. They acknowledge that 'the greatest tensions and challenges, but also the opportunities, arise from the interactions between these concerns', (WMRF, 1991, Executive Summary). These documents are notable in setting out an approach to the environment entirely absent from the previous guidance: 'moving to a more desirable and sustainable environment is ... a major underlying theme that we think should have a strong influence on the future of the Region' (WMRF, 1991, para. 4.6). This new emphasis is supported by reference to the UK's sustainable development strategy, *This Common Inheritance* (HMSO, 1990), stating that the principles contained within that document of resolving mobility pressures, recognition of resource limits and pollution control should perhaps steer the West Midlands regional guidance.

Later, four possible future directions for the region's spatial strategy were presented: an environment-led approach, a market/economy-led approach and two possible directions for a social needs-led approach (WMRF, 1992). These directions were discussed at a conference held with over 50 organisations in 1993. The intractability of the economy/environment dimension was recognised: 'if environmental sustainability is taken seriously it will have repercussions on the amount, type and distribution of economic growth in the region' (Saunders, 1993, para. 13.1). Although there was superficial agreement amongst participants in relation to such issues, 'it seemed at times as if participants had simply added an environmental label to their existing luggage' (ibid., para. 15.5). It was recognised that as understanding of such issues increased, 'this particular area of consensus may turn out to be rather less solid' (ibid.). The resultant Regional Planning Guidance policies became more specific on air, soil and water quality, and on the conflicts between the objectives of economic growth and environmental sustainability (GO-WM, 1995).

The most signficant strategic organising idea which emerged out of the RPG process was the concept of transport corridors as a way to reconcile demands for development whilst minimising environmental damage, in effect a policy of transit-oriented development. Thus corridors were being employed in a different way than in the Lancashire case. Here the aim was to push as much development as possible to locations around public transport nodes within and beyond the conurbation. The corridors idea had been around since before the abolition of the West Midlands Metropolitan County Council. It was given renewed currency by the perceived need to minimise the use of private cars. However, although the corridors idea had broad support, the shire counties in the region saw it as having less relevance to their spatial strategies, for two reasons. First, it could signify development incursions into the green belt, and second, it centred on travel into the conurbation which made up a small proportion of total journeys in counties somewhat distant from the conurbation, such as Shropshire. In addition, some authorities beyond the conurbation saw the potential for development along corridors as being minimal in comparison with the total land needed. The idea incorporates an assumption that inward commuting to the conurbation is of great importance, which was not borne out by recent trends towards greater labour market self-sufficiency in the counties. There were also doubts about the capacity of public transport routes to cope with significant increases in traffic resulting from such a strategy, especially in relation to travel at peak periods such as the commute to work.

The metropolitan districts in the West Midlands were amongst the quickest UK authorities to get their unitary development plans adopted. This speed of preparation was a deliberate strategy. Only Solihull Metropolitan Borough Council struggled to get its plan adopted, the reasons for which are discussed in Chapter 4. In rolling forward these plans, the districts generally felt that there was a coherent view across the authorities and that the 'fundamental policy emphasis is correct' (district planner). The focus on stemming decentralisation and promoting opportunities in the inner city will thus remain. This is likely to be coupled with an environmental sustainability rhetoric, which could incorporate a social needs approach through a focus on quality of life rather than standard of living.

The development of Birmingham City Council's Unitary Development Plan (UDP) illustrates the process of plan preparation and the tensions inherent in spatial policy formulation in the West Midlands conurbation in the 1990s (Table 3.5). In terms of content, Birmingham City Council's UDP takes forward the conurbation-wide focus on urban regeneration and economic development issues.

The UDP strategy highlights the need for the plan to promote itself in relation to three elements: to consolidate the position of Birmingham in the UK, to promote a distinctive role for Birmingham in the region and to promote a multicultural, social and physical environment for Birmingham's citizens (BCC, 1989). The twin aims of the UDP, and indeed the city council generally, were to facilitate economic revitalisation and inner city regeneration. Interviews with officers of the city

Table 3.5   Key stages in Birmingham City Council's UDP production

Plan stage	Date
Strategy paper	February 1989
Consultation draft	January 1990
Deposit draft	April 1991
Inquiry	January/February 1992
Inspectors' report	September 1992
Adopted plan	July 1993

council conducted in 1996 revealed that these two aims were still at the heart of BCC strategy.

In most of Birmingham City Council's policy outputs of the 1990s, the environment is treated in a way which recognises the importance of the physical environment to citizens' quality of life and the decisions of firms. This is typical of the traditional notion of environment amongst town planners (Marshall, 1994, Healey and Shaw, 1994). The Birmingham UDP also sets priorities for itself in terms of space. Certain areas of the city are privileged in terms of policy attention. The city centre is priority number one, followed by the remainder of the inner city and then 'other areas of need', This spatial prioritising is not just rhetoric; it was reflected in implementation through the actions of the city council, notably in a very real focus of resources on the city centre.

The measures of success outlined in the plan reflect a focus on physical development: '*Confidence within the inner city will be reflected by the scale of investment and the amount of new building taking place. This in turn will act as a barometer for the success of the strategy as a whole*' (BCC, 1989, para. 2.15). This property development focus was an attempt by BCC to develop alternatives to the declining manufacturing base in the city, of which the UDP was just one response. Birmingham, and the city centre in particular, was marketed as the principal alternative to London in the UK office location market. The city was positioned as a key location in a pan-European business tourism market, being promoted as 'Europe's Meeting Place'. These efforts to appeal to investors, conference organisers and the professional classes that surround both decision processes led to large-scale renewal of public spaces and buildings in the city centre and the development of the National Exhibition Centre, a convention centre and a range of other attractions. This form of boosterism attracted the criticism that BCC's focus on the city centre and on property development was disadvantaging the city's existing residents. The focus of attention on the central area was also seen to be to the detriment of the physical renewal of other parts of the city and it was felt that the benefits accruing from such a strategy would be confined to small sections of the population (see Loftman and Nevin, 1994). Alternatively, in the light of the transformation of the city centre, the actions of the city council could be seen as a successful response, given the limited range of policy tools at its disposal and its relative powerlessness in the face of international property speculators.

Conclusions

To conclude this chapter we return to the main concerns of this book, as detailed in Chapter 2. First, we consider the notion that we are in a unique period of transition. Our localities reflect evidence of evolution in policy agendas and in the processes of policy preparation. There were, however, few indications that a sharp transformation has occurred. The processes involved were much more organic, and continuity of policy agendas was more the norm (see Imrie and Raco, 1999, for similar conclusions in other localities). The incorporation of environmental agendas was the key change in policy content, but there was little change beyond one of a shift in policy rhetoric and little evidence to suggest that much changed in the way decisions were taken within localities, or in the frames of reference of key policy makers.

Second, in relation to territory and place there was a re-emergence of attention to strategy making at the regional level in Lancashire and the West Midlands. This re-emergence predates UK central government's regional agenda. The alliances in the north-west were new, whilst the West Midlands alliances were given added emphasis by regional programmes emanating from the European Union. The region was also becoming the level where public and private sectors were increasingly coming together to discuss issues of mutual concern. Between 1979 and 1997, this was driven in part by a desire to bypass a hostile central government, but also out of a recognition that economic, environmental and social issues required consideration in the round in a way which cuts across policy sectors. The absence of a county-level tier in metropolitan areas after 1986 gave this added significance. The new regional arenas were bringing new players from the business sector into a more active role in policy formation, usually in non-public arenas. The existence of these closed arenas, and the fact that much of the participation in regional arenas comes from producer and amenity groups who are also most active in development plan arenas, prompt many to suggest that this just perpetuates a form of corporatism in providing more opportunity for key players with the resources available to influence public policy to meet their own ends. However, the social capital developed in these arenas did at least provide a basis on which to build as the regional level took on renewed importance in the UK under the Labour government.

Our third concern is how economic, environmental and social issues are being integrated in policy and decision making. Some of the alliances cited in this chapter were a direct result of stakeholders seeing the links between issues and the need to cut across policy sectors. Certainly, economy–environment trade-offs were being flagged up in policy documents, and ecological issues were sometimes being integrated into discourses surrounding spatial change throughout our three areas. However, the plan preparation processes studied were often set in train before local authorities had come to grips with the full implications of a sustainable development agenda. Existing structure plan policies reflected attempts to integrate key sectors (development land allocation, transport, environmental quality) around a central focus on 'environmentally sustainable economic development'. Yet discussion later in Part II will highlight the fact that key integrative links required for sustainable futures have been omitted, or that policies were based on fragile assumptions about powers and resources, for example in the shift to development locations served by public transport. Tensions between economic and environmental issues were often not resolved even within the confines of development plan policies. Many local authorities stated that they would put sustainability at the heart of their next development plan, possibly around an integrating concept such as environmental capacity. At present, except in environmentally protected areas, strategic emphases on economic promotion remained with local authorities fearful of implementing strategies that may disadvantage them in the competition for jobs.

The social agenda was typically still marginal to plans and spatial strategy, although attempts to relate environmental issues to people's everyday experiences were leading to a focus on quality of life or environmental justice notions. Some authorities had sought to put social issues at the heart of spatial strategy, but in general there was little strategic thinking in relation to social issues beyond a partial directing of development to areas containing high proportions of the long-term unemployed. Although the planning system is at the heart of this strategy, the planning system's regulatory lever of the right to develop is a limited tool in this context.

Fourth, we examine who was participating in planning debates. Plan preparation processes are unique in having opportunities for public involvement and this is cited as a rationale for their continued existence. However, structure plan processes are notoriously poor in engaging a wide public in their preparation, and few groups beyond those traditionally seen in technical planning arenas, such as the development industry and elements of the environmental lobby, were present. Local plans arouse more interest among the general public than structure plans and many local authorities had consciously encouraged this interest. Many local authorities instigated innovative attempts to involve groups going far beyond those traditionally involved in such debates. This proved to be a useful educative experience for all concerned and did affect the strategic direction of plans. In essence, however, the major issues of contention were often resolved through a bargaining process between development lobby groups (mainly the House Builders Federation), civil servants, local government and, to a lesser extent, environmental lobbies. These negotiations frequently took place beyond the arenas of the development plan, increasingly often at regional level, even when such issues required a legitimating sanction through the policies and procedures of plans. So, whilst there was some widening in the range of participants in planning debates, land-use planning remained a public sector-dominated activity despite an increase in activity in plan inquiries and in ad hoc arenas at regional level.

Finally, did the plan-making practices of the planning system provide a resource for territorial strategy making in bringing many of these issues together? In both Lancashire and Kent, structure plan preparation proved to be important in providing arenas for statutory interests to discuss strategic issues. The formal statutory development plans system does not, however, appear dominant in setting the agenda for strategy making. The key determinants of change in localities arise separately, frequently through the preparation of bids for monies and the processes of networking between officers and members, and with partner organisations. Any relevant outputs from such processes are then lifted into the planning system when the need arises. The functional divisions within local authorities often emphasise this, with planning departments split into statutory functions, responsible for plan preparation, and non-statutory functions. There may be good reasons for this division, but it often distances policy formulation from implementation, and regulatory and investment nexuses, in undesirable ways.

The extent to which the development plan remains an important place for discussing spatial strategy and is capable of uniting conflicting economic, environmental and social concerns is a key question explored in the remainder of this book.

4   Cascading Numbers: Finding Space for New Housing

Containing spatial conflicts over new housing development

The allocation of land for new housing has been a prime task of the British town planning system since its infancy. The scale of land required to meet housing needs and the intensely conflictual nature of site identification sustains its central importance. This chapter looks at the way decisions on housing land release were made in our three areas, in what arenas, by whom and using what criteria. Throughout the 1980s and 1990s, this particular policy task was given a high priority: to identify appropriate locations for new housing and ensure that sufficient land was available to meet society's housing needs. The key actors involved hardly changed in this period. However, the policy approach developed into a sophisticated accounting technology and the relations between the actors developed distinctive characteristics. By the 1990s, allocating land for new housing had become a relatively closed, hierarchical policy area, resulting in tensions arising locally when the full impact of these decisions on the quality of local residents' lived-in environments were realised. This raises two questions which are examined in this chapter: firstly, how concerns about the quality of place and space have been interpreted and, secondly, how this hierarchical decision-making process structures the relationships of the stakeholders involved.

Up to the mid-1970s, housing provision and settlement design in the UK was set within clear spatial strategies which provided blueprints for town extension or new town development. This plan-led regulatory process provided certainty for public sector infrastructure providers and private sector developers. Managing housing development was considered to be a technical process, in which town planners identified sufficient sites for housing, based on population projections for their area (applying a local household size ratio), previous local supply capacity (based on recent trends) and the preferred locations of the implementors. However, this process was weakened as the pressure for development and the growing strength of the residential development industry challenged locations allocated in plans, demanding more and more appropriately located sites (Hall *et al.*, 1973, JURUE, 1977). There were also tensions between the demand for sites for owner-occupation and the needs of social housing provision. By the 1980s, these pressures had increased, and were made more complex by the privatisation of utility providers. The development plan remained the key tool for allocation, backed by development briefs which provided more detailed site-specific criteria which developers were expected to adhere to, such as site capacity, site constraints, layout, design, tenure and type of dwelling. Where the sites allocated were large or owned by the local authority, extensive negotiations would be carried out with the developer and/or landowner to decide the phasing of development, the mix of housing development and any additional design features. The development plan had thus become an inter-organisational tool to manage the development of housing to meet local requirements (Healey, 1983).

The extent to which the development plan was used as a tool to reflect local housing concerns was slowly curtailed after the election of the Thatcher government in 1979. The rapid decline in the public sector house-building programme from the late 1970s meant that the local authority role became primarily one of regulating housing land supply by the private sector. Meanwhile, the national government continued to support private sector provision through the encouragement of owner-occupation, using legislation, ministerial statements and subsidies. The private sector residential development industry was increasingly dominated by a few national 'volume' builders and strong regional companies (Ball, 1983). It supported a nationally organised lobby group, the House Builders Federation (HBF). The industry exhorted local planners to be faster and more flexible in making regulatory decisions. Persistent lobbying by the HBF led to the requirement that local authorities undertake land availability studies to provide regular updated local inventories of sites appropriate for housing development.

The 1980 Local Government and Planning Act required each authority to have available a five-year supply of housing land at any one time, with two years' supply ready for immediate development. This legislation formalised the previous loose housing land assessments carried out by planners, and gave an open invitation to the HBF to be involved in drawing up the annual statements of housing land availability in each local authority area (Rydin, 1988, Hooper, 1985). These requirements were restated in Planning Policy Guidance Note 3 (DoE, 1992c), which set out the 'residual method' of calculating dwelling requirements. This highly structured process pitted the housebuilders' knowledge of market demand against the local authorities' need assessments and environmental considerations in determining the location of new housing development. National government had therefore factored the key protagonists into a continuous dialogue on the amount, location and flow of housing sites, in a form which came to be known as the 'housing numbers game'.

The planning task in finding space for new housing was redefined gradually through the 1980s. By the 1990s, the plan-led system potentially allowed local authorities more control over the location of housing sites, but it often proved difficult to take a strategic housing overview at district level, where local residents perceived such sites as a threat to their quality of life. The national government response to local mobilisation against housing growth was initially to stand back and let the local planning machine take the strain. Thus local political action had the power to introduce local variations into the housing numbers game as the policies cast in general, aspatial terms at national and regional level were drawn into place-focused local arenas. This reflected the effective lobbying of relatively resourceful residents who place a high regard on the amenity value of their immediate environment.

However, because of the highly specified procedures and detailed policy criteria which evolved in this policy area, debate flowed down vertically through a spatial hierarchy of intervention and responsibilities, typically clustering around formal development plan arenas (see Figure 4.1). The key actors within these public arenas were local authority planners, the HBF, the Council for the Protection of Rural England (CPRE) and the Government Office for the Region (GOR). Each tier of governance had a different function in this process. At national level, the government not only regularly updated the relevant planning policy guidance (PPG) notes, it also issued population and household projections by region and conurbation every three years. The spatial implications of the household growth projections were the critical element in the draft regional planning guidance, which the regional association of local authorities prepared on behalf of central government. This disaggregation of the household projections to subregions,

National government
planning policy guidance
regional planning guidance
household projections
planning inspectorate

Regional level
government offices in the regions
regional associations of local authorities

County Councils
structure plan
examination-in-public (EIP)

District Councils
unitary development plan
district plan
public inquiry

Figure 4.1   Housing decision arenas in the planning system

and then to districts, started the complex 'numbers game'. The Regional Planning Guidance Note, issued by the government, specified the number of new dwellings required over the 15-year period of the guidance for local actors to 'test' during the preparation of local plans. However, the negotiations between the regional representatives of local authorities, the GOR, the HBF and the CPRE set the parameters for debates on housing growth at the local level (Hull, 1997; Hull and Vigar, 1998). Increasingly in the 1990s, the national government was prepared to intervene to ensure that the administrative tiers of government accept the hierarchical cascade of housing growth responsibilities (see Figure 4.1).

What resulted was a competitive process amongst local and regional stakeholders. Each stakeholder was wary that shifts in government policy ideas would be used by the other interests to their own advantage. The HBF was quick to test any innovation or use of discretion by local authorities in the way they interpreted government guidance in relation to housing and housing related decisions. They followed a consistent line, arguing for plans to tie local authorities to policies agreed at national government level, and for the exact translation of regional guidance targets into local plans. The environmental arguments of the CPRE were used almost as a counterbalance to the market approach of the HBF. Stable relationships and ways of working have built up between these stakeholders. Other actors impinged on the 'housing numbers' game from time to time. At subregional level, these tended to be those promoting large-scale mixed-use projects justified on employment generation grounds, but with significant residential components which affected the trading of housing numbers between local authorities.

Absorbing growth: urban regeneration versus greenfield locations

Towards the end of the 1990s, the 'housing numbers' game became increasingly criticised for the oversimplistic linkage of the household projections to the demand for new housing land. Rarely had market demand factors, such as house and land price indicators, been incorporated in any way (Coopers and Lybrand, 1985). Debates, which started outside the planning system, on 'sustainable development' raised questions about the environmental impact of the continual release of greenfield sites for housebuilding. The 1992-based household projections published in 1995 identified the full effect of counterurbanisation and the impact of changing lifestyles and aspirations. To allay some of the resultant conflict and ensure sufficient release of land, the Conservative government in 1996 set a national and regional aspirational target: that 50 per cent of new dwellings should be built on brownfield sites (DETR, 1996e). The new Labour administration increased the target to 60 per cent in 1998 (DETR, 1998h).

For most of the twentieth century, certain spatial organising ideas had influenced planning decisions on the allocation of land for housing. Concepts of contained settlement growth, the segregation of land uses within urban areas, the segregation of urban areas from each other and from rural areas by green belts, and the protection of special landscape areas, had enduring influence (Hall *et al.*, 1973; Healey, 1983; Healey *et al.*, 1988; Wannop, 1995, Goodchild, 1992). The success of urban containment in restraining urban sprawl has been acknowledged, but its effects in delivering urban regeneration remain disputed. The movement of people out of metropolitan cores continued throughout this period (Champion, 1996), supported by transport investments which allowed journeys to lengthen in space but not time. However, despite increasing demands for more attention to the qualities of places in considering housing land allocation, as opposed to the narrow focus on distributing 'housing numbers' (CPRE, 1999), the entrenchment of the 'numbers game' in the policy community proved hard to displace.

The debates in the 1980s and 1990s were therefore almost entirely focused on the amount and location of housing. Until the mid-1990s, few questions were asked in planning arenas about the affordability of the proposed market housing for the projected households or about the declining quality of the existing urban housing stock. In line with the principles of private provision, housebuilders were encouraged to provide a cross-subsidy from market housing for social housing needs, in the context of applying for planning permission. By the end of the decade, only a trickle of affordable housing units had been supplied, partly because the right to negotiate was restricted to the larger sites (Tetlow, 1997). However, the New Labour administration gave a new priority to social issues, and more encouragement to such negotiations (DETR, 1999b). Slowly, the policy discourses presented in this chapter were beginning to change by the end of the century, with a wider search for housing information to assess housing needs, to justify the innovative use of the existing planning tools for the phasing of land release and the setting of social housing targets for each district authority.

The local political pressures which enveloped discussions on housing land allocation and which affected policy outcomes will be discussed below. First, each case study will discuss the distinctive ideas which have structured the policy agendas and the discussions on the allocation of land for housing, and how these have been changing. Secondly, the nature of the policy community membership over time will be analysed. Finally, the institutional relations between the key actors and how they have responded to national government policy and institutional change will be discussed.

The West Midlands: 'old wine in new bottles' – repackaging the tools and concepts of the 1970s

There was substantial continuity in the housing discourse in the West Midlands, through successive County Structure Plans in the 1970s to the Unitary Development Plans (UDP) of the 1990s. This reflected a long-standing policy consensus around the regeneration of inner urban areas which, from the 1970s, required that housing site releases on the urban fringe should be related to the rate of urban regeneration. This consensus was coupled with a long-standing commitment to the West Midlands' green belt, which wraps around the conurbation. The green belt provided a peripheral, expansion-restraining tool (Elson, 1986). The concept, as applied, also allowed 'appropriate' development to jump over the buffer zone, whenever sufficient argumentation could be upheld at a public inquiry to the effect that there was a lack of land for new housing within the West Midlands conurbation (Healey *et al.*, 1988).

The first round of UDPs carried forward the broad intentions of the West Midlands 1986 Structure Plan, to regenerate the inner urban areas and to encourage the reuse of derelict and disused land, through the phasing of housing development. The strategic guidance (PPG10) for the conurbation supported, in principle, the controlled release of housing land to aid urban regeneration, but failed to give any guidance on how to achieve this in a market-dominated economy (DoE, 1988c, para. 5). This guidance and planning framework proved ineffective in preventing areas beyond the conurbation from exceeding their Structure Plan housing site allocations by a considerable margin, allowing developers to pick and choose sites outside the conurbation (GOWM, 1994, p.18). In addition, despite some very successful projects, urban local authorities were often lacking the resources to facilitate inner urban land assembly and clearance. Significant land recycling in the region was eventually achieved largely because of the additional resources the two urban development corporations brought into the area.

Nearly a third of the dwelling numbers required between 1988 and 2001 were replacements for dwellings expected to be demolished in Birmingham and Sandwell. In the 1970s and 80s lack of housing land in these two districts put pressure on the metropolitan county council to open up the green belt in Solihull, Birmingham and Wolverhampton (DoE, 1988c, para.13). Solihull was already a key development location in the conurbation. However, by the late 1970s, local resistance to new development was strong, and supported by local authorities (Healey *et al.*, 1988). Solihull Metropolitan Borough Council's (SMBC) phasing policy, however, failed to convince a government inspector at their first UDP inquiry in 1991, who concluded that insufficient land had been made available for housing. At the second inquiry, the strategy was supported by a detailed environmental impact appraisal of different development scenarios. The second public inquiry took place against the background of new planning guidance for the whole of the West Midlands region (RPG11), which increased the number of dwellings to be built in the conurbation between 1991 and 2011 (see Table 4.1). Within this context, SMBC were able to negotiate a settlement which reduced their regional share of the housing requirements, in favour of a greenfield site allocation for economic activity adjacent to the M42.

Table 4.1   'The regional numbers': the annual average rate of new dwellings
required in the West Midlands, 1991–2011

County	PPG10 1988	RPG 11 1995	RPG 11 Review 1996	Revised RPG 11 1998	Change 1995–8 (%)
Herefordshire	—	2 800	800	825	+3
Worcestershire	—		2 100	2 065	—
Shropshire	—	2 200	2 400	2 400	+9
Staffordshire	—	3 300	3 500	3 520	+7
Warwickshire	—	1 850	2 000	2 035	+10
Shire counties total	—	10 150	10 800	10 845	+7
Birmingham	1 715	2 050	2 200	2 325	+13
Coventry	385	450	500	555	+23
Dudley	569	680	600	620	–9
Sandwell	577	850	900	890	+5
Solihull	577	480	500	505	+5
Walsall	523	450	500	505	+12
Wolverhampton	346	390	500	505	+30
Metropolitan county	4 692	5 350	5 700	5 905	+10
Region		15 500	16 500	16 750	+8

Source: Derived from DoE (1988c) and GOWM (1995), Table 1 Housing Provision
1991–2011.

New ideas on how to achieve sustainable development were being
voiced in planning and environmental arenas by the beginning of the
1990s. The region's existing planning policies for urban concentration
were thought to support this agenda. The operationalisation of these
sustainable development ideas at the regional level was discussed as a
key issue in the regional 'debate' on strategic planning held in 1993
(see Chapter 3). The metropolitan districts favoured 'recycling' the idea
of transport corridors from the 1970s. This proposed that development
corridors, based on rail routes, would radiate out from the inner city,
providing development opportunities at the transport interchange nodes
within the corridors (GOWM, 1995). Overlaying this, as far as housing
locations were concerned, was the development of a prototype 'sequential test'. This stated that priority should be given to accommodating
new housing development within the metropolitan area, and next at
free-standing towns beyond the green belt. Greenfield locations were to
be used only in exceptional circumstances. This 'test' was later
employed by national government in Planning Policy Guidance Note 6

(DoE, 1996c) to identify appropriate sites for large retail stores, following intense criticism of the detrimental impact of out-of-town retail developments. The revised 1992-based household projections fell into this wider debate just as revised regional planning guidance (RPG 11) was about to be published in 1995. Because of the potential for intense conflict over the number of houses required in the region between 1991 and 2011, the Government Office in the West Midlands asked the West Midlands Regional Forum of local authorities (WMRF) and various regional collaborators to undertake a technical analysis of the revised household projections. This was to include wider housing market issues (such as vacancy levels, migration and the structures of housing provision) and settlement capacity studies (WMRF, 1996, Annex 1, para. 3.1). The report presented by the WMRF concluded that two policy measures were necessary if future housing development was to be sustainable: firstly, the reintroduction of a phasing mechanism and, secondly, the setting of social housing targets for each district authority. The phasing mechanism proposed that a greenfield site on the edge of the conurbation should only be released if the developer

● either redeveloped a derelict inner city site,
● or proposed a substantial provision of affordable housing on the site (more than 50 per cent),
● or if there was less than a five-year supply of housing land available.

The WMRF argued that, with the equivalent of eight years' supply of land already allocated, further allocation would give builders the freedom to 'cherry pick' the greenfield sites from a wide portfolio and thus negate the urban regeneration policies.

Expanding relational resources at regional level   Discussions concerning site selection in the West Midlands were dominated by negotiations between mainly Labour-controlled conurbation districts and Conservative-controlled county councils. This issue was a contentious one for councillors, creating inter-authority tension, with set-piece battles over housing issues throughout the 1970s and 1980s (Wannop, 1995; Hall *et al.*, 1973; Healey *et al.*, 1988). The primary arena for this interaction was the planning system and in particular the development plan. Some metropolitan districts were not thought to be serious enough about using housing land as a means to achieve urban regeneration. As national government shaping of the decision-making process increased, the regional local authorities in the 1990s sought to present a more united front. Some agreement was reached between local authorities on key issues, such as phasing the release of greenfield sites to encourage urban regeneration and the use of full regulatory powers to ensure a diversity of provision for different housing needs. Tensions still remained, however, over the extent to which the housing needs of the conurbation should spill over into the shires.

It was important for the local authorities to be involved in, and to understand, the intricacies of these debates, if they were to resist national government direction and/or effective lobbying by the HBF. There were two implications of the housing numbers debate which the local authorities sought to address. Firstly, they wanted to secure regional agreement on the definition of a 'sufficient' number of new dwellings to provide for. This calculation was for a 20-year period, taking into account not only the household projections but also changes to the existing housing stock. Secondly, local authority unity was needed on how to play the game of fixing regional numbers to specific sites and the handling of the local political fall-out for the districts concerned.

The united local authority front was secured through some clever 'institutional footwork' (metropolitan district planner). Despite the good working relationships between both the 'coal face' planning officers and the Chief Engineers and Planning Officers Group (CEPOG), agreements reached did not always extend to their political masters. The existence of the West Midlands Regional Forum and the supportive attitude of the Government Office (GOWM) helped to relieve the entrenched positions of the different actors. The mediatory role played by the GOWM was apparent in the regional discussions between 1993 and 1996 which led to the revised dwelling requirements in the 1997 revision to the regional planning guidance statement. The WMRF had suggested 285 000 dwellings were required by 2011, the HBF argued for 400 000 and the CPRE for less than 200 000. The GOWM was keen to skew the housing requirement figures towards the metropolitan area by applying relative constraints on land release in the shire counties. The WMRF had argued for an approximate 50/50 split on housing growth between the conurbation and the shire counties which the GOWM feared would lead to a shortfall in dwellings in the metropolitan area. The HBF's argument that more houses were required would have put more pressure on the greenfield sites in the shire counties. The GOWM came under pressure from the national government to tie development plan housing land release to the revised national household projections. They increased the regional housing requirements by 25 000 in the 1995 version of RPG11, and by another 25 000 in the revised RPG11 in 1998, nearly reaching the mid-point between the WMRF's and the HBF's opening figures.

The HBF had long argued against the simple equation between the restriction of land release on the urban fringe and urban regeneration, and claimed that the phasing policy could merely perpetuate counter-urbanisation (WMRF, 1996). It challenged the local authority consensus at regional level on both the numbers of new dwellings required by some future date and the need for a phasing policy. It was selective in applying lobbying pressure at district level. Where the housing market was buoyant, as in Solihull, the HBF and their members countered any loose argumentation by local authorities, forcing Solihull's local plan through two local plan inquiries.

The WMRF widened the regional debate in the mid-1990s, by putting the issue of social housing at the centre of the debate on how the household projections should be translated into land allocation requirements. This issue had been bubbling up at local plan inquiries, where districts had proposed plan policies reserving parts of housing sites for special housing needs. In most cases these had been diluted, under pressure from HBF and the GOWM, through policy wording which sought only to 'encourage' the provision of social housing needs in suitable locations. The WMRF's advice for the RPG11 housing review in 1996, which proposed social housing district targets, therefore caused concern for both GOWM and the HBF. The WMRF was supported by the wider constellation of interests involved in the housing review, which included local authority planning and housing departments, the Housing Corporation, the West Midlands churches and environmental pressure groups. The GOWM was not prepared to use the planning system in the revised RPG11 to link housing needs so directly to resource requirements. Despite this, the policy community in the West Midlands was leading national policy in this respect by widening the debate to include the likely demand for housing in relation to the projected income mix of the new household projections.

This case study illustrates how the three regional reviews on housing strategy in the West Midlands expanded the relational resources between organisations in two ways. Firstly, in each review, 'intellectual capital' was generated, helping to reach agreements on policy agendas, housing numbers and phasing. Secondly, the strategic positioning of the WMRF in the mid-1990s was a determining factor in the creation of horizontal 'social capital' at the regional level. The WMRF worked to maintain alliances and arrive at solutions above the lowest common denominator, which would otherwise arise from the tendency for local political priorities to undermine regionally agreed strategies.

Kent: promoting a sustainable balance between environment and employment

The county of Kent provides some contrasting sets of housing market conditions to those of the West Midlands conurbation. Parts of Kent are very attractive locations for housing, yet the demand for housing encounters institutional and cultural pressure to protect high-quality landscapes and village ways of living. Landscape protections (areas of outstanding natural beauty, special landscape areas, the green belt and so on) cover a large percentage of the county (see Chapter 3). Local residents' and lobby groups mobilise to protect areas from development. For these reasons, finding space for new housing is a highly political issue, but one that works its way through the planning arenas in a way different from that of the West Midlands. The story of how the strategic debates unfold in the planning system and their spatial implications is first introduced below, followed by discussion of the way the policy community is structured and how the institutional relationships are played out.

The strategic housing issue for Kent County Council (KCC), from at least the 1970s, was how to contain housing growth in areas where housing demand was particularly buoyant (as these tended to be those areas with landscape protection designations) and also to steer as much of the 'mobile' element of housing demand to approved growth points. The Maidstone/Medway area and Ashford were designated as 'medium growth areas' in the 1970 Strategic Plan for the South East (MHLG, 1970). At the time, Maidstone and Medway were scheduled to be developed first, since they were then considered to be sufficiently far away from Greater London to deter commuting. Ashford's growth was seen as contingent on the rate of employment growth which could be attracted and the timing of the Channel Tunnel development.

Two key spatial arguments stood out in strategic planning in Kent. The first was that employment growth and housing growth should be kept in balance. This was the key to the planning of the future growth of Ashford in the 1984 Kent Structure Plan and the Structure Plan Third Review (KCC, 1993a). The growth of Ashford was to be driven by employment but supported by an adequate provision of housing so as to avoid 'overheating' of the market in the latter part of the 1990s and early twenty-first century. This principle was also to be applied to the longer-term commercial proposals to redevelop sites in Dartford and Gravesham districts. The structure plan strategy was to focus attention on land for new housing first, in order to maintain a balance between employment requirements and labour supply. This view was supported by the Government Office for the South East (GOSE) which called for 'a distribution of development that will help to establish a sustainable relationship between homes, workplaces and other facilities to minimise unnecessary travel' (GOSE, 1994, para. 5.10).

The second strategic spatial concept was the strong presumption against new development in the metropolitan Green Belt and in national and county-designated landscape conservation areas. These environmental constraints were strictly applied in the past. This removed much of west and mid-Kent from consideration for large-scale development. Maidstone Borough Council was supported on two occasions by planning inspectors appointed by the national government, who argued that additional housing land allocations would create unacceptable pressure for housing development in areas designated for their special landscape or agricultural quality.

This context of restraint shaped the way KCC dealt with both indigenous growth and in-migration. KCC accepted the argument for in-migration, but always resisted the overprovision of new dwellings, though unsuccessfully on several occasions. Regional housing reviews in 1989 and 1994 increased Kent's housing requirements to the extent that KCC was set a target of 116 000 dwellings to be constructed between 1991 and 2011. KCC's deposit Structure Plan Third Review proposed a figure of 109 300 dwellings between 1991 and 2011, which was in line with government guidance up to 2006, and thereafter at a reduced rate. Just as KCC was about to adopt the Structure Plan in 1996, it was directed by the secretary of state to increase its allocation to 116 000 and thus to provide for the full share identified in regional planning guidance.

The solution brokered during the examination-in-public of the Structure Plan in 1994 was to steer most of the additional growth to

Table 4.2   Housing provision requirements in Kent,
1991–2011 (net dwelling units)

	Kent CC Structure Plan		
Districts	*Second review:* *1990 (1991–2001)*	*Third review:* *1993*	*EIP report:* *1994*
Maidstone	2 700	9 100	10 600
Tonbridge & Malling	1 700	7 600	7 700
Sevenoaks	1 800	3 100	3 100
Tunbridge Wells	2 800	5 200	5 700
Dartford	3 000	8 000	10 500
Gravesham	2 000	4 000	4 600
Medway towns	8 200	16 000	16 000
Swale	4 300	12 100	13 200
Ashford	8 000	14 500	13 900
Canterbury	5 800	9 300	10 300
Dover	3 600	6 100	6 100
Shepway	5 000	7 800	7 800
Thanet	3 000	6 500	6 500
Kent county	51 900	109 300	116 000

Source: Derived from KCC (1990, 1993a), Bathos and Mumford (1994).

Dartford and Gravesham in the Thames Gateway area (see Table 4.2). This was in recognition of the development opportunities and the new infrastructure proposed to regenerate this area (see Chapter 3). In this regard, the Kent Thames-side Partnership proposals (see Chapter 3) emerged at an opportune time for many Kent local authorities because they served to relieve some of the development pressure on the Maidstone/Medway Gap and west Kent more generally.

The interrelationship between employment-based development potential, housing potential and environmental capacity has, as already discussed, been at the heart of the regulation of land use in Kent. The regeneration of the Thames Gateway provided a strategic opportunity to upgrade the quality of the environment and to enhance the economic base of the area. This allowed a continuation of strong planning policies in Kent which had, through the 1970s and 1980s, minimised the use of what KCC planners called 'fresh land' by maximising the use of land within the existing built-up area. In Dartford's case, preference had been given since the early 1980s to the development of sites damaged by past mineral working and industrial activity. Regional guidance supported this sequential approach to new housing developments in north Kent where the reuse of derelict and contaminated sites was the first priority and greenfield land was only to be released as a last resort (GOSE, 1996).

Social housing issues, however, were missing from regional debates throughout the 1980s and 1990s. In the early 1980s, the Secretary of State for the Environment deleted a draft structure plan policy which addressed local housing needs and gave preferential treatment to certain household groups, on the grounds that issues of housing need and site suitability should be considered at district level. This continued to be a particular issue of concern for the districts in north and east Kent. In the mid-1990s, the Government Office for the South East had no specific policy line on this issue except to suggest that the 'larger opportunity sites' in the Thames Gateway should provide for a 'reasonable mix and balance' of house types and sizes to cater for a range of housing needs (ibid., p.10).

To conclude, since the early 1980s two structuring ideas dominated the discussion on the spatial implications of the 'numbers game' in Kent. First was the importance of securing a balance of employment and housing development at each approved growth point. Housing growth provision was therefore entwined with debates on economic development. In Kent Thames-side this evolved into a spatial strategy that used new employment and retail development to create new demands for housing in the area (KTP, 1995; Hull and Vigar, 1998). The second key structuring idea was the long-standing restraint of development in the areas of landscape and high-value agricultural land in the buoyant housing market areas of west and mid-Kent. These environmental issues had been a high priority for the people of Kent and, as the next section will show, specific housing proposals were actively debated through the local plan procedures, making housing a highly political local issue.

A consensus on key structuring principles   As a government actor, KCC was not able to impose itself at the regional level to anything like the same extent as the West Midlands metropolitan authorities. KCC had helped to shape the housing numbers required within the county, but in the complex political context of London and its surrounding hinterland, KCC had to take a supportive role within the regional planning mechanism, SERPLAN. On housing issues it therefore followed the SERPLAN growth management strategy of designated growth points beyond the metropolitan green belt to absorb its share of regional household growth (see Chapter 3).

In those instances where KCC acted strategically on housing issues, its approach was firmly linked to economic development, as at Ashford and Maidstone and more recently at Kings Hill (see Chapter 5) and in Kent Thames-side. Negotiations over the latter two developments largely took place outside development plan arenas. However, the regulatory principles of what could be allowed and where within the buoyant areas of housing demand in Kent were both well established and accepted by all the regional actors. In areas of weak market demand, however, new mechanisms were needed to allow partnership arrangements to form to address the complex issues involved. The Kent Thames-side initiative is one example which has led to a new partnership approach between KCC, the two district authorities and the major landowner in the area, Blue Circle Industries (see Chapter 3). Housing issues here were conceptualised in terms of the effect of private sector housing investment in helping to kick-start other private investment and enhance the value of land.

In areas of weak demand, such as the Thames Gateway, private sector developers needed government resources and commitment to provide the certainty they required before being able to commit themselves. Neither the HBF nor the CPRE were active in the area development partnerships in Kent. The CPRE found that their strong interests in environmental protection were matched by the county and district authorities. The HBF had regular contact with the Kent Chief Planning Officers Group through meetings on a quarterly basis. They expected discussions on market demand and district housing totals to take place within the structure plan arenas. They reserved their lobbying effort for these and regional level arenas.

Besides its strategic project-based housing developments, KCC was involved in quelling district and local stakeholder opposition to increased housing growth in specific locations. The place-related aspects of the RPG targets became politically charged, with the county lobbying MPs and using its influence in the House of Commons. Political mobilisation on housing growth issues was prevalent at every political level. For example, Maidstone Borough Council found its additional housing growth politically difficult to accept and contested the housing figures strongly at the EIP. However, the panel allocated even more housing to the Borough in the 2006–2011 period than even the County Council had argued for.

In addition, there was a feeling amongst the local planning policy community that Ashford had tended to be used as a 'sink' (district planner) for housing land allocations in the 1970s and 1980s. Ashford Borough Council considered that it had been set unrealistic allocations in successive structure plans given the then prevailing low market demand conditions. In turn, such allocations infuriated housebuilders keen to ensure that the full extent of Kent's housing demand was realised. The HBF questioned the policy of directing allocations away from areas of high market demand to those of low demand without additional resources being provided to improve market conditions in the areas of low demand.

In the 1990s, local politics played a part in tempering the excesses of housing allocations. Many district authorities undertook extensive local consultation on their housing growth alternatives, yet still received strong opposition during plan inquiries from local groups and residents. In Ashford this led to a proposal for the development of a new community to the south-east of the town in their district plan. Ashford Borough Council was praised by the public inquiry inspector for the way it had handled the local opposition to housing growth:

> The step-by-step approach by which Ashford BC have finally produced their housing allocations ... and the way in which their technical analyses were subjected to wide ranging consultation and criticism followed by consideration and approval by their elected members, cannot be faulted. (Inspector's report into Ashford Borough Council's district plan (unpublished) quoted in Ashford Borough Council, 1993, p.29)

The most significant aspect of the spatial strategies under discussion in Kent was the acceptance by the main stakeholders of planning policies which protect the environment and promote the sustainable development of balanced communities. This reflects the stability of the relationships between key actors at the county level, who have all been together long enough to know what each of the other actors expects of them. This contrasts with the West Midlands, where strong officer networks were necessary to maintain a political consensus on these issues.

Lancashire: an uncertain housing future?

The 1990s marked the end of a 40-year period during which Lancashire was used by Manchester and Liverpool as a reception area catering for their population overspill. It was assumed at regional level that net in-migration would cease from Greater Manchester but that a steady flow of in-migrants from other parts of the country would continue (NWRA, 1995). The story in the Lancashire case highlights the political bargaining between the districts and the county council to steer the location of housing growth, and the way the HBF was able to exploit this disunity. We first begin with the broader spatial debates within the plan-making arenas on growth and regeneration, before analysing the institutional manoeuvring to deflect future housing growth.

In the 1990s, housing debates were strongly influenced by two wider discourses: urban regeneration and sustainable development. Measures to combat both the economic and environmental 'degradation' of the predominantly nineteenth-century east Lancashire towns dominated county council strategy from the early 1970s (DoE 1996a). This concern was reflected in the strategic issues of the adopted structure plan (see Chapter 3), which aimed to steer some of the market demand from the west of Lancashire to the east. It was hoped that new housing investment could be attracted to the urban areas as land became available through demolition of poor-quality housing. There was, however, concern that low market demand and the quality of the environment in these areas would deter investment without substantial resources to change market conditions and perceptions (LCCPD, 1995, p.44).

This issue was taken up at the structure plan examination-in-public. Concern was expressed at how the county council's strategy for investment along a north–south growth corridor would affect attempts to achieve the sustainable regeneration of east Lancashire: 'Any extensive development of growth points outside the main urban areas in a County with the regeneration problems of Lancashire would risk jeopardising that regeneration and creating undesirable encroachment on the countryside,' (Critchley and Smith, 1995, p.19).

The Regional Guidance Note for the north-west (DoE 1996a), the structure plan and the examination-in-public report recognised that the reuse of inner urban sites and the utilisation of the existing stock were priorties, but failed to provide political support for action. This was a well-documented issue in the structure plan's technical working papers on housing and in structure plan policy which encouraged housing on recycled urban land and the reuse of redundant buildings.

A long-standing planning concern within the county, particularly at district level, was the protection of both the best physical environments and agricultural land. This included the national designations of high-grade agricultural land in west and north Lancashire, the area of outstanding national beauty in north-east Lancashire and the green belt designations. These constraints were factored into a broad-brush settlement appraisal as part of the consultation draft structure plan, taking into account infrastructure capacity, regional economic policies, district environmental policies and market demand for housing. The broad housing numbers proposed in the consultation draft reflected this appraisal and suggested that housing demand should be capped in South Ribble and West Lancashire districts (see Table 4.3). There was thus a physical environment discourse, similar to that in Kent, wrapped around the debates on the housing numbers game in Lancashire. Despite the strong strategic steer given to regional competitiveness, there were few debates linking the housing allocations to potential inward investment sites. This is in part explained by the dominant role played by the Commission for the New Towns (CNT) and the scale of their existing permissions for new housing in the region. The winding down of the CNT at the end of the 1990s encouraged both Chorley and Preston Borough Councils to seek to reduce their future housing supply commitments and the associated infrastructure costs they might have to bear (Hull and Vigar, 1998). The result of the two concerns of urban regeneration, particularly in the towns of East Lancashire, and the physical environment discourse resulted in a strategy to redirect housing demand along the central, west–east regeneration corridor from Preston eastwards.

Trading housing figures in public inquiry arenas   Lancashire was in a similar situation to Kent, as a county in a larger region, where regional housing issues were discussed as an adjunct to other issues through a number of overlapping networks. But, unlike the case of Kent, there was not the same embedded support at regional or county level to protect national designations at all costs. In addition it was unclear how the concept of a 'transport corridor' should frame planned growth. At the regional level, Lancashire County Council (LCC) had influence in the North West Regional Association strategy and the regional guidance preparation steering committee meetings, yet there was little strategic discussion on housing issues at the regional level beyond the scale of the population movements to be expected from the Manchester and Liverpool conurbations. This contrasted with the visible interaction between the urban districts and rural counties which came together to agree agendas and resolve problems in the West Midlands.

The Lancashire Structure Plan was put out to public consultation simultaneously with the production of the draft regional advice to GONW. This focused attention on the examination-in-public of the structure plan, as the main political arena for the testing of the regional housing figures. The examination-in-public (EIP) provided a forum for the HBF, the CPRE and the districts to advance their particular viewpoints on the amount and location of housing growth.

Both the HBF and the CPRE used the EIP to challenge the scale of housing growth that the county council was proposing. The CPRE, the Countryside Commission and certain districts regarded the target of 66 000 dwellings as excessive. GONW considered it represented the upper limit of what should be contemplated, whilst the HBF wanted a figure nearly 10 000 higher. The panel chairman sent LCC and the HBF away to agree the different elements of housing demand. LCC had agreed with some districts prior to the EIP that local capacity constraints on housing were needed to enable land to be reserved for other community needs. Precisely which districts these agreements covered seemed to change between successive planning documents, but South Ribble, Blackpool, Chorley and West Lancashire were most affected. Here there were extensive areas of green belt and high-grade agricultural land. Reductions made for some of these districts, against trend housing demand projections, required compensatory measures to be made elsewhere. Initially, additions were made to the totals for the districts of Ribble Valley, Hyndburn, Pendle and Wyre (see Table 4.3).

Preston Borough Council tried to influence the structure plan housing allocations by progressing their local plan concurrently, since they were wary of accepting such a level of allocations with the winding down of CNT and the expected withdrawal of capital finance for infrastructure. At the time, 5000 units of their original allocation were covered by existing planning permissions, received by CNT from national government. For Lancaster and Chorley Districts, infrastructure funding was also the key to accepting their 'share' of new housing. In the latter's case, 20 years of growth in central Lancashire, arising from the development of the New Town, had raised public opposition to development on greenfield locations.

Table 4.3   Changing housing numbers in Lancashire, 1991–2006 (net dwelling units over plan period)

District	Trend -based	Structure plan, 1993	Structure plan deposit, 1994	EIP, 1995
Blackburn	6 000	6 000	6 000	5 980
Blackpool	4 000	4 000	4 000	4 170
Burnley	4 050	3 250	4 050	3 130
Chorley	5 900	5 900	5 900	7 310
Fylde	4 850	4 000	4 000	5 170
Hyndburn	2 600	3 300	3 300	3 150
Lancaster	7 600	6 400	6 400	8 300
Pendle	3 000	3 950	3 950	3 180
Preston	8 250	8 350	8 400	7 180
Ribble Valley	700	2 100	2 100	2 410
Rossendale	2 850	2 800	2 800	2 490
South Ribble	6 700	4 500	4 500	4 710
West Lancashire	5 700	4 550	4 600	4 620
Wyre	4 850	6 050	6 050	5 620
Lancashire	66 000	65 150	66 000	67 420

Source: Derived from DoE (1996a) and LCCPD (1995a).

In contrast to the situation in Kent, both the CPRE and the HBF were active in influencing public sector interpretations of the regional household projections. The CPRE argued that the indigenous housing needs of the population, in particular single-person households, should be a priority. The HBF countered that housing policy was best left to the market, and that smaller households should not be assumed to demand smaller houses. The HBF and regional house-builders sought consistently to increase the county's assumptions on in-migration, vacancy and second homes, while reducing household size assumptions. Interestingly, the EIP panel tried to satisfy both these pressure groups' concerns in their final analysis. On the one hand, they erred towards caution in translating the projections; on the other, they increased the total housing requirements by some 1400 dwellings. This included an allowance for second homes, a higher vacancy rate and a contingency allowance in case some of the land was not available during the plan period.

The EIP provided the forum for negotiation and compromise on the apportionment of subregional household growth. In a classic prisoners' dilemma situation, with no detailed housing strategy in place and a wish to protect their own interests, the districts used a variety of arguments to volunteer each other for more allocations and ended up 'knifing each other in the back' (property interest). If they had all held out and 'joined and fought together' (property interest) then the outcome might have been different (Hull and Vigar, 1998). Thus the local authorities that had been subject to New Town allocations in the past argued for a reduction in their allocations to counter the growth assumptions implicit in past allocations. Other district authorities, which failed to anticipate the scale of the negotiation on housing figures at the EIP or to prepare their technical arguments sufficiently, felt excluded from the strategic decisions brokered in the EIP arena. This subsequently led to considerable difficulties in the allocation of housing land in development plans for many of them, such as Lancaster City Council, as they encountered considerable public opposition to many sites which they were then forced to put forward. Lancaster was forced to accept an additional 1900 dwellings between the consultation stage and the adopted plan.

Whilst the EIP allowed a compromise to be reached between the growth scenarios of the county and the HBF and the particular local concerns of the districts, there were feelings of mistrust between the participants, which hindered the formation of alliances and strategic visions. As a landowner, the CNT was considered to be more of an asset stripper than in the past, but as a key player in releasing sites for inward investment and housing it had to be given respect. The EIP panel increased the range of housing sites to be provided by some of the districts, which felt powerless to prevent the HBF from developing the easy sites at the expense of the brownfield sites. One planner commented, 'what happens is the best sites are continually creamed off, so you top up and the best sites are creamed off again' (district planner). The housing numbers game in Lancashire was thus played out in a different way from the other two case study areas. In the absence of strong direction from the county council, and without a clear consensus on spatial strategy, Lancashire's growth allocations were decided by political negotiation during the final consultation stage on the structure plan. As with our other cases, this case shows how, within the strong structuring of the housing land policy discourse and practices provided at the national level, there was significant variation in local interpretation and politics.

The planning system and releasing land for housing

The case studies illustrate the impact of contrasting relations between the various parties in the housing land allocation process. The discussion of housing numbers and locations took place in a relatively structured way in a hierarchical series of arenas for interaction. These 'cascade' down (a metaphor often used in the 1990s) from the DETR through the Government Regional Offices to the county and then the districts, as in Figure 4.1. Around each of these levels of governance, the policy community widens out horizontally (against this vertical dynamic) to debate issues of relevance to the actors at that level. The key actors involved in the vertical 'cascade' of housing numbers always included representatives of central government, local authorities and the house-builders who debate the 'technical' issues of amount, location and flow of new dwellings. This technical interaction was structured by cross-cutting issues and practices laid down by national government. Occasionally, the horizontal networks of actors were able to intersect this vertical discourse to voice local political concerns about ways to accommodate market growth and, to a limited degree, bend the discourse to suit their own ends.

The policy discourse of 'housing numbers' was resolved through the public arenas of the planning system, involving a fairly narrow policy community. The main task was to translate the implications of the government's household projections into land allocations in local plans. Sufficiency of land supply was decided through discursive negotiation and the testing of 'technical' household projections. Two planning arenas were important to this debate: the preparation of regional planning guidance which allocated dwelling numbers among counties and districts, and the local development plan which allocated housing sites. The regional associations of local authorities were nominally in charge of collating draft regional advice to present to the secretary of state. The institutional capital available to each of these associations was variable, however, with different impacts in each case.

The HBF tried, first, to tie the local authorities to equating the regional household projections with new building requirements. Second, they lobbied to secure the release of sufficient sites in buoyant local markets. The inherent flexibility of the English planning system sometimes worked against the mechanistic cascade of central government policy. The disaggregation of the household projections at each level of the planning hierarchy provided an opportunity to review this 'top-down' policy process against local housing demand and housing capacity assessments. The review process was a competitive game played between the HBF, individual proactive local authorities and the regional association of local authorities. Where a regional or sub-regional consensus on housing policy was built up, as in the West Midlands and Kent, the 'cascade' process worked smoothly, providing policy certainty from regional level down to local plans and development control. If strategic level agreements could not be reached, the negotiation shifted downwards to the local plan level, where the regulatory task encountered a wider range of values and concerns. The task of political management was much harder at this level.

Here the debates raised specific spatial concerns. Residents put great store by protecting the amenity and environmental qualities of the places where they lived. Local authorities could not ignore the strength of local feeling where it was well-articulated. In Kent, the protection of the green belt and areas of outstanding natural beauty was taken as non-negotiable by the public sector. Only in circumstances where development would remove a despoiled environment and provide the anchor for area-wide redevelopment could land from the green belt be released for housing development. Both Solihull and Chorley, growth areas in their respective subregions, argued for a break in the extrapolation of past housing trends to protect their attractive high-quality living environments. Districts in the West Midlands and Lancashire were trying to position themselves as high quality environments to secure the label of 'non-negotiable' territory for housing development.

During the 1990s, the housing requirement figures which emerged from the 'technical' debates within the 'closed' planning for housing policy community were subject to intense questioning by environmental groups, politicians and the media. To stakeholders outside the planning system, the housing figures appeared to cascade down from the national government, allowing little local autonomy, with the debates highly constrained by decisions made by the administrative tier above (Murdoch *et al.*, 1999). At the local political level, elected councillors, in many cases wary of protests from their electorate, instructed planners to negotiate to reduce their housing numbers by employing convincing planning arguments. This trading in numbers was very noticeable in Lancashire, with the local authorities which were ill-prepared, losing out in negotiation. In the West Midlands, the local authorities pushed the debate to the regional level in an attempt to stabilise the conflicts.

Kent developed a more coherent spatial strategy, linking housing growth points to underpin their economic development policies. Thus each case developed a different approach to this highly political issue, within the nationally structured debates and procedures for the release of housing land.

In each of the case study areas, it was difficult to integrate economic concerns, voiced in terms of creating jobs (see Chapter 5), with growing environmental and social concerns. Particularly in Kent, environmental concerns provided the first sieve with which to discount areas from accepting housing growth. Thereafter the growth was steered around the county and located to sustain the economic development strategy. The power of environmental designations provided a similar undercurrent to policy development in the West Midlands. The 1970s idea of transport corridors was a way of brokering agreement over future housing land allocations beyond the immediate conurbation. However, the WMRF embraced a wider discussion of the issues, employing consultants to explore the complex dynamics of the way housing markets work. It tried to expose the myth of the housing 'trickle down' effect which asserted that, if more four-bedroomed homes were built on greenfield sites, affordable housing and starter homes would be released at the bottom end of the market. This research also suggested that the continual over-provision of housing sites would eventually draw investment away from areas of low demand in the centre of conurbations. A vicious circle sets in as, when residents cannot sell their homes, they end up renting them out, the community structure changes with a younger, more itinerant population mix, and eventually collapse can occur. It has been difficult for planners to give voice to what then became, in effect, social policy issues in a planning system constrained by a narrow land use focus. The review of the 1992-based household projections therefore provided the WMRF with the opportunity to take the housing debate into issues of affordability and accessibility. It attempted to assess future housing need and present unmet needs, linking this assessment to the capacity of existing stock and to issues of regeneration and sustainability.

The integration of environmental, economic and social concerns did not develop as far in Lancashire or Kent, although both attempted to control growth in relatively buoyant markets on sustainable development grounds. Kent took a strong policy line on the reuse of derelict and despoiled sites in order to protect what it called 'fresh land'. The brownfield–greenfield debate was a rhetorical issue in Lancashire and the West Midlands, but neither area was able to use planning tools to control the release of greenfield land.

Allocating housing numbers was moulded into a narrow debate among a small policy community in the 1980s and 1990s. The introduction of a plan-led system in the early 1990s increased the number of housebuilders interacting in planning arenas. However, overall the range of active participants hardly changed from the 1970s. The 1993 Regional Conference in the West Midlands was the one arena which tentatively extended participation to various local groups. The West Midlands is also the one case study where joint working between housing and planning officers became the norm in the consideration of housing policy issues.

The planning system provided the key arenas for the determination of policy through the different spatial scales. The main actors clustered around these arenas, developing practices at national and regional level which clothed a highly political issue in the mantle of technical calculation. This in turn set the ground rules within which the local politics of housing land development was played out. The 'housing numbers' approach was essentially a form of demand accommodation, or 'predict and provide', as it became known in the transport field (see Chapter 6). There was substantial continuity in approach throughout the 1980s and 1990s, suggesting that the contextual changes identified in Chapter 1 had little impact in this policy area. The key actors in this policy sector were entwined in a complicated relationship with the planning system. On the one hand, they clung to the historical system rigidities and certainty, which helped them prevent other actors achieving their goals; but, on the other hand, they championed system discretion where it would ease achievement of their own objectives. The HBF always objects to housing allocation levels in such arenas, but its public face masks its general acceptance of the 'rules of the game'. The planning system thus mediates the considerable tension between the main actors over local housing land issues. This tension was heightened by the greater emphasis on the development plan in the 1990s (see Chapter 1).

Nevertheless, local practices vary, both in their capacity to articulate spatial strategies and in their ability to build consensus on key parameters among key actors. This has allowed some innovation as, for example, in the West Midlands Regional Conference procedure. By the end of the 1990s, it was clear that the 'numbers game' itself was up for reconsideration. The secretary of state identified the approach as an example of 'predict and provide' in 1998, and 'monitor and manage' was put forward as an alternative (DETR, 1998h, CPRE, 1999). The devolution thrust was used to shift the focus of attention in developing housing land allocation policy to the regional level. The national government's (DETR, 1998b) proposals to widen stakeholder involvement in preparing regional planning guidance also posed a threat to current HBF influence and may contribute to 'widening' the policy agenda and policy community. There has also been increasing emphasis on the significance of attention to 'place quality' rather than merely housing numbers (DETR, 1998j).

In conclusion, the procedures and practices of allocating land for housing generated an inertia which restricted attempts to widen those involved in housing land debates. It also inhibited making links to the environmental, social and economic issues surrounding housing stock and the need for renewal. Finally, however, the 'housing numbers game' showed signs of having played out its utility. With more stakeholders getting involved, it will be harder to keep the political choices within the framework of technical calculation. With more local power to frame policy agendas, it will be difficult to isolate the location of housing from other dimensions of place quality. It remains to be seen how far the preparation of regional planning guidance in the twenty-first century will provide regional stakeholders with the opportunity to set their own housing strategy. It will be interesting to evaluate, as new practices develop, how far regional housing decisions are made on the basis of politics and horse trading or whether agreement can be reached on the spatial ordering principles to steer regional growth. In allocating land for housing, local authorities will reflect local concerns about the negative impacts on local environments and the public sector resources required for infrastructure. Their decisions will always be political, but, if trust and new ways of working and networking can be invigorated by regional government, regional agreements on housing land allocations and settlement change can be used to negotiate between the centre and the local level.

5 Jobs, Sites and Portfolios: Allocating Large Sites for Economic Development Purposes

Creating jobs or competitive assets?

This chapter focuses on the role of the planning system in promoting and regulating the provision of sites for large industrial developments. The sites in question are either for single-company purposes or for industrial estates or business parks. Although the scale of land involved is much less than in the housing field, the location and quality of such sites is critical to their attractiveness to companies. Increasingly, the provision of such sites has been emphasised in national and regional policy, in terms of their key role in promoting economic competitiveness in a globalising economy. Typically, such sites were on greenfield land adjacent to motorway access points. In this activity, therefore, the planning system is both linked to national and local economic development agendas and faced with mediating conflicts between perceived economic development priorities and the increasingly powerful environmental requirement to conserve greenfield land and reduce road travel.

Until the 1980s, the tension between economic development considerations and environmental ones was framed primarily as one between providing sites for job-generating industry and conserving agricultural land. Behind this lay deeper oppositions of images of urban working classes and industrial pollution versus the rural landscape and way of life (Hall *et al.*, 1973; Williams, 1975). Greenfield site allocation could be justified so long as the highest quality farmland was protected and there was a need for jobs. It was also accepted that, from time to time,

the national economic interest (that is, the 'needs' of nationally important companies) could justify specific site allocations. This chapter illustrates the shift from this 'framing discourse' in two directions. On the
economic development side, the emphasis changed from a focus on
'job needs' to overall local economic 'competitiveness'. On the environmental side, the change was from protecting farmland to conserving
landscape and reducing road-based travel. All our cases were affected
by these changes. The West Midlands developed innovative approaches
to both coalition building and agenda development which influenced
other localities and national planning policy itself.

Whether justified by job needs or by economic competitiveness, the
supply of large sites, meaning anything from around 10 to over 50
hectares, was a key issue for regional and local economic development
in the 1980s and 1990s. These sites were seen as particularly important
for relocating larger firms, either inward investors from another region
or country, or firms moving to a less congested part of a region.
(Throughout our study period, attracting large inward investment companies was a key objective of economic development strategies,
prompted by the belief that these would replace the jobs lost from traditional manufacturing. That this strategy could itself be criticised was
rarely addressed in our cases). However, demand for such sites was
limited in amount and highly selective geographically. By the 1990s,
servicing such sites with adequate infrastructure required either the
commitment of developer-investors or successful bids for subsidy from
central government or the EU. Competition within and between regions
for site development funding and associated infrastructure created an
uncertain climate for investors and a confused context for funders.
Local authorities with economic difficulties sought to allocate sites and
capture funding in their areas, while regions competed to attract major
companies with nationally funded investment packages. This generated
pressures for the strategic selection of major sites.

Until the 1990s, there had been little concern in the arenas of the
planning system about overallocation of sites for industrial purposes. In
many parts of the country by the early 1980s, providing sites for
employment generation had become a strong political priority, supported by government encouragement of the needs of business. 'Fast-
tracking' major allocations for inward investing companies was largely
accepted as necessary in the pursuit of jobs. The main constraint had
been environmental conservation and 'bad neighbour' considerations.
However, by the late 1980s, 'clearing' site allocations through the

planning system had become more contentious, because of the increasing pressure from environmental lobbies, as well as the competition between local authorities for sites. The Department of the Environment's emphasis on 'plan-led' planning also limited the flexibility of the planning response. In contrast to the housing field, the Department of Environment shared a concern for providing employment land with another government department, the Department for Trade and Industry. The tension between these two departments was never strategically resolved during the 1990s, and planning policy guidance gave little direction concerning how to address strategic policy frameworks for site allocation. It was left largely to local planning processes to work out how to proceed.

In parallel with these policy developments, the production relations of the supply of sites changed significantly. Until the mid-1980s, the public sector dominated the supply of sites, particularly the conversion of greenfield sites. English Estates, an agency originating in north-east England with a remit to develop industrial sites in areas of job need, and the New Town development corporations were very significant in this process (Fothergill *et al.*, 1987). In the Thatcher years, this policy was steadily reversed, with public subsidy incentives to the private sector to supply sites in areas of weak market activity. These incentives included enterprise zones, the Urban Programme, the urban development corporations, specific urban grants, the European structural funds and the Single Regeneration Budget (Oatley, 1998). Whilst the public sector continued to purchase many derelict sites (Watson, 1992; Healey, 1994), from the mid-1980s it became a significant seller of sites for industrial development, as it came under pressure to dispose of assets for financial and policy reasons (Adams *et al.*, 1994, p.210).

The shift in development initiative from the public to the private sector went in parallel with a change in the conception of the industrial developer. Until the 1980s it had been assumed that user demand drove supply and that companies seeking property for their own needs were the main 'developers' of industrial property (Fothergill *et al.*, 1987). In the 1970s, however, the financial institutions moved into investment in industrial estates, and encouraged property developers and investors to branch out into this market. By the 1980s, many local authority economic development teams and the urban development corporations shifted their attention from attracting companies as such, to attracting developers to invest in the production of industrial estates. The lure of Enterprise Zone and other subsidies added further encouragement to such investors and developers in the boom conditions of the mid-1980s (Healey, 1994, Ball and Pratt, 1994). National planning policy guidance accepted this dynamic as a desirable manifestation of market processes and exhorted local authorities not to discourage such 'speculative provision' (DoE, 1988b, para. 12).

As a result of this encouragement, and the 1980s property boom, a large supply of speculatively built industrial property came onto the market, particularly in the form of 'parks' of one kind or another (Axford, 1994, p.32). However, by the 1990s, a more sombre situation prevailed (Ball and Pratt, 1994; Adams *et al.*, 1994; Healey, 1994; Tsolacas, 1995). The south east of England was left with a higher proportion of vacant industrial floorspace in the early 1990s than either the north west or the northern regions (Axford, 1994). However, the developer emphasis of the 1980s, coupled with the flexibility provided by Enterprise Zone regimes and the new 'B1' business class which allowed buildings to change use between light industrial and office uses without planning permission, allowed sites allocated for industry to be used for other commercial purposes, notably warehousing, retail and office uses. This had the effect of reducing stocks of land dedicated for industrial use. In this context, many local authorities, and eventually the Department of the Environment itself, sought a more managed approach to industrial land allocation in development plans.

This experience shifted attention among local economic development agents to user demand once again. Developers ventured only cautiously into the industrial arena, and then only with committed occupiers and typically a lot of support from a public sector agency (Healey, 1994, Tsolacas, 1995). The needs of companies replaced the demands of developers in local policy makers' conceptions. The 'competitiveness' agenda concentrated attention on the kinds of sites which large inward investing companies sought. The problem then was to find a way to supply such sites. By the mid-1990s, enterprise zones and urban development corporations, which had become the main sources of supply of 'brownfield' sites, were mostly winding down, yet the new environmental politics meant that it was a contentious matter to allocate greenfield sites. This thrust local authorities into a second competitive arena, that of capturing funding for site development for 'brownfield' site development. It was therefore increasingly difficult to separate regulatory planning policy from that of investment policy. This generated an institutional challenge to devise ways of linking the arenas used for planning policy development to the work of the Department of Trade and Industry, the Department of the Environment's Urban Policy section, regional and local development agencies and English Estates, which, by 1993, had evolved into English Partnerships. Sites also needed transport and other infrastructure, drawing in yet more central and local government departments and agencies. This tension persisted into the design for the New Labour administration's ideas for regional development agencies and regional planning guidance (DETR, 1998b, 1998d). Thus, by the 1990s, negotiating new locations for industry had become a complex policy dilemma, both institutionally and in terms of devising new policy discourses.

Yet national planning policy gave little attention to the issue. The major innovation of the 1980s was the change to the B1 Use Class referred to earlier. This change caused great anxiety to local authorities wherever office development was a more attractive market, as local authority planners feared that their 'stock' of job-generating industrial sites would be used up. However, the needs of large companies and big inward investing firms could always be protected by the invocation of a 'national interest' override.

Planning Policy Guidance 4 (DoE, 1988b) stressed that a supply of land should be available to meet all demand for industrial and commercial development. PPG 1 argued in the same year that 'weighty national or local need' could 'outweigh important planning objections' (DoE, 1988a). Planning authorities were exhorted not to obstruct 'economic prosperity', to provide a 'sufficient' amount and a 'variety' of sites to meet any demand, to have a positive view of speculative development in supplying sites and to encourage 'high technology industries' in urban areas to assist in urban regeneration. By 1992, however, the environmental sustainability agenda had moderated this accommodating attitude. There was little substantive change in the revised PPG 4, but it acknowledged the new environmental priority to reduce the need to travel, and recognised that it might be necessary to reserve locations for industrial development if land was scarce (DoE, 1992b, para. 11). The revised Planning Policy Guidance Note 1 of 1997 (DoE, 1997) advised local authorities to 'take account of economic considerations' in their development plans by providing for 'choice, flexibility and competition' (DoE, 1997, para. 46).

Despite such exhortations, and in sharp contrast to the housing field, where the rules of the 'numbers game' were carefully specified (see Chapter 4), it was left to local planning authorities to work out how to approach the task of industrial land allocation. As the following account illustrates, a form of 'numbers game' also appears in this policy area, using a language of a 'stock of sites'. But, rather than a 'top-down' allocation based on national and regional demographic assessments, these numbers were typically built up from local authority 'wish lists', aggregated up into county and regional totals and then expressed in structure and local plans. By the late 1980s, this aggregative approach was no longer adequate. Local authorities were therefore faced with developing more sensitive and sophisticated approaches. A new discourse emerged, focused on consideration of the different dynamics and needs of the various industrial property submarkets. This replaced the concept of a 'stock' of sites with the notion of a 'flow' through a 'development pipeline'. This new discourse focused in particular on the need to have a sufficient flow of sites 'cleared' through the planning system and linked to necessary funds for site preparation and servicing in order to provide the top end of a 'portfolio' of sites with sufficient variety to reflect the nature of the subregional economy. However, as subregional economies are different in their production relations, development situation and governance context, the discourse evolved in different ways in each area. The three case study areas illustrate these differences in a context where government planning policy lacked the policy straitjacket which characterised the housing field. The chapter reviews, first, the evolution of the policy discourses in the three areas, and then examines the institutional relations through which the discourses were developed.

Premium sites, regional selectivity and area transformation: policy agendas and discourses

The evolution of the policy agendas for large economic development sites in our three areas illustrates the struggles which take place in situations where potentially deep conflicts exist between different institutional networks and policy communities. In our cases these conflicts were exacerbated by the context of economic competition among firms for commercial opportunity and access to subsidy funding. The West Midlands case illustrates the emergence of a coherent discourse, which reframed thinking among many players and was effectively disseminated among them. It also helped to develop national planning policy. In the Lancashire case, the evolution of the policy discourse was more diffuse, lacking the strategic efforts at discourse transformation which characterised the West Midlands. In Kent, the reconstruction of the discourse was being forced by the pace of change in economic conditions and government investments over which local authorities had limited control. In the West Midlands, we focus on the regional level, in the other two cases we focus principally on the county level.

The West Midlands: developing a 'portfolio' approach

Land for industrial development has long been a key issue for politicians and business in this industrial heartland region. Until the 1970s, the concern for industrial sites around the conurbation was driven by the expansion needs of existing companies. However, by the 1970s, the major companies were consolidating or retrenching, and had less need for new sites. This allowed a 'comfortable consensus' to build up between the conurbation and the shires, which accepted that the priority was to attract industry into the urban areas, to replace jobs and reuse vacant sites. This strategy underpinned the conurbation structure plan of the then West Midlands County Council (Healey *et al.*, 1988). By the early 1980s, however, it became increasingly clear that the regional economy was in deep recession. The area around the periphery, and in particular in Solihull, where the major national motorway routes intersected (M5, M6, M40, M42), along with the National Exhibition Centre and Birmingham Airport, continued to attract companies interested in one of the best locations nationally for industrial and commercial activity (see Figure 3.5). However, many parts of the conurbation, and particularly the Black Country to the west, inner Birmingham and Coventry, were badly hit by the rationalisation and closure of large companies, with 'knock on' effects among the many smaller firms. This focused the attention of the West Midlands Metropolitan County Council on a new task of economic development. Attracting inward investment became a key priority.

By the late 1980s, it became evident that a more sophisticated approach was needed to the industrial land issue. Firstly, it was increasingly clear that the justification for large land allocations on greenfield sites could not be made in terms of an overall amount of land needed for firms, as there was a good deal of vacant industrial land in the conurbation. Secondly, the conurbation was potentially in competition with surrounding counties for attractive development sites. The shire counties around the conurbation, which had traditionally resisted industry as a threat to their landscape and class composition, now welcomed clean, high-skill production activities. Some means of limiting the competition between local authorities was needed if the conurbation was not to lose out to the shires. By the mid-1990s, the impetus for collaboration had moved to the regional scale as the region felt it was losing out to other regions in attracting inward investment because of the lack of well-located large sites.

In its efforts to address the issue of the location of economic development sites at a regional level, in a situation of acute potential conflict over locational issues, the West Midlands drew on its traditions of elite collaborative working at the regional level (see Chapter 3) to evolve a widely shared sophisticated approach to industrial land market management. This involved a shift from the conception of allocating hectares of land, 'cascading' from regional allocations into structure and local plans following the model developed in the housing field, to an emphasis on a 'portfolio' of sites, with a flow of strategic sites available at any one time, reserved for 'inward investment'. The justification for the allocation shifted also, from an emphasis on creating jobs through allocating sites ('jobs on sites') to a concern for the quality of sites in the eyes of inward investing companies. Throughout, the discussion was contained within a spatial understanding of the conurbation pushing at its boundaries in search of land for new economic development investments. Locational choices were therefore substantially constrained. In this context, key concerns centred on ways to keep the site allocation process within the framework of the planning system, and hence 'legitimate', and how to protect sites from alternative development.

This discursive shift is evident in the treatment of sites for economic development in the sequence of development plans and regional guidance from the early 1980s to the mid-1990s, each one providing an arena for developing and reworking the ideas. The relation between the formation of the strategic guidance and the development of the content of the unitary development plans (UDPs) increasingly became an interactive one, rather than a hierarchical cascade. As all key stakeholders were involved in the regional consensus-building effort, a common approach developed which permeated both the conurbation UDPs and the regional guidance.

The first signs of a shift emerged in the inquiry into the West Midlands Structure Plan, approved in 1982. The objective, as in previous policy, was to increase the amount of industrial land allocated. 'Major locations' for development were specifically identified and there was consideration of differentiating among the larger sites allocated. The revised Structure Plan (1986) had a policy on 'prime locations', which were to be protected from alienation to other uses. By 1988, this discussion of 'prime locations' and 'land for high technology industry' had evolved into the concept of a 'premium site'. The regional planning guidance (DoE, 1988c), affirmed that most industrial sites were to be found within the conurbations. It also stressed the need for 300 hectares by 2001 for 'high quality development'. This is specified as requiring sites for

> high technology development … [with] easy access to the motorway system; proximity to the conurbation or Coventry; ready access to its workforce, preferably by both public and private transport (but sites need not immediately adjoin the built-up area) … in attractive settings and developed to a very high standard: low density, low site cover, high quality building, extensive landscaping and generous parking. (DoE, 1988c, para. 9)

This is a clear signal that the free-standing business park model was envisaged. The environment is treated as an implicit constraint (on greenfield land allocation) and an asset (an attractive landscape). The criterion of accessibility to public transport derived from social and labour market considerations, not environmental ones.

The requirement for 300 hectares was linked to two principles. The first, a form of 'phasing' policy, required that 'a new site should be released when monitoring indicates that the existing site will be over three-quarters occupied within three years' time' (ibid., para. 7). What was required was therefore a 'flow' of sites rather than a 'stock' in a particular time period. The second principle specifies three broad locations for major development: along the M42, near the NEC and the regional airport, in the Black Country, and in the Coventry area. All these allocations were in and around the conurbation, implicitly reflecting an 'outward expansion' strategy.

The discourse evolved further as the conurbation authorities began preparing their unitary development plans, for which new 'intellectual capital' was generated. The concept of a 'balanced portfolio of sites' replaced the emphasis on quantity of land with a focus on site quality. The West Midlands Regional Forum (WMRF) also initiated a study to identify the 'premium sites' indicated in the regional planning guidance. This approach is illustrated in Birmingham City Council's UDP. Underpinning this plan was a sophisticated analysis of the 'industrial land market'. This was divided into four submarkets: 'premium', 'best urban', 'good urban' and 'other urban'. The notion of a flow of sites through the 'development pipeline' was related to each of these, in order to estimate the site allocation requirements during the plan period. The plan allocated two large sites. This approach was followed consistently in the other UDPs, with a further two large sites being allocated in Solihull. All the sites were peripheral, greenfield locations. The development of ideas continued into the 1990s, when the regional guidance was revised (see Chapter 3). One theme running through the revision was the recognition that the process of identifying the 'premium sites' across the region was fraught with technical difficulty and political disagreement. This led to the view that the sites had to be selected at a regional level. By this time also, the 'premium site' category had been further differentiated to identify a 'top of the range' category of 'major investment sites (MIS)'. The problems of justifying greenfield (and green belt) land allocation, of co-ordinating with infrastructure investment and of obtaining funds for brownfield decontamination and clearance had all become more acute, while the arguments against greenfield land allocation had become more robust. This meant that the competition between local authorities could not be resolved by a 'fair shares' allocation of sites among them.

By 1991, the process of revising the regional planning guidance reaffirmed the concepts of 'a balanced portfolio of development opportunities' across the region.' (WMRF, 1992, para. 4.13) and premium industrial sites, though there was slow progress in bringing these sites forward (ibid., para. 4.19). The issue then moved into the arena of the 1993 Regional Conference, set up under the aegis of the WMRF (see Chapter 3). By this time, transport issues, particularly concern about investment in motorways around the Birmingham conurbation, were causing considerable anxiety to the business community (see Chapter 6). Local authorities were primarily concerned about the location of sites. They also worried about industrial sites being switched to other uses, and feared that growth in the freestanding market towns of the shires would undermine urban regeneration and the development of 'brownfield' sites. There was widespread recognition that the identification and phasing of premium sites was not working, as the triggers for allocating the next site in the 'pipeline' had not been activated. Developers had to fight sites through the regulatory system on a site-by-site basis, in the arena of the planning appeal system. The procedures for site identification were proving lengthy and only one site, in Solihull, had so far obtained planning permission, in this case via the appeal process.

Although the approach was continued in the new draft regional guidance (RPG 11) (DoE, 1995a), environmental criteria were to shape the search for new sites. Two new large sites were explicitly mentioned. By this time, a company was actively seeking one of the sites, with the support of economic development agencies. The regional planning guidance (RPG 11) also made the criteria for the location of all larger sites much more explicit. In addition, the RPG argued that the region needed 'major investment sites': 'up to two large sites for new industrial and commercial investment, each by a single large multi-national organisation … [of] a minimum size of 50 hectares' *(*ibid., para. 7.19*)*. A key concern was to protect the sites from subdivision into smaller lots. Such sites could therefore 'break' the environmental criteria and locate on greenfield sites, in order to ensure that the region had sufficient assets to compete in the 'market' of capturing major inward investing companies.

These policies and criteria in Regional Planning Guidance Note 11 reflect a strong effort by the Government Office and the WMRF to mobilise a strategic regional approach to the industrial land allocation process. The result was, once again, considerable specificity in site allocations and in policy criteria. However, ensuring that these major sites were processed through the development plan system presented a major challenge, although several key stakeholders shared this objective. Stakeholders in both the local authorities and the private sector wanted clear and stable policies, to progress sites through anticipated environmental contention and to reduce inter-district competition. The overall objective was to identify the sites in the context of the regional planning guidance, which would then allow them to be treated as 'material considerations' in planning applications, given that most of the unitary development plans had been approved before the 'major investment sites' were selected. It was also necessary to sort out how infrastructure and other investments would be provided, so that a quick response could be made to any potential inward investor. The Government Office had a crucial role in these considerations, as it had to make decisions on the allocation of investment for site preparation. It would also have to decide how to link decisions about sites to the planning process, and to the development plan framework in particular. As with the local authorities, the Government Office was caught between its role in promoting the competitiveness agenda and its role as arbiter in the planning system.

Developing regional selectivity in Lancashire

In contrast to the West Midlands, parts of Lancashire have been living with economic difficulty for many years. Generating jobs and bringing in new industrial activities were long-standing objectives of local and regional planners and politicians. So too was the objective of conserving the county's high-quality agricultural land and its valued landscape assets. Economic development thus co-existed with a strong environmental concern, leading to a well-established county strategy of concentrating development around the urban areas.

By the 1980s, a key problem for the county was that the supply of large well-serviced sites was becoming depleted as the Central Lancashire New Town was wound up. Because the new towns in the county supplied large, well-serviced industrial sites until the 1990s, the county council itself had channelled its own energetic economic development activities through Lancashire Enterprises Ltd. (latterly Enterprise plc) which provided direct support for firms (see Chapter 3). However, by the late 1980s, the county and the districts faced competition both from the south of the region (around Greater Manchester and Warrington in particular) and from each other for subsidy to prepare sites with appropriate conditions and services. In parallel, the new environmental discourse began to permeate discussions in local government policy making more generally. The overriding priority of economic development (and 'jobs') was challenged, as strong and well-organised environmental groups contested the allocations, arguing that sites should be located within urban areas, on brownfield sites and near public transport routes.

Until the 1990s, the discourse was dominated by the simple equation: 'sites = firms = jobs'. With unemployment an issue across most of the county, each district sought some large sites (known as 'strategic industrial development locations'). As in the West Midlands, districts calculated their 'wish list' of job needs, translated these into amounts of land and aggregated them into county totals. The structure plans then confirmed these allocations, to give the appearance of a hierarchical 'cascade' of land needs. Although the county council had maintained for many years a strategy of 'urban concentration', the larger sites were shared among the districts. The application of the 'urban concentration' strategy was in any case loosely interpreted. The approach, affirmed in the Central and North Lancashire Structure Plan of 1983 and reasserted in the 1986 Lancashire Structure Plan, sought to remove any constraints to the supply of sites. The objective was that 'Sufficient industrial land will be provided to ensure that no opportunities for generating and attracting new economic activity will ever be constrained by lack of land' (LCC, 1986, p.8).

Thus, by the late 1980s, there was an established policy discourse about the need for larger sites, for inward investment, near good-quality trunk roads, with flexibility to accommodate the unexpected investment opportunity that might want to locate on an allocated site. The strategic sites were scattered around the main urban areas, giving each district some opportunity within the 'pool' of available sites to attract firms. This approach was well understood by district planners, within the overall context of the urban concentration strategy.

From the late 1980s, the discourse began to change, with a much stronger statement of spatial strategy and a more sophisticated approach to the provision of sites. Discussions over a regional economic strategy (Pieda, 1993) introduced the language of selectivity, justified by regional competitiveness considerations and by the need to capture limited public subsidy for site preparation. Mirroring the analysis in the West Midlands, the strategy concluded that the region needed three or four 'flagship sites' for inward investment which were available by 2000, and a similar number by 2011. These should be reserved for this purpose and protected from subdivision, as in the West Midlands' 'major investment sites'. These ideas were translated into the draft regional guidance, *Greener Growth* (NWRA, 1995). While the strategy in the draft Guidance claimed to be supported by principles of sustainable transport, urban regeneration and environmental upgrading, the priority of economic competitiveness potentially overrode these. The region 'needs to provide sites which can compete effectively for inward investment in all market sectors'. This required a 'balanced portfolio of sites for attracting private investment, especially inward investment' (p.8). The implication was, as in the West Midlands, that some new large greenfield sites would need to be allocated, despite the policies of urban concentration and regeneration.

To identify 'large, attractive strategic sites', a set of criteria derived from the regional economic strategy was used. Sites were to be reserved for 'key purposes' rather than letting them be used for warehousing or retail uses. In addition, another category of 'key employment sites' was proposed, to be located more in line with the environmental sustainability criteria which the guidance rhetorically asserted, within a general approach aimed at creatinga 'full' and 'mixed' portfolio of sites for inward investment and indigenous firms. The overall result was very similar to that developed in the West Midlands, though less clearly articulated and with some confusion over the terms used to describe the sites ('flagship sites', 'large strategic sites' and so on).

The Lancashire Structure Plan revision was developing in parallel to these regional evolutions. The strategy of urban concentration had now partly been recast in the language of 'strategic corridors' (see Chapter 3). The Draft Plan (1993) proposed three major new 'strategic locations for development'. These sites were expected to provide for a range of activities, in mixed-use developments, including a large amount of industrial land. In addition, an area was identified for a 'regional business location'. This was a direct response to the regional economic strategy's proposals for major 'flagship' sites, reserved intact for a big inward investment. The plan text was written up to provide a 'cascade' of allocations from the county level to district allocations, justified by arguments about rates of take-up of sites and trends in employment 'needs'. In practice, the amounts of land were largely worked out by negotiating upwards from the specific sites available, along with the three new locations. The regional business location was treated as an addition to the amount, since it was to be for regional purposes, not county or local needs and demands. The amounts were then detailed in the district plans, which listed sites by size, but made little use of the 'portfolio' concept.

In contrast to the case of the West Midlands, there was no sign of a common discourse among the levels of the planning system about the analysis of industrial land supply or the meaning of the regional business location. The regional planning guidance which eventually emerged from the Government Office for the North West in May 1996 (DoE, 1996a) introduced yet more labels for the types of site discussed. It recognised that overprovision of sites was likely to hinder efforts to concentrate on land reclamation funding, which the Government Office was responsible for allocating. It also supported the new image of a transport 'spine' and introduced the concept of a portfolio of sites including three or four 'regional employment sites' per county and one or two 'major inward investment sites'. There are strong echoes of the West Midlands regional guidance here, as well as an emphasis on allocating the sites through the framework of the development plan system, following national government policy. The guidance also reflected the need to have consistent strategies when bidding for EU funds, and the increasing challenge from environmental groups for development to be concentrated on brownfield rather than greenfield sites.

For Lancashire, this created no problems, as its sites were already progressing through the structure plan and district plan process. Nor was any large company knocking on the county's doors seeking such a site, in contrast to the West Midlands. The major problems were between the county council and the district authorities over the siting of the regional business location, along with the challenge to the sites which came from the environmental lobbies. Three new 'strategic locations for development' had been identified for some time, and rolled forward relatively smoothly through the structure plan process. The regional business location was more of a problem, as three sites competed for this designation. One was a large, brownfield, former defence industry site. The other two were greenfield sites. The sites fell in the areas of two districts, and the county council and the Commission for New Towns had land-owning interests in the two greenfield sites. As in the case of housing (see Chapter 4), the arenas of the structure plan examination-in-public and local plan inquiries were used to agree which site to allocate, the chosen one being one of the greenfield sites, largely owned by the CNT. The districts had some problems keeping up with the shifting ideas. One district changed from backing one site to another during the process. Planning officers admitted to some confusion by this time as to the meaning of these various site 'labels'. Nevertheless, as one participant noted, 'This allocation is an example of how the planning system should work. The demand for the site is recognised by the Government Office for the North West and INWARD [a regional development agency]; the Structure Plan picks it up and the Local Plan picks it up' (New Town Commission official).

However, the process was hardly a 'cascade' from regional guidance to local plans. It was more a process of simultaneous negotiation in different arenas of both allocations and criteria, which occurred over time, during which contextual factors and the interests of the players were changing. In this situation, the EIP inquiry became the arena of resolution.

Co-ordination, competition and transforming locations in Kent

Kent has serious problems of economic decline in the north and east of the county, but parts of the county are at the heart of the London commuter belt, and some lie along one of the most strategic axes in trans-European transport networks, reinforced by the Channel Tunnel (see

Chapters 3 and 4). Kent is thus very obviously positioned in multiple economic spaces: in very local labour markets with diverse economic situations; in a sub-regional context, which divides the county into the very attractive and environmentally well-defended Garden of England and a depressed periphery; regionally, in the shadow of London; along a corridor to Europe; and within a core region between three European capitals, London, Paris and Brussels. It has intricately differentiated local labour markets, which evolve in the shadow of these diverse economic relationships.

In this context, tough policies of environmental restraint in the middle and west of the county have long co-existed with the promotion of economic development in the north and east (see Chapter 3). Until the mid-1980s, the primary strategic development location was Ashford, which served as a pivotal location between the protected middle and west and the declining east. Planning policy concentrated economic development sites in Ashford, with a spread of small sites among the many small towns. The objective was to pull development impetus away from the affluent western core of the county and attract inward investment. The conception of the Kent economy reflected in these policies assumed an internal division into two primary economic spaces, one affluent and the other disadvantaged, within a region in which the county overall had a peripheral location.

Through the 1990s this approach shifted. A proliferation of large site allocations was increasingly justified, not in terms of local job need, but on the basis of the provision of a choice of quality sites, to attract firms seeking sites throughout the region. One, Kings Hill, promoted by the county council on an airfield it owned, was located in the more affluent part of Kent. This substantial development allocation was justified as creating a top quality business park, to compete with others proliferating across the south east during the 1980s development boom. The other sites were in north and east Kent, promoted by efforts in the 1990s to regenerate large sites, through the Thames Gateway and east Kent initiatives (see Chapter 3). The development of these sites required a transformation in the image of these areas held by potential investors and developers. Attention to the wider qualities of places was thus a key requirement if the overall county strategy was to be achieved.

To achieve such transformations, it was necessary to obtain funding on a considerable scale and over the long term. This was available from national and EU sources, but only for small parts of projects, and typically linked to the formation of partnerships between public and private actors. By the 1990s, therefore, area transformation projects and partnerships had come to play a key role in the allocation and development of large sites for economic development purposes in Kent. However, there were significant problems arising from the fragmentation of governance effort among these partnerships and delays to the Channel Tunnel and associated infrastructure. These were made obvious in the property crash at the end of the 1980s, when the extent of the competition between the major sites became evident. In all these developments, Kent County Council (KCC) sought to play a key role in developing strategy, providing information on land take-up, mobilising lobbying and co-ordinating economic development and planning strategy. But the county council lay ambiguously within the dynamics of the multiple economic spaces in which it was positioned. It struggled to maintain a significant role in economic development strategy and in binding the major projects (and frequently their associated partnerships) into a legitimate approved planning framework.

KCC was particularly concerned to maintain development commitments allocated at Ashford and at Kings Hill. Ashford's strategic importance was re-emphasised and recast in the context of the Channel Tunnel and the hoped-for economic benefits from stronger links to Europe. Major development was proposed in the second review of the Structure Plan in 1990. This review (1990) referred to Ashford as the emerging 'commercial hub of East Kent', but acknowledged that any further development allocations beyond the 1990 Plan were not needed. However, the recession and uncertainty about the Channel Tunnel Rail Link route and stations prevented a significant change in demand for employment land in Ashford. Meanwhile, site allocations proceeded in other locations potentially more favourable to investors, such as Kings Hill and the Thames Gateway.

The Kings Hill development was a major opportunistic initiative by the county council. Strategically located near the M20/M25, on the motorway network to the Channel Tunnel, it could be claimed as a 'brownfield site', since it was formerly an airfield. A high-quality business park development with residential and leisure development was proposed. The location was included as a major development opportunity in the 1990 second Structure Plan review, justified as of benefit to the whole county. However, construction was progressing as the recession of the early 1990s hit the south east of England. By the time of the inquiry into the third review of the Structure Plan in 1994, county council officers had scaled down the proposal and introduced a larger housing element. The allocations at Kings Hill attracted the highest number of written objections to the third review. By the 1994 examination-in-public, it was seen to be contrary to policies encouraging development in the east and north of the County, policies to reduce car dependence, to preserve visually attractive areas in Kent, and in competition with other development locations (notably Ashford and the Thames Gateway). Since the site had already been approved in the previous structure plan and had been given planning permission, it was essentially a fait accompli. The inquiry inspector backed KCC's case for the need for a choice of sites and the uniqueness in terms of quality and infrastructure access of this particular site. However, by the mid-1990s, it was market conditions which delayed development, not planning policy. It was only in the late 1990s that the development impetus at Kings Hill really picked up.

If the recession of the early 1990s threatened Kent County Council's ability to capture economic opportunity, it was also being challenged in its role as a strategic shaper of development opportunities in the county. This was increasingly driven by the logic of regeneration subsidy and European funding, and by the national government's major regeneration project for the Thames riverside. However, KCC was a major player in partnership efforts aimed at drawing down funds from such projects (see Chapter 3).

The East Kent Initiative was locally driven, arising from the vigorous mobilisation of Kent councillors, officers and a few business people in order to obtain assisted area status and thus eligibility to bid for regional assistance and urban policy funds. The initiative reviewed the sites available in its area, most of which were in the slowly emerging district-wide plans. But there was a considerable tension between the various investment schemes being proposed through project initiatives, and maintaining site allocations through structure and local planning processes.

The tensions were more obvious in north Kent, where the central government's Thames Gateway Initiative overrode the county's own activities in planning and economic development. Through the initiative, large development sites were provided. As in east Kent, these developments proceeded in parallel with the third review of the Structure Plan. Sites allocated in these processes were then 'lifted into' the structure plan, just as they were in the 1994 regional guidance (see Chapter 3). These allocations were then legitimated through the language of 'competitiveness' in the regional guidance for the South East (DoE, 1994a).

The competitiveness agenda had been slow to filter into Kent policy communities and was expressed rather weakly in the concern with a 'sufficient choice' of sites. The third review Structure Plan deposit draft (KCC, 1993a) gave a good deal of attention to the county's position in Europe and to the priority of sustainable development, but did not use the 'portfolio' approach. It was not until the mid-1990s that North Kent Success, the East Kent Initiative and Kent County Council's economic development department began a review of the range of sites available. In this work, personnel from Birmingham City's Economic Development Department, and from INWARD in the north west, helped to shape new ideas and practices.

Thus the policy agendas about large sites for economic development were somewhat diffuse in Kent, and much more related to area development than to the competitiveness agenda as such. It was led less by the interests of business groupings and much more by the public sector, and notably the county council, the districts and central government. But although in Kent County Council the economic development and planning sections worked well together and environmental concerns were never far from the consciousness of those thinking about the location of major economic developments, the county had problems in keeping economic development initiatives in line with planning strategies. Most of the major investments pouring into KCC's territory – the major motorway investments, the Channel Tunnel, the Channel Tunnel Rail Link and the big flow of funds into north Kent – were directed by national policy considerations and the preoccupations of Westminster and Whitehall. KCC had to struggle to make the most of the opportunities, minimise the adverse impacts and keep some degree of co-ordination in a situation where districts, partnerships and other initiatives were encouraged to flourish. In this context, the power of the planning framework to shape the location of development was severely constrained.

Co-ordinating, mobilising and repositioning: reconfiguring institutional relations

These accounts show that there were significant shifts in all three cases in policy agendas and their supporting justificatory discourses between the mid-1980s and the mid-1990s. The changes varied, however, in their coherence and in their relation to the arenas of spatial planning discourse. In the West Midlands, the discourse was strategically coherent and centrally focused around planning policy, although there were difficulties in keeping actual site allocations in line with agreed policy. In Lancashire, there was much less coherence in the new discourse, which was largely imported into the planning arenas. This led to conflicts over policy interpretation as well as site allocation, but these conflicts were nevertheless resolved in the arenas of the planning system. In Kent, however, the new policy agendas were much more diffuse, with the county struggling to marry a strategic discourse with site allocations which were arising through multiple area initiatives. One reason for these differences was the different economic situation of each case. A second reason lay in the different institutional histories of the three areas, and the arenas, networks and institutional capital which were significant in shaping policy agendas.

Transforming policy discourses requires considerable institutional work. In this case, it meant a change not merely in rhetoric, but also in the way sites came forward for consideration within planning frameworks, and the language used to justify the sites. This required processes for selecting and prioritising sites, and ensuring that these priorities were sustained through to site development. The institutional challenge of transformation was thus to build strategic consensus around a recast policy agenda and to disseminate this among all those with a key role in implementation. Only in one of our cases was this reasonably effectively achieved, through a combination of a past history of regional collaboration and skilled institution-building work.

Mobilising the regional arena in the West Midlands

The innovation in policy discourse which evolved in the West Midlands was underpinned by drawing together the key players in economic development into an increasingly coherent arena focused around the planning system and the production of regional planing guidance. Long-standing networks related to planning and development issues were mobilised to convert the West Midlands Regional Forum (WMRF) of local authorities into a key policy development arena (see Chapter 3). Because of the coherence of the planning and economic development policy communities in the region, the discourse was able to evolve wherever arenas were available. Thinking strategically, key actors mobilised the relationships to ensure that the momentum moved from one arena to another even though the formal institutional context changed.

In the early 1980s, the West Midlands Metropolitan County Council, with its planning, transport and economic development powers, was the key arena where economic development strategy was shaped. With strong political support, both in the region and among the Labour Party networks at the time, the county developed its approach to economic development, established an Enterprise Board (which became the West Midlands Development Agency, WMDA) and carried through these ideas, with only limited tensions, into the structure plan (Healey *et al.*, 1988; Wannop, 1995). Both members and officers developed a strong commitment to 'carrying the strategy' into other arenas after the abolition of the Metropolitan County in 1986. For some, this meant taking the ideas into the metropolitan district councils. But economic development officers in Birmingham City Council, always a little in tension with the county, saw the opportunity to raise the discussion of strategic sites beyond the conurbation to the region. Using abolition to generate a sense of crisis, the leader of the council supported his officers in their efforts to reactivate the WMRF. The preparation of regional planning guidance (DoE, 1988c) provided a focus for this work, which involved both officers and members of the constituent authorities in building a consensus about strategy.

Two issues emerge clearly from these efforts. Firstly, the long-established political and officer networks in the region helped build up the capacity to come to a common view and to deal with difficult issues, such as the balance between urban regeneration and peripheral development. As a metropolitan borough planning officer commented: 'You will have difficulty in understanding the trust and ways of working at various levels and the networking between people. Joint Committee and Chief Officers Groups are longstanding. This makes us unique.'

The offices of the government departments in the region were closely involved in these relationships, the West Midlands regional office of the Department of the Environment/DETR being widely regarded by headquarters as having 'gone native'. Secondly, Birmingham City Council's economic development department provided much of the intellectual capital for the work. Their ideas were developed further in the context of the WMRF, and diffused into the thinking of the other local authorities, as discussed earlier.

In the 1980s, policy arenas were mostly dominated by public sector players although, by 1987, the city council had set up an Employers' Forum which, with the help of consultants, had produced a report on economic regeneration. The 1990s saw a reinforcement of the regional web of relationships and a widening out from the public sector to include business groupings, including WMDA, the Birmingham Chamber of Commerce and the regional Confederation of British Industry (CBI). To reinforce these new relationships, a West Midlands Regional Economic Consortium was established, under the aegis of the WMRF and serviced by the Forum's secretariat. The result of this consolidation and expansion of networks around economic development issues was that a web of relationships existed through which policy concerns and strategies could diffuse with ease. Despite the involvement of business groups, the public sector officers, and in particular planning and economic development officers, played a key role in building up the networks and holding them together. One reason for this was that the business community in the region was itself fragmented. Even the larger companies and the chambers were not accustomed to work as a collective interest group. The CBI played an important role in bringing the business community together, but there were other arenas within which the private sector could consider economic development and planning issues, notably the Chamber of Commerce, the Training and Enterprise Council and Birmingham 2000. Yet business representatives were often unclear about the role of the planning system and did not always maintain positions asserted in the regional forums. They continued to lobby on an individual basis directly to the Government Office.

The Forum and the Regional Economic Consortium provided the key arena for policy discussion. The participation of senior representatives. was critical to the success of such arenas:

> The Forum is the mechanism by which authorities come together to work out a regional approach ... It operates much as a consensual model so most of its output is 'lowest common denominator', but this masks a lot of hard work and good relations despite policy differences among authorities ... we have to work together and present a united view. (Metropolitan district planning officer)

The commitment of the Government Office and its involvement in the Forum helped to reinforce its role. A planning officer noted that 'they don't play one local authority off against another'. But some officers

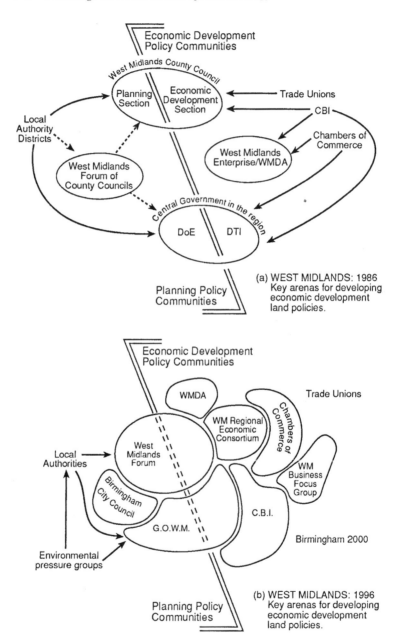

Figure 5.1   Economic development arenas 1986 and 1996

played a key role too. A senior economic development planner at Birmingham City claimed, 'I am up to my neck in networks. I seem to be indispensable to them all.' The result of this network building effort is illustrated in Figure 5.1.

While the West Midlands County Council existed, the WMRF was relatively marginal to policy development. Although there were reasonable links between the county and the metropolitan districts, with business groups and the unions, and with central government's offices in the region, each arena was largely separate. There was some tension between planning work and the activities of local economic development and, even more so, the work of the Department of Trade and Industry in the region. By the mid-1990s, a regional web of relationships had configured themselves around the WMRF, within which planning officers and the policy development mechanisms of the planning system had a major role (see Chapter 3). This was held together by several factors: the commitment of the Government Office, the common interests of the local authorities and the business community in promoting economic development, the commitment and strategic foresight of a few key players, the traditions of good relationships among those in the public sector and the movement of some key players from the public to the private sectors. Nevertheless, the commitment and the capacity for consensus building was always under threat from interest conflicts and the distraction of other priorities. The arena of the Forum, with its informal status, did not carry much power in its organisational form, in contrast to the Government Office, which had formal regulatory and investment power. The Forum's power lay in the continuous active work of key participants, through good analysis and policy ideas and through clever institutional 'footwork'.

It is also clear that, although the web of relationships had been widened out in the 1990s, there were significant stakeholders who were not included. The trade unions had disappeared from the nexus, and environmental groups were never included. Social considerations were largely treated in terms of obtaining jobs and locating them somewhere accessible to areas of high unemployment. Local authority officers and members were expected to 'carry' these concerns into the arenas of policy discussion. The concerns of the environmental groups were also 'carried forward' in the implicit recognition that any release of green belt land would have to be legitimised through the planning system and that this could engender considerable environmental conflict. The WMRF began considering environmental strategy in parallel with its economic development discussions, but there seems to have been little connection between the economic development and the emergent environmental sets of relationships and discussions. Thus the policy community which dealt with the allocation of large sites for economic development purposes in the West Midlands was a form of 'territorial sectoralism', building up a horizontal web of relationships in and around the region, but with strong corporatist tendencies, as in the housing field (see Chapter 4).

Re-positioning in regional and EU networks in Lancashire

Until the 1980s, Lancashire County Council (LCC) had little need of the kind of strategic alliances which developed in the West Midlands. It was the main articulator of economic development strategies and actions in the county, underpinned by the work of Lancashire Enterprises Limited (see Chapter 3). Both the County Council and the district councils had a deep commitment to saving and attracting jobs. Despite a strong commitment to conserving rural landscapes, economic development considerations took priority. The only other significant player was the Commission for the New Towns, which was, as already noted, a major supplier of large sites for economic development. In the 1990s, however, the pre-eminence of the county council's role in policy was challenged from several directions. The first was the developing regional coalition building around economic development (see Chapter 3). The second was a growing environmental lobby, partly championed from other parts of the county council, such as the Environment Unit. The economic development policy makers therefore had to reposition themselves. In a significant shift of strategic attention, LCC began to participate actively in the regional coalition, and to develop its links with the EU, using the Brussels office of Lancashire Enterprises Limited (LEL) to do so. This further strengthened LEL's role as the representative of business interests in the area as far as LCC were concerned In any case, most other large businesses preferred to cluster around the Government Office and the training and enterprise councils and their disbursements of grants and contracts. The county council, LEL, the Government Office for the North West, the Commission for the New Towns and the districts were therefore the key players in this policy area in the 1990s.

In contrast to the West Midlands, the Government Office North-West (GONW) kept itself largely aloof from the alliance building of the local authorities and the business community at the regional level. Along with INWARD, the north west's regional development and marketing agency, and the national Invest in Britain Bureau, it had an important role in major promotional initiatives. The main priority for the GONW lay in the south of the region, and the relations between planning and economic development were little developed until the late 1990s. The North West Regional Association (NWRA), in which Lancashire County Council played a key role, was viewed more as a politicised lobby group than as a partner in a strategic coalition. The GONW therefore did not play a strong role in developing the North West Regional Business Strategy, and took its time to digest the implications in relation to planning strategy. Yet the Government Office was very important to the local authorities and many of the business interests in its role as a channel for EU and national funds, for which a strategic underpinning was increasingly required. Its lack of engagement in regional coalition building and strategy development in the Lancashire context contributed to the uneven diffusion of the new strategic ideas about business sites among the planning policy community in the county (see above).

The power of the New Town presence in the county was on the wane in the 1990s. The Commission for the New Towns, the successor body of the Central Lancashire and Skelmersdale New Town Corporations, remained a very important landowner and site developer and had a strong belief in the strategic importance of such a role. In the past, its strategy had been commensurate with that of LCC, but it was now under pressure to dispose of sites more rapidly, which reduced its capacity for a long-term strategic approach, against the wishes of many officers in the Commission. By the 1990s, the CNT acted more as an independent partner in project development with other agencies and landowners than as part of a coherent grouping.

The relations between LCC and the district authorities were increasingly those of autonomous agents, negotiating areas of mutual interest, rather than a hierarchical relationship. District officers and members had their own arenas for discussing common issues. A fairly small circle of people were involved in these forums. It was in the context of the District Planning Officers Group that planning officers joined forces to promote the brownfield site as a Regional Business Location, challenging the county council's preferred greenfield site (see above). District officers and members also met in the NWRA and in policy forums set up by the county. LCC and LEL nevertheless provided a useful strategic and mobilising resource for the districts, although there was some suspicion of county council motives in promoting development projects. It was also recognised by the districts that their planning policies needed to nest within a county framework. However, there was some concern by other interests that the districts could in effect 'drift away' from what had been agreed in strategic policy arenas.

There were other stakeholders who had some presence in the development of the planning policy agenda over large development sites in Lancashire, but their influence was limited. Environmental groups were well-organised and had contributed to raising the salience of the environmental agenda in local politics and in the county council policy agenda, but they had little leverage over the priority given to job-generating economic development. Individual landowners used the structure and district plan arena to push for particular sites (for example, the Hospital Trusts and British Aerospace), but there was little sign of any involvement of landowners and business interests in prior discussion about strategy, in contrast to the West Midlands. The voice of local residents and other stakeholders concerned with the areas where the sites were to be located was largely silent.

In effect, Lancashire county's preoccupation was with building political networks, rather than making links among stakeholders in Lancashire. Its objective was to position the county to capture influence and resources in the context of the regional coalition building through the North West Regional Association, and to make links with European commissioners who controlled regional development programmes. Compared to the West Midlands, the NWRA was less closely linked to the business community's own alliance-building efforts, despite the existence of some key 'cross-over' people, such as David Taylor, who moved from Lancashire Enterprises to AMEC Ltd, a large construction and development company, and then on to be the first head of English Partnerships. Although the arenas of the NWRA, the North West Business Leadership Team and the North West Partnership (an alliance of the two bodies) helped develop and promote the new discourse of strategic development sites, the coherence and web-like form of the coalitions in the West Midlands was absent.

Within Lancashire, there was little emphasis on building up webs of relationships which could link across the different sectoral policy agendas. Instead, the county council tended to act as a proactive hub for particular policy objectives. One result was that different groups linked into the county council through different networks, which connected uneasily within its own internal organisation. This gave considerable importance to the formal arenas of the structure planning process, and particularly the examination-in-public, as shown above. It was in this arena that county policies were tested and the problems of integration between the different policy sectors brought out into the open. But the planning system was not seen by the economic development players as an important resource for them. LEL officials talked disparagingly of the planning system as 'the last bastion of Stalinism', implying irritation at the constraints which planning regulation could place on economic development initiatives.

In the Lancashire context, therefore, a narrow nexus of stakeholders continued to dominate the economic development agenda, though in an increasingly uncertain and fragmenting institutional context. They were losing their links with some previous partners, notably the new town corporations, and were faced with competing arenas. It was in this context that the strategy of repositioning the county council in regional and EU arenas can be understood. LCC was involved in a major effort at political mobilisation at this level. Within its own organisation, and within the institutional landscape of Lancashire itself, a largely sectoral set of relationships persists. As a result, the planning system was not as central to the economic development agenda as in the West Midlands. The translation of economic development policies into the planning system thus tended to open up complex conflicts at the level of both strategy and specific allocations which were not always easy to resolve.

Fragmentation and repositioning in Kent

As in Lancashire, Kent County Council (KCC) had been the central player and nodal point in planning and economic development in the county. It was a key locus for defining spatial strategy, co-ordinating planning policy around the structure planning process, providing information, mobilising lobbying and building partnerships for economic development. In contrast to Lancashire, however, it operated in the backyard of national government, with powerful electorates defending environmental quality (see Chapter 3). Until the late 1980s, KCC could act with a degree of autonomy, building strong relationships with its districts. The Kent area at that time was marginal to ministers and civil servants concerned with the political and economic voice of the south east. In the 1990s, however, it was catapulted into the political and administrative limelight, as a result of the Channel Tunnel and Thames

Gateway projects. The county council sought to maintain its nodal position in the face of pressures from national government initiatives and regional planning policy, and the multiplying area development initiatives with their own autonomy and links with the districts. In this context, as in Lancashire, getting involved in European networks, in this case through the Euroregion and INTERREG projects, offered the prospect of strengthening the county council's nodal position. Compared to Lancashire, KCC placed more emphasis on internal network-building within the county, and building links with the business community. It initiated some partnership efforts, including the East Kent Initiative and North Kent Success, and drew public and private stakeholders into the third review of the Structure Plan.

Kent County Council members and officers had worked effectively to lobby for Kent interests in the 1980s in the campaigns for assisted area status, the Channel Tunnel route and the locations of the stations. In this they collaborated with the districts. Kent had a strong District Planning Officers Group, which brought the county and the districts together on planning issues and helped to sort out conflicts. However, the districts were ambiguous about their relations with the county. They worked well together, and the county's encouragement of forums for inter-district discussion probably helped this, but the climate of competitive funding increasingly encouraged districts to act alone in bids for Single Regeneration Budget and other initiatives. This created tensions in county–district and inter-district relations which were exacerbated by county council members' predilection for directing resources to certain parts of Kent.

KCC also had a tradition of good working links with other key stakeholders in economic development issues. This social capital was deliberately mobilised in the 1990s structure planning process, which was developed through dialogue with major stakeholders. This, and the new emphasis on 'plan-led' planning, helped position the structure plan as a key tool for managing an otherwise ad hoc process. However, the reality in relation to economic development was less co-ordinated than this suggests. There were good links between the county council and Kent Training and Enterprise Council, and major business players spoke well of the county council, but there were tensions between the planning function and the county's economic development initiatives, the Kings Hill project being a good example. The business links helped to facilitate building what was often referred to locally as a 'partnership culture' in Kent in the 1990s. However, business people were sometimes confused about the relations between the partnerships. Nor did partnership necessarily help to reduce conflicts. At the Structure Plan examination-in-public, good partners had a habit of turning into adversarial lobbyists.

Despite these complex linkages, there was no strategic stakeholder forum comparable to those at the regional level in our other two areas. KCC acted as a hub, drawing in the various stakeholders. However, stakeholders on the 'spokes' were repeatedly drawn into other hubs around the specific partnerships, and around national government itself. Thus, by the 1990s, the relatively simple hublike pattern of the 1980s had become a complex and fragmented institutional terrain. It is in this context that moves were initiated by the county in the mid-1990s to create some kind of economic forum. However, the county level was not necessarily the most appropriate one for some of the major business players, for whom lobbying national government brought considerable returns in investment and planning regulatory outcomes in the 1990s (Hull and Vigar, 1998). Thus Kent's role as a nodal point in economic development was compromised by the multiplicity of economic relations which were layered across its area.

One problem for areas like Kent was that regional level organisation in the south east was weaker than in the West Midlands and the north west. There was no equivalent to the regional business forums in our other cases. This partly reflected the scale of the south east as a region, which makes alliance building difficult. But it also arose because, for most businesses, the regional interest was equated with the national interest. Clustering directly around national government politicians and civil servants was likely to be more effective. At regional level, the local authorities' regional planning association, SERPLAN, and the Government Office were primarily concerned with housing land allocations, not economic development issues.

In relation to economic development and large site allocation in Kent, therefore, there was no active coalition of stakeholders shaping policy agendas as in the West Midlands, nor was there a tight nexus of planning and economic development activity in the control of the county and its close partners, as in Lancashire. Kent County Council had no option but to live in a fluid, and increasingly fragmented, institutional context. One reason for its exposure to such fragmentation was its political and geographical relation to national government, which increasingly operated through ad hoc project initiatives. There were other important reasons. At one level, Kent lived in the shadow of very large development projects which inherently generated uncertainty as to the nature and scale of development impacts. At the level of the sub-region, these big projects landed in localities with much local diversity, in landscape and in their local economies. This made it difficult for a strong local voice to develop to articulate either the interests of businesses seeking opportunities or local people seeking job-generating activity. It may prove very difficult to build and sustain such relationships at the level either of the county or of the region.

The planning system and economic development

This account of the policy discourses and institutional relations surrounding the allocation of large sites for economic development illustrates the acute tensions which have to be resolved in the context of the planning system. One is a matter of priorities, economic development versus environmental quality. Behind this lies a tension between the different dynamics and institutional relations of investment programmes and regulatory regimes, in this case between the dynamics of a promotional approach to economic development, involving significant investments of subsidy funds and public sector sites, and that of the regulatory system and its requirement to consider the wide-ranging impacts of development projects, locally and subregionally. Underpinning this tension between developmental and regulatory objectives is the institutional landscape of the policy communities involved in economic development. At national level the Department of Trade and Industry and the Department of the Environment's, now DETR's urban policy division struggled against the regulatory constraints of the DETR's planning division. Often in local authorities, economic development sections and departments were institutionally and culturally separate from the plan-making and development control work of the planning system. Meanwhile, business lobbies and their networks influenced government through largely separate channels from those of the environmental lobbies. Despite the evidence of widening networks in our cases, the organisation and financial tools of the public sector continued to undermine efforts to integrate the economic development agenda into a broader approach to territorial development. The New Labour administration, through the DETR, made a significant shift by adopting the rhetoric of strategy and integration between economic, social and environmental policies (DETR, 1998a,

1998b, 1998c), but by the end of the decade it was still not clear how the rhetoric would shape specific policies.

Nevertheless, there were clear shifts in the policy discourses and some evolution in both policy arenas and policy communities. As regards the discourses, although there was little specific national planning policy guidance, all three cases had moved from a needs-based approach to assessing land requirements, linked to providing a fair share of opportunity around areas with high unemployment, towards greater selectivity, focused on providing a choice of sites and a 'portfolio' of provision. By 1997, central government too was moving in this direction (DoE, 1997, para. 46). This reflected a shift in perspective from the worker seeking a job to the company seeking a site, although in all the plans the site allocations were translated into needs-based calculations of site areas to legitimate the landtake proposed. This shift embodied an interpretation of competitiveness to mean competing for relocating companies. There were clear differences in the local development of this shifting discourse between the three areas, with the West Midlands developing the most sophisticated, coherent and widely diffused approach. There were growing commonalities, but these were not the result of national planning policy. Rather, they were a response to a mixture of local economic circumstances, lobbying by business groups and the national government's general orientation towards a 'competitiveness' agenda. These all helped to mould planning policy towards large site allocations and, more generally, to limit the power of other objectives to constrain the sectoral independence of the economic agenda.

This suggests that the planning arenas had only limited significance in the allocation of large sites for economic development, but the role of the system in legitimating land allocation for business purposes in a context of increasingly well-articulated contrary arguments should not be underestimated. In the West Midlands, the legitimisation problem was etched into the consciousness of planning and economic development policy communities as a result of past struggles over the green belt. Because of this, articulating regional level planning guidance became a core arena for developing major site allocation policy. In Lancashire and Kent, in contrast, policies developed elsewhere were 'lifted' into the regional guidance, structure and local plans. In Lancashire's case, the actual site definitions could progress through the plan-making process. In Kent, where there was potentially real pressure for development, as well as substantial newly available funds for area regeneration programmes, the specific site allocations themselves were developed outside the plan-making process, and then placed inside the plans.

In all three cases, the hierarchical order of national planning guidance, regional guidance, structure plan and local plan allocations was a mirage, although carefully reconstructed in plan texts. In effect, what was happening was a multi-level negotiation, in attempts to make strategic policies and actual site allocations more consistent with each other. In the West Midlands, the major investment sites were being identified in the regional planning guidance process following revisions to regional policy. Actual site release then had to pass through procedures for departure from the plan. In Lancashire, site allocations were contested in both structure and local plan inquiries, and resolved simultaneously, through the decision of the structure plan examination-in-public inspector. In Kent, a process of 'rationalising opportunism' was taking place, as sites were 'adopted' from their origin in specific area initiatives and projects, and given some kind of logic in county and district planning terms. These planning arenas allowed the policies to encounter vigorous opposition from objectors concerned either about compromise to environmental objectives, or about competition with other economic development initiatives. This is where the hierarchy of planning arenas had its real value, as it allowed regional agreements, agreed structure plan policies and national planning policy criteria to override these objections easily. These practices served to reinforce the sectoral autonomy of economic development considerations, though most key players were aware that the task of legitimisation was becoming more complex as the environmental sustainability agenda at national, regional and levels became more assertive.

The diffusion of common policy discourses and the translation of economic development strategies and site allocations into the arenas of the planning system were less problematic where there were well-established policy communities linking the two. This was strikingly the case in the West Midlands, with its store of institutional capital actively renewed for the purpose. In Lancashire, there was no such coherent and broadly-based policy community around economic development, although efforts were being made to create one at the regional level. Kent was in a similar position, but with a much more complex regional, national and European institutional context in which to act. Kent sought to maintain a nodal role in the emergence of such a policy community, but its efforts at co-ordinating the various players in the local authorities and the business community were uneven and unstable. In all cases there were efforts to expand policy communities, to include more business players in the West Midlands and Kent, to reach to wider arenas in Lancashire and Kent. But these widening moves primarily focused on linking to potential sources of funds (the Government Offices, the European Union and the networks encouraged in funding criteria) and to partnership with business groupings (to help in lobbying for funds, as well as in gaining access to private sector funds). What was developing could perhaps be described as a form of 'fund-seeking corporatism'. It remained largely sectoral in its emphasis, and vulnerable to challenges grounded in the discourse of environmental sustainability and community development. For many in the economic development policy communities, the planning system provided a convenient set of arenas through which to legitimate their policies and site allocations. This allowed them to neglect building direct networks and alliances with policy communities with different objectives, political strategies and cultures.

There were tendencies towards a more territorial focus in economic development strategies in the West Midlands, and at the regional level in Lancashire, but this was not well integrated with other policies. Sites were largely treated as disembedded locales, a collection of 'sites-with-attributes' in a despatialised portfolio of location opportunities for developers and companies. Environmental considerations entered into these strategies as a rather vague constraint or as an asset used in area or site marketing. Social considerations were subsumed under the legitimation of 'sites = jobs'. As a result, there was very limited consideration of the qualities of the places within which the sites 'landed' and how these might be affected by such projects. At the level of detailed location, sites had to be 'fitted into' their particular locations, through attention to policy criteria found in regional guidance and development plans. Place-making at the area level was not a major preoccupation of the planning policy community, at least as far as large site allocation was concerned.

The situation in Kent, in contrast, was more sensitive to places. Both the structure plan policies and the various project initiatives were evolving in a political context where there was a strong understanding of both a broad spatial strategy and a fine-grained appreciation of the qualities of places, and how impacts interrelate to affect them. This infused planning and economic development thinking in Kent much more profoundly than in the other two cases. This implicit frame of reference acted to co-ordinate and focus policy and action in this case, even though there were no major strategic alliances and the power of the plan-making processes to determine the location of major development sites was limited. In the other two cases, the social links were largely made through the 'sites = jobs' equation. Kent's place-transformation agenda implied that new social groups would come into the areas earmarked for change. This led to a greater emphasis on the qualities of places.

Thus, in the field of allocating large sites for economic development purposes, the changes in the economic context, and to some extent the developments in national and EU funding, were encouraging a more territorial focus, but this did not result in a more broadly integrated policy agenda or the building of more inclusive policy communities. The pressures for inclusivity were channelled into the arenas of the plan-making process, producing substantial objections at the inquiry stage. But the institutional context sustained sectoral policy communities and reduced the leverage of pressures for more policy integration and wider participation.

6 Transport at a Metaphorical Crossroads: the Gradual Penetration of a Sustainable Development Discourse?

Discourses of transport policy-making

> We are at a huge metaphorical cross-roads. We have a population that wants more and more transport facilities, yet they want more and more green space, they want more parking but they don't want to pay for it, we have shopkeepers who want more parking but they don't want the cars on the road'. (Kent County Council transport planner)

The focus of this chapter is upon the different policy agendas and discourses that surround local transport planning and investment, and on the subsequent contestation over policy amongst stakeholders. Criticism of UK transport policy accrued throughout the 1980s and early 1990s, focusing on a perceived overemphasis on road construction without appropriate regard for environmental and mobility issues. Ultimately, this has led to a gradual but fundamental shift in policy direction in central and local government.

Throughout this time the importance of land use planning in addressing issues of concern in transport planning was continually emphasised. This concern was slowly addressed in policy advice from central government in the 1990s and the merging of the Departments of Environment and Transport in 1997 crystallised this still further. At local level transport policy sits within the development plans framework. Land use planning policy and transport policy should therefore have similar objectives and strategies. In practice, however, transport policy and land use policy are formulated by different public officials with differing professional norms and approaches working in separate policy communities, with strong links vertically to central government civil servants, yet separated functionally in local government. This chapter explores the rise of a new sustainability discourse in the context of these distinct policy communities of land use planning and transport.

There is no question that transport has become a more politically contested issue in recent years. This seems to relate to two main factors. First, as part of a wider liberalisation project, Tory administrations throughout the 1980s privatised and deregulated many transport services. Second, growing awareness and understanding of sustainable development agendas has meant that concern over the use of private vehicles has gained a great deal more political leverage. To understand the impact of these two factors it is necessary to look at recent central government transport policy and the policy agendas of other stakeholders through this period.

Transport, regulation and the state

Throughout the 1980s, transport was subjected to the same ideological imperatives as other areas of government. An essentially anti-collectivist approach undermined state intervention, underpinned by principles of allocative efficiency rather than notions of the public interest. Transport, like other policy areas, underwent extensive processes of deregulation and privatisation. Much of the associated discourse behind these processes revolved around notions of personal mobility and freedom, and the belief that the private sector could provide more efficient and cost-effective services than public agencies. The state's role shifted from one of transport provider to transport 'enabler'. As in many other areas of public policy, this 'deregulation' led to the creation of a plethora of new agencies such as the Highways Agency and various public transport regulatory bodies. In addition, bodies such as the Monopolies and Mergers Commission entered transport arenas more often in order to regulate newly created markets. The European Union has also become more important in a variety of roles: as regulator of markets, environmental legislator, policy developer and financier of projects.

However, in terms of responsibilities, transport planning still exhibits the centrism characteristic of the British state. Central government through the Department of Environment, Transport and the Regions (DETR) determines the financial and regulatory framework for transport planning, despite network management issues being devolved to the arm's-length Highways Agency and attempts to introduce an element of market provision. In addition, local government is highly dependent on the centre to realise its strategic objectives due to the capital-intensive nature of much transport planning activity.

Discourse shifts in UK transport policy

The transport policy emphasis of the Tory administrations of the mid-to-late 1980s and early 1990s was heavily biased towards market provision in public transport and increased investment in road construction. Deregulation was prompted by the neoliberal philosophy of the administrations. Heavy investment in the roads programme reflected two discourses widely promoted at this time: first, a personal freedom discourse, which was narrowly interpreted as a freedom to drive a car without hindrance; second, a business competitiveness discourse (interpreted as, '*Roads for Prosperity*' in a white paper (DoT, 1989) which introduced a considerable expansion in government's programme for new road construction.). As a result the roads programme expanded considerably from the mid-1980s until around 1994 (see Figure 6.1.).

This focus on roads investment came under increasing challenge in the late 1980s and 1990s. Goodwin *et al.* (1991) suggest that two streams of thought within the transport planning profession converged at around this time. Previously one stream argued that car use should be curbed for environmental and/or social reasons, the other that provision was needed to provide for an inevitable growth in road transport usage, the 'predict and provide' approach. This argument was long-standing and echoed Plowden's conceptualisation of 'traditionalist' transport planners (adherents to the 'predict and provide' philosophy) and 'non-traditionalists' who argued that the social costs of road building override the need for new roads (Plowden, 1972). Goodwin *et al.* (1991) suggested that a 'new realism' was occurring in relation to the extent to which government could keep providing for predicted traffic growth and thus a consensus could be said to be emerging amongst traditionalists and non-traditionalists. The principal elements of the 'new realist'

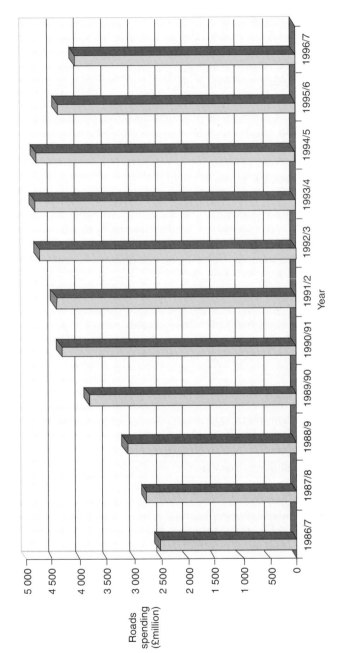

Figure 6.1   UK public expenditure on roads infrastructure, 1986/7 to 1996/7
Source: DETR (1998l), Table 1.1.6.

approach focused on less road construction, the adoption of a package of solutions to given problems and, in general terms, on managing travel demand rather than providing for it (Owens, 1995). The 'new realism' in the transport planning profession was reflected in a changing central government approach by the mid-1990s. This change can be seen in cuts in the roads programme from 1993 onward; the release of more funds for public transport and cycling projects; the adoption of a package approach towards local transport provision; the publication of revised Planning Policy Guidance Notes, Planning Policy Guidance Note 13 in particular (DoE/DoT, 1994); consultation exercises on transport policy in 1996 and 1997; and the publication of a transport white paper (DETR, 1998c). Despite this apparent policy change, 'the philosophy of provision to accommodate demand ... [was] still a powerful force in transport policy' (Owens, 1995, p.43; see also Richardson and Heywood, 1996). Thus local authorities felt that public transport projects were not being accorded the same priority as road schemes they put forward within their package bids (May, 1995; CPRE, 1996) while other funding mechanisms, such as urban regeneration monies, were being used by local authorities to fulfil long-standing commitments to road projects (CPRE, 1998b).

The local context

The policy framework for transport is set by regional planning policy guidance in all areas, structure plans in county council areas, and unitary development plans in unitary authority areas. Following 1997 local government reorganisation there were thus 133 'highways authorities', as they are legally known in England and Wales. The continued existence of passenger transport authorities and executives (PTAs and PTEs) provide a further institutional layer and a voice for public transport issues in conurbations. Within this institutional framework, local transport plans, whose primary function is to set out a funding framework for the area, provide an indication of the priorities of local authorities. (Local transport plans were introduced in the 1998 transport white paper. Previously, this function was achieved through transport policies and programme statements and package bids.) Such investment strategies are typically produced by transport engineers and the policies of development plans are given variable attention in devising the bid documents. This separation may create problems as the proposals of development plans get 'translated' into the implementation-focused outputs of the transport engineers, and in turn proposals get adopted from the transport engineers' policy communities into development plans. Investigating this potential fracture is explored in this Chapter.

Local policy agendas and discourses

The departure point for this chapter is that the old paradigm of 'predict and provide' in transport policy has been usurped by a 'new realist' approach which emphasises managing the demand for road transport. Awareness of this shift is achieved through an analysis which identifies a number of discourse strands: 'predict and provide', 'roads for prosperity'; demand management, sustainability, and accessibility. We also examine how local transport policy reflects patterns of relationships between local government and other stakeholders, and the influence of the wider local polity on transport planning in our case study areas.

Lancashire: rhetoric and reality in transport policy implementation

The Lancashire case centred on investigating the contradiction implied by the high level of road building proposed by Lancashire County Council (LCC) in the 1994 Structure Plan and LCC's promotion of a sustainability agenda in the same plan and in other policy arenas.

As detailed in Chapter 3, Lancashire's strategic spatial policy is framed by regional guidance, and implemented through the Structure Plan and local plans. Work in environmental arenas such as the Lancashire Environment Forum (LEF), the production of two green audits (LCC, 1991, 1997a) and the Lancashire Environmental Action Programme (LEAP), is also crucial to understanding the development of policy agendas in Lancashire. In short, LCC progressively sought to incorporate environmental issues into the core of its strategic spatial strategy making. The incorporation of such an agenda resulted, however, in a number of conflicts with other agendas, notably economic competitiveness. The relationship of transport issues to these broad themes is explored below.

The attempt to integrate a sustainability agenda into spatial strategy making is evident in the draft regional planning guidance developed by local authorities in the north west for the Secretary of State for the Environment (NWRA, 1995). The strategic emphasis contained in this advice aimed to promote new development along two axes: a north–south spine running from Cumbria through to Cheshire and an east–west link running from Merseyside across to Manchester. Transport issues were thus placed centre-stage. The advice sought to promote an integrated approach to transport and land use planning, and attempted to guide development to locations which would minimise the need to travel. This emphasis was maintained in the final guidance (DoE, 1996a). Despite these admirable intentions, there is evidence to suggest that they were not carried through to implementation in the plans and decisions of local authorities (Hull *et al.*, 1996; Davoudi *et al.*, 1996).

The consultation draft of the replacement Structure Plan (LCC, 1993) took forward the principles embodied in the previous Structure Plan (LCC, 1986): accessibility for all sections of society and roads for economic development purposes. The 1993 plan introduced at least a rhetoric of sustainability, and a demand management discourse was newly evident (see Chapter 3).

The deposit version of the plan (LCC, 1994a) changed few of the transport policies of the consultation draft, although there were some changes in the language and tone of the document. The first obvious change lay in the titles of relevant sections. Although this may at first seem trivial, it reveals something of the underlying thinking of the county council, or at least its response to changing messages from central government. Thus the section entitled 'managing traffic' became 'managing transport' to incorporate an emphasis on all modes, not just roads. The 'Infrastructure' chapter is retitled, 'Transport – Managing the Demand'. This chapter was also reordered: policies for road transport were moved and placed after those for public transport policies in the deposit version. Accessibility maps were dropped from the 1994 version, emphasising a shift away from mobility and social access concerns as a central issue and towards demand management and sustainability rhetorics. There remains a continuing emphasis on the importance of road transport to the county's economic competitiveness. A long list of road schemes is appended to the plan which appears to contradict its sustainability and demand management emphases.

The proposed road schemes contained in the Structure Plan led to lobbying from a range of sources, particularly a coalition of environmental groups comprising Lancashire Wildlife Trust, Lancashire Council for the Protection of Rural England and a number of local Friends of the Earth groups. Sources within Lancashire County Council also expressed concern over the scale of road building, arguing that it was not in keeping with the general aims of the plan. This view was partly supported by the inspector at the plan's examination-in-public (EIP), who recommended the removal of the two most expensive schemes in the plan, for two reasons: first, changes in national government policy meant that the likelihood of their being funded was remote yet, while they were still in the plan property would remain blighted; second, considerable environmental impact was associated with the schemes. However, many stakeholders were surprised that so many road schemes were left in the Structure Plan by the inspector. The reasons for their inclusion in contravention of the plan's sustainability emphasis are discussed later.

Policy outcomes: providing roads for prosperity   Job creation is at the top of the county council's strategic issue list. The perceived competitiveness of Lancashire, especially with regard to its peripherality to the south east of England and to mainland Europe, is of great concern to the county council. This concern results in jobs issues overriding other considerations: 'greening, environmentalism, is seen as a component [by the county council] rather than as an all-embracing issue and it can be over-ridden by other components ... the most important of which is economic development' (pressure group representative).

This is confirmed by a county council officer:

> The administration wants to achieve both [economic development and sustainable development objectives] and on occasions there are conflicts, but when it comes to the crunch, jobs always win. We here in the [planning] department and through our Structure Plan have been doing the best we can to embrace the new agenda of environmental sustainability and we've managed to achieve that in our plan in all respects except for the road programme proposals which members wish to see pursued on the back of this idea that it will create jobs. (County planner)

So influential members believed that continued road construction was essential to maintain the county's economic competitiveness. This view was widely held, with little difference discernible amongst different political parties, a feature of transport policy both at national and local government levels. Such a view became powerful when it coincided with the agenda of the designers of schemes who were committed to getting them implemented: 'The county surveyor in turn has already designed the scheme three or four times as it's probably been in the drawer for 30 years, there's a lot of [personal/intellectual] investment

... in those things' (county planner). This notion of 'bottom-drawer' schemes and the promotion of them by scheme designers is a powerful one and was found in each of our localities.

The momentum behind road building was perpetuated by the importance attached to specific road schemes by electorates and members, and the lack of control the county council had over the provision of other services:

> In any political system there are deals done behind closed doors between members. So you have some members saying you vote for my bypass and I'll vote for your so and so. In terms of tradable goods ... road schemes are one of the few things that can be traded between members. (County planner)

Added to this is the need for members to be seen to be delivering to their electorates. Whilst bypass schemes, for example, carry a great deal of political weight with electorates, demand management measures can be unpopular. So the combinations of the two pro-road building discourses become magnified by the clientelist actions of local politicians: 'the reality is that each individual scheme is, as it were, *owned* by a County Councillor ... its the scheme they have been selling on the doorstep every election time to their constituents' (county council planner, emphasis added).

An alliance thus arose as the momentum of an, albeit waning, 'predict and provide' paradigm amongst transport engineering professionals became coupled with the belief that roads were essential to maintain jobs in the county. This was magnified through the clientelism and parochialism of county and district councillors. Thus LCC put forward in its 1994 Structure Plan a set of road proposals that were quickly rendered contrary to national policy by shifting concerns in central government. Schemes were 'lifted' from the working practice of the engineers and transplanted into strategic documents as a result of local political pressure and the power of the engineers, even though they may not have fitted the overall objectives of the strategy. This had three consequences: first, uncertainty prevailed over many schemes which were dependent on funding that might never arrive, which in turn blighted property; second, as a consequence, the contents of the Structure Plan became unrealistic and the document lost validity amongst its users; third, the Structure Plan's objectives of a 'sustainable Lancashire' were undermined when so many road proposals were put forward by the county council itself.

The difficulties the county council faced in implementing transport policies should be recognised, however. Through the 1980s, local government lost a great deal of authority with regard to public transport and other services. The county council had contributed to improvements to the local rail network in the 1990s through the opening of new stations, but its powers over public transport provision were severely limited. This loss of functions provided a real challenge for officers in the context of the parochialism and clientelism referred to earlier:

> There is a need for us ... to put things into the political shop window that [members] can actually trade with behind closed doors, and things that are achievable because there's so little money coming in to build the new roads. We as officers have got to put these fancy goods in the shop window: things which will appeal to them, things which fit with the new agenda, and things which they can actually afford. (County council planner)

Meanwhile, other players such as business groupings, parish and district councils and other elements within LCC, such as economic development officers, continued to push for an improved road network. Transport debates were thus conducted against a background of various coalitions of actors, many of which were rooted within different elements of LCC itself. The coalition promoting a demand management approach to transport, and a sustainability discourse more generally, failed to get sufficient influence over Lancashire's transport policies. There was little evidence that work carried out in environmental arenas such as the LEF, or the work of environmental pressure groups in Lancashire, influenced transport policy formulation in the county to any great extent. This was explained through the separation of these activities from the day-to-day practice of the engineering department in LCC. Whilst the planners were key players in the LEF, engineers were not. Whilst the planners were making attempts to develop a more sustainable strategy for the county, the engineers were still working to an older more established paradigm, that of a technical approach to meeting transport demand.

West Midlands: restricting private vehicle use in England's 'Motor City'

The West Midlands provides an interesting case study of transport issues, for a number of reasons. First, the transport issues and policy emphases in a conurbation are different from those of our other two areas. Second, it has a different institutional structure and history. The lack of an administrative tier between national and district levels since the abolition of the West Midlands Metropolitan County Council in 1986 has implications for the treatment of issues and the making of policy. The West Midlands conurbation does, however, have one formal intermediate-level institution, a public transport authority and its executive arm, Centro, operating across the former Metropolitan County area. The relationship of Centro to the districts provided an interesting area of exploration and one unique to this case study. Third, and perhaps resulting from the first two points, the West Midlands is an area with a recent history of innovation in the tackling of transport issues, principally through the development of 'integrated transport studies' and the 'package approach' (see p. 164). Fourth, the West Midlands has traditionally been the heartland of the UK vehicle production industry. This colours the way transport policy issues are discussed in the conurbation.

In this account, attention is focused principally on the development of transport policy in the largest of the metropolitan districts in the West Midlands, Birmingham City Council (BCC). From this analysis the relationship between activity in the transport policy sector and the wider city polity is explored. The contribution of one significant debate to this relationship is examined in detail. Events subsequent to this policy moment will be documented to illustrate how Birmingham and other districts searched for new ways to address issues of policy concern. Through this search, elements of a 'new realism' emerged locally. As in the Lancashire example, a key focus in this account is placed upon the representation of environmental issues throughout this period in the policy outputs of BCC.

As detailed in Chapter 3, the conurbation reshaped its strategic land use and transport focus in the 1990s. In transport terms, this 'new' focus attempted to integrate land use and transport planning more closely, placed a higher priority on public transport which included the development of a light rail scheme, the Midland Metro, and acknowledged that there were limits to road building.

Regional guidance for the West Midlands sets the context for transport policies in the conurbation (see Chapter 3). A key concern in preparing the regional guidance of the early 1990s was the growing distances between home and work, producing congestion, air and noise pollution, unnecessary movements by car and thus increasing demands for road improvements (WMRF, 1992). Managing traffic demand was seen as critical to addressing this concern, even if it was not expressed explicitly in demand-management terms. There was wide consensus over this approach amongst the participants of the regional planning guidance process, although for different reasons: that is, the 'roads lobby' saw it as a way to get 'essential traffic' moving again, whilst the environmentalists saw it as a way to tackle the damage caused by vehicles to the built and natural environment. Although there is evidence that the full implications of a commitment to environmental sustainability on transport policy were not considered in any depth, there was total agreement on three principles: 'road building cannot solve traffic needs, better and fuller co-ordination of all forms of transport are needed, [and] public transport must be given higher priority' (Saunders, 1993, para. 17.1).

In the final regional planning guidance (GOWM, 1995) there was a very strong rhetorical line on transport issues. The guidance sought to affect a modal shift away from private transport 'to reconcile the demand for travel with environmental concerns, including impacts on human health and climate change' (ibid., para.10.2). The development of a transport corridors approach was a way of achieving this (see Chapter 3). The corridors idea was developed principally to accommodate housing growth, but the need to minimise the use of private cars from such developments pushed transport issues to the top of the agenda and led to revisions in the emphasis of the policy.

A new approach to funding local transport initiatives, the 'package approach', originated in the West Midlands conurbation in the early 1990s. This approach was designed to look holistically at transport issues across a wide area to encourage synergies to be released from an accumulation of small schemes. It was submitted jointly on behalf of all the metropolitan authorities. That this idea came from the West Midlands conurbation is in keeping with the collaborative approach to land use and transport planning which had been present for many years, but gained momentum following the abolition of the Metropolitan County Council in 1986. The philosophy behind the packages is that 'transport is not an end in itself, but rather a means to wider social, environmental and economic ends', and that 'many transport issues transcend district boundaries' (WMJC, 1995, p.6). There were difficulties associated with the package approach, in terms of co-ordinating all the local authorities, resultant internal policy conflict within the package and the fact that the package was a 'bid' and would not receive funding in its entirety (Truelove, 1994). These criticisms could also be levelled at transport policies and programmes and in part apply to the replacement funding mechanism, local transport plans.

Transport policy in the conurbation was informed by work undertaken as part of integrated transport studies. These originated to 'provide a more broadly based and politically defensible transport policy' (Wenban Smith, 1994, p.64). Four studies covering the entire conurbation were undertaken between 1988 and 1991. These were underpinned by modelling and projection processes in an attempt to provide locally relevant travel trends data. Their conclusions were consistent across all four studies: the demand for travel by private car could not be met; demand management alone could not tackle the problem of the growth in demand for car travel; and investment in public transport was needed alongside improvements to a defined 'Strategic Highway Network' throughout the conurbation. This was labelled a 'balanced approach'.

The studies attracted some criticism. Newson (1992) noted that the predicted growth in transport demand in the Birmingham Integrated Transport Study (BITS) was based on assumptions which were not realised in the years immediately following its production. This appears to relate principally to two points. First, Birmingham witnessed continuing decentralisation of businesses and households from the inner city. Second, the modelling for the BITS was undertaken at a time of national and local economic growth. Subsequent recession meant that increases in car ownership and movement were not as great as predicted. These criticisms reflect concerns that the modelling underlying the 'predict and provide' ethos is flawed. In this case it meant that BITS substantially over-estimated the growth in vehicles entering Birmingham City Centre.

Despite these criticisms, the integrated transport studies provided useful data on which to base transport policies in the conurbation and helped to promote a renewed emphasis on public transport, following a certain despondency in the metropolitan districts as a result of losing control over the provision of bus service deregulation in 1986. The highlighting of the need for some specific road improvements did, however, give certain sections within local authorities the ammunition they needed to argue for more road building. One specific episode in south Birmingham is explored later, by way of illustration.

Transport policy in Birmingham   The principal statement of transport policy and spatial strategy in this period was the Birmingham Unitary

Development Plan (UDP). Although adopted in 1993, it was crucial in expressing BCC's thinking regarding transport and land use issues in the five years of its development. The UDP was set within the context of the conclusions of the BITS. The UDP recognised that road building could not meet all transport demands and that, even if implemented, such a policy would produce, 'a poor economic performance ... with serious environmental impacts' (BCC, 1990a, para. 5.15). However, the boosterist nature of BCC policy noted in Chapter 3 translated into the transport policy sections. Thus the first principle was to reserve 'the highest priority for transport provision which underpins the economic well-being of the City Centre' (BCC, 1989, para. 3.43).

The plan included proposals recommended in BITS to define a Strategic Highway Network (SHN). The development of the SHN idea attracted a lot of criticism from residents who contested the strategic importance of some of these links. This debate was carried through the UDP preparation process and was a major feature of its public inquiry. The inquiry inspector noted that, although the SHN was an abomination to many people, this attitude in part reflected a misunderstanding between BCC and the objectors.

Despite the emergence of a demand management rhetoric, a sustainability agenda had yet to emerge in BCC at this time. There was no reference to making sure new development was linked to public transport infrastructure, for example. In addition, the plan contradicted itself. It sought to promote energy efficiency alongside more road building, and had no means to monitor the environmental impacts identified. There was also a lack of policy attention and specific proposals to improve facilities for cycling and walking.

Many of these issues came to a head in south Birmingham. The debates that resulted proved to be pivotal in transport policy making in the conurbation and contributed to change in the wider local political environment. Plans to upgrade part of the SHN in south Birmingham were proposed by highway engineers working in BCC in 1991. The completion of the M40 from London to Birmingham alerted highway engineers to possible increases in traffic arriving on the southern edge of Birmingham. The solution proposed by city council engineers was to upgrade to dual carriageway existing roads, and to build a tunnel under Kings Heath and a new flyover to facilitate through traffic from the M40 heading for the city centre. The proposals were scaled down following initial disquiet over the scheme and a new proposal involved widening three arterial roads into the city centre from the south of Birmingham. Over 200 businesses and homes were to be demolished.

The engineers and those in favour of the scheme argued that increasing the penetration of cars into the city centre would benefit the city as a whole and characterised local protest as 'NIMBYism': 'strong local pressure [exists] for local interests to take precedence over city-wide interests' (BCC, 1990b). The interpretation of scale and the prioritisation of interests, in line with the UDP policy of prioritising the revitalisation of the city centre, meant that local interests should give way to a wider, ill-defined set of interests. BCC argued that business interests, both actual and potential, would only be attracted to Birmingham if road access to the city was swift and relatively congestion-free. Residents asked who these other interests were and what specifically were the benefits to them. Residents of south Birmingham argued that effects on existing businesses and the disbenefits for the city in terms of their destruction would outweigh the less tangible effects of better access to the city centre.

The proposals were rejected by the public, and eventually by local politicians, following a period of intense local debate. Thus, although demand management ideas were present in BITS, it was not until this event in South Birmingham two years later that city engineers were forced to confront alternative ways of addressing transport issues. The rejection of the SHN proposals led to the South Birmingham Study, which created a framework by which the 'top-down' national, regional and city-wide perspectives were complemented by 'bottom up' perspectives on the local environment, community and political concerns. As a result, long-standing radial route improvement lines were removed, freeing areas from blight and allowing reinvestment in property. The key to resolving these perspectives was the demonstration that the SHN could be managed so as to perform a strategic function without additional road construction. Indeed, in some places the SHN was eventually narrowed. The outcome was a framework rather than a master plan which allowed the new approach to be developed flexibly over time, with the participation of the local community in the decision making process.

The study, and wider considerations within the local authority, also had implications for the functional and political make-up of the city council. Some members who supported the scheme were ousted and a younger element from within the Labour Party came through. In many ways the scheme supporters were attracted by the window of opportunity that arose in persuading central government that its project, the M40, had consequences for Birmingham and that these needed ameliorating. They were thus responding in a typically clientelist way in trying to get as much central government cash for Birmingham as possible. If they did not take this opportunity, money would be lost for Birmingham. The 'predict and provide' models had enabled BCC to show that they needed government money to ameliorate the effects of a central government scheme, albeit one BCC had lobbied hard for. The rigidity of budget heads at central government level was in part responsible for the way this intragovernmental politics was framed.

In addition, at officer level, BCC had inherited the Highway Construction Team (and an associated set of schemes) from the West Midlands County Council on its abolition, 'without the mechanisms to control their activities' (metropolitan district planner). The team had a large influence on transport policy, despite being concerned only with roads and their construction. Following the south Birmingham study, a new city engineer was appointed from a city (York) with a history of car restraint strategies. His role was seen as being to 'sit on the engineers and make sure they don't move policy back' (pressure group representative) towards road construction. In addition, the Directorate of Planning and Economic Development within BCC was economic development-led. The subsequent separation of planning from economic development was a key moment in the development of wider BCC strategy. It was recognised that 'separation [was] probably a good idea' (metropolitan district planner). In a similar appointment to the new city engineer, the director of planning was appointed from Bath City Council, again an authority with a conservationist rather than pro-development stance. There was a tension here between promoting an integrated approach to spatial strategy through large departments and the dangers inherent in having regulatory and policy functions together.

Thus the debates in south Birmingham became linked to a wider debate about urban strategy, the relationship between officers and members of the council and who planning and transport policy in the city was for. The emphasis on the city centre, the promotion of the service sector, and the resultant attempts to appeal to 'men in suits in cars' (pressure group representative) led to a particular configuration of policy. BCC argued that they should pay attention to the needs of potential stakeholders in the form of businesses that may not even yet know Birmingham exists but who might locate to the city. Opposition groups claimed that citizens of the city are the people who should take priority. Plans for the re-development of the Bull Ring in central Birmingham brought this to a head. The outcomes of these episodes, for which BCC was much criticised (Loftman and Nevin 1994), led to a subtle refocusing of policy on the needs of residents rather than business.

The 'predict and provide' discourse was evident in the Birmingham UDP: 'there is an increasing contrast between the quality of inter-urban roads and those within the built-up area … the completion of the M40 link to London … will throw this into stark relief in the south of the city' (BCC, 1990a, para. 5.10). So old approaches to transport planning were present in relation to specific proposals in the early 1990s, despite the presence of demand management arguments in the BITS study. The south Birmingham study highlights the fact that engineers were conforming to a 'predict and provide' modus operandi and focusing on accommodating road traffic. Engineers were thought to have 'cooked up a story' (pressure group representative) with regard to traffic levels from the M40 in order to get a 'bottom-drawer' scheme constructed: 'Bottom drawers are so full of highway schemes … that the package … in the last couple of years is full of these schemes and not necessarily those you would come up with if you started with a blank piece of paper' (metropolitan district planner).

BCC's principal long-standing concern is with urban regeneration and economic revitalisation. To that end, 'the central purpose of the transport element of the strategy is to support economic revitalisation and urban regeneration by providing good quality transport infrastructure' (BCC, 1989, para. 5.13). So it appears that, as in Lancashire, economic issues were dominant and influenced the way policy issues were perceived: 'economic recovery is the principal objective to which changes to the transport system must be directed' (ibid., para. 5.14).

Thus in Birmingham environmental issues were still marginalised in the 1990s in the policy outputs of the city council. This situation partly arose from the history of institutional responsibilities in the conurbation. Following the abolition of the West Midlands County Council, various issues were assigned to particular districts. As a result, Dudley Metropolitan Borough Council became the lead authority with regard to environmental issues. Whilst this potentially created a 'policy champion' role, it may have served to further distance environmental issues from other issues. In transport terms, demand management as an issue was raised early in the conurbation compared to our other case study areas through work undertaken as part of the integrated transport studies. The demand management principle was subsequently embodied in UDPs. The early emergence of demand management may reflect the levels and intractability of congestion in the conurbation as compared to Lancashire and Kent, and also a degree of 'policy learning' on the part of policy makers following events in south Birmingham and elsewhere. However, on closer inspection, we note that principles of demand management apply only to certain areas, where congestion is greatest. Thus there is a geography to the demand management discourse: 'a strategy emphasising traffic management ... would produce a significant benefit for the city centre but little elsewhere' (BCC, 1990a, para. 5.15). Demand management is therefore driven by a perception of the problem as 'congestion', not that car driving is damaging to the environment and citizens' health. This reflected the weak nature of the environmental discourse in the city and the strong technocratic emphasis prevalent in issues of transport policy formulation.

Partly as a result, transport policy in West Midlands districts other than BCC was represented as being, 'still on the old track' (planner). This was, as in Lancashire, compounded by the parochial actions of members attempting to get investment, in the form of new roads, for their electorates. Through the 1990s, however, local politicians started to see a need to change direction, partly because areas of the conurbation were becoming congested despite investment in roads and so the 'gridlock scenario is very real' (metropolitan district planner). In addition, much reduced levels of central government funding for local transport schemes provided an opportunity for officers to engage with members about dropping many of the pet schemes they had lobbied for in recent years. Such parochialism on the part of local authority politicians also had the potential to further undermine any attempts at consensus through the package approach, as horse trading over schemes and proposals could have undermined strategic policy direction and the aims of the packages themselves. However, in the main, the package approach was very successful. The adoption of the approach by central government in 1993 indicated a shared view that transport issues should be approached in a way which sets them in a wider context.

The emergent 'new realism' in the West Midlands   A new agenda had therefore begun to permeate transport planning across the West Midlands so that, 'we are now doing things that were unthinkable a few years ago' (transport planner). However, it is congestion, rather than environmental issues, that is driving a 'new realist' agenda: 'politicians are starting to see we can't go on as we are, and that we can't build our way out of trouble even if the money was there' (metropolitan district planner).

Whilst some statements of policy in the West Midlands had a strong environmental emphasis, 'when fundamental issues affecting economic growth are involved, the needs of the economy and the current lifestyles of residents are given priority' (Marshall, 1994, p.3). In many ways transport policy did not shift earlier because congestion was not that bad. This partly reflects efforts in road building in the past. Innovation in demand management in the conurbation, for example, was unlikely as there was neither a consensus that this was the way forward nor was there a 'context of desperation' (academic interviewee) provoked by severe congestion. Thus by the end of the 1990s the conurbation had 'still got the big bullets to bite on' (metropolitan district transport planner). The big bullets referred to here are the more draconian measures at discouraging car use such as removing car parking spaces in the city centre. Thus opposition from some councillors and businesses, afraid that policies to exclude cars from the city centre would damage retail and office markets, continued to delay the adoption of the environmental discourse.

Kent: playing political games in London's backyard

Kent provides a different context in which to assess how the 'new realism' was taking hold in the 1990s. This was particularly interesting given certain similarities in spatial and socio-economic profiles between the county and Lancashire: a number of small towns with large rural hinterlands, but with a major conurbation nearby.

Kent is unique in the UK. It accommodates 80 per cent of road traffic from the UK to Europe. Partly as a result of this, considerable infrastructure investment has taken place in recent years, notably the Channel Tunnel, international passenger stations at Ebbsfleet and Ashford, the Dartford Bridge, motorway extensions and widening (M2/M20/M25) and the Medway Tunnel and associated link roads. These developments have contributed towards a perception that Kent is moving from being 'The Garden of England' to becoming a 'Gateway to Europe' or from a 'peninsula' of England to a 'corridor' in Europe (see Chapter 3).

The planning framework for Kent is set by Regional Planning Policy Guidance Note 9 (RPG9) (DoE, 1994a), and in the Thames Gateway area by RPG9a also (DoE, 1995c). RPG9 seeks to affect a west-to-east shift in development, taking the pressure from west of London and facilitating development in the east. RPG9a expands upon RPG9 and sets the framework for developments in the Thames Gateway, part of which includes north Kent. RPG9a is largely concerned with economic regeneration, although transport issues feature prominently in two ways: first, with respect to capturing development opportunities through the provision of passenger stations on the Channel Tunnel Rail Link (CTRL) at Stratford and Ebbsfleet; second, in relation to moving people within the Gateway area for which a light rail system, the Medway Metro, has been proposed for north Kent.

The 1993 Kent Structure Plan put the environment centre-stage in policy. It marked a departure from previous plans in stating the main requirement as being 'to improve the quality of life and standard of environment within Kent' (KCC, 1993a, p.11). Environmental issues were defined as the conservation of the built and natural environments, as in previous plans, but were widened to encompass ecological issues.

Transport policies in previous structure plans were primarily intended to support economic growth. Subsidiary aims were to 'meet social needs by securing a reasonable level of mobility', and to contribute to road safety and minimise the damage to the environment (KCC, 1984, p.74). The 1993 Structure Plan had a more sophisticated view of the tensions between providing for accessibility for all, economic growth and protection of the environment. It is clear that a policy shift has occurred, as Policy T1 of the 1993 plan attempted to go some way to resolving this difficult balance by prioritising walking, cycling and public transport modes. Nevertheless, there are very many new road improvements contained in the plan and considerable controversy surrounded upgrading the A259 in the south of the county and the Thanet Way in north Kent. The Kent Structure Plan, although well in advance of many others in the UK at this time in terms of its treatment of sustainable development issues, went through a process of 'greenwashing', as the Lancashire plan also did. To this end, sections were moved and policies reordered to reflect a new rhetorical emphasis on environmental issues.

By the mid 1990s, investment strategies such as transport policies and programmes and package bids were being developed very much within a 'new realist' paradigm. This may have resulted from a deeper understanding on the part of Kent County Council (KCC) of central government's policy intentions at this time as compared with Lancashire County Council, for example. KCC officers were in good contact with civil servants in Whitehall and dialogue with central government civil servants and ministers was highly developed. In transport, the concentration of regulatory and investment power amongst civil servants and ministers made it vital for local authorities to understand changes in thinking at the centre. Thus:

> We [KCC transport planners] spend as much of our time ensuring they [DETR Civil servants] are well fed when they are here and we try and break down barriers, and try and develop rapport. Over the TPP [a now defunct investment mechanism] we see them almost weekly; [they are] almost part of our team so they understand when they sell things to their bosses and we understand their problems. (County council transport planner)

This process of officers stitching up funding arrangements is not necessarily so clear-cut, however, and local political priorities can override it. For example, in deciding on the area to select for the county's fourth package bid, indications from the Department of Transport (as it then was) suggested that they would prefer the Thames-side area as it linked with a number of central government transport and regeneration objectives. KCC members, however, wanted to put forward the Thanet area, although Thanet was much less likely to get funded as the perception amongst central government actors is that it is less worthy than other areas within Kent. Officers put this information to members, who still wanted to select Thanet as they wished to capture votes in this area: 'So we [officers] say, "Yes, that's right, but you won't get your transport problems solved", and they say "Well, we don't care"' (county council transport planner). If the bid for funding failed then they could blame central government.

More generally, following considerable investment in new road infrastructure in the late 1980s/early 1990s, transport policy in Kent shifted dramatically away from road building through the 1990s. Road building in the county in the early 1990s was explained by reference to public demands:

> We are public servants and we go in the way [the] public wants us to, [we] never had call to question the way we were tackling transport until recently.

We have no big urban areas causing difficulty, our customers were happy with the road system and they are a car-borne population, we have [a number of small–medium-sized] towns, a great deal of movement geared to the car; only recently have the true environmental costs been realised. (County council transport planner)

However, by the mid-1990s, the mood in the local transport policy community and beyond was for change. KCC officers' reading of policy change was important, but also vital was a shift in the broad base of local public support. As a result, and in contrast to our Lancashire case, Kent members appeared willing to abandon road schemes based on support from electorates: 'local people more and more are screaming for less and less roads' (county council transport planner). Electorates saw that road construction did little to alleviate congestion and yet detrimentally affected local environments.

Despite this change, in one or two areas, as in the Lancashire case, the clientelist actions of members presented a barrier to moving away from road building. This was represented by an officer as follows:

Everyone is signed up to the idea of changing from road schemes to other systems, absolutely, once they have their road scheme. 'Totally accept that, unequivocally, we must shift, but don't forget Stage Three of the [...] Ring Road.' They've all got their one pet scheme. (County council transport planner)

This desire for new links was often driven by a very local 'roads for prosperity' discourse: traders saw the relief of congestion as making a particular town centre more attractive, thus helping its local economy. Such public pressure meant that in Kent there was a consensus over the broad direction of policy but problems arose in relation to detail. The policies in plans and investment programmes adopted a sustainable rhetoric in relation to transport. The problem for policy makers occurred when schemes affected people directly in the places where they live and work. So policy was developed with comparatively few problems, but it was in the details of individual projects where access was denied or open space or parking spaces lost that difficulties were caused. This was partly resolved by officers explaining strategy to members and its relationship to demands for schemes in their own patches, and then using these members to convince others of the merits of a particular strategy. However, some members were more open to such persuasion than others: 'there is a gulf in thinking between high vision and the district man [sic] who is very concerned about [for example] those five residential parking spaces' (county council transport planner).

So in Kent there were signs of a policy shift, but it was having difficulty biting in particular places in relation to very immediate local concerns. There was a feeling that there was some way to go before people made connections between their own lifestyles and public policy and decisions: 'the public isn't ready for that yet, and we are here to serve, shopkeepers are our public' (transport planner). There remained a feeling that Kent had solved some of its easier problems through the building of new roads, but that more intractable ones were arising in urban areas and the demand management discourse had some way to go before people felt inclined to give up the freedom to drive their cars.

The transport policy community and the wider polity

The cases presented above highlight the changing policy agendas and discourses surrounding transport issues in three localities. As Chapter 2 highlighted, analysing the importance of the networks and alliances that hold stakeholders together and how they are actively constructed is critical to understanding such change. The alliances encountered typically cluster around certain functions of local government, issues, policy (sub)sectors, spatial areas, professional bases, and political parties.

The discussion and development of transport policy in all three case study areas was dominated by the public sector. The strongest links between organisations were between local government engineers and civil servants at regional and national levels, with relationships cemented through regular contact, often associated with bids for finance (see figure 6.2). This bond appeared particularly well developed in the Kent case, where senior local government officials were perceptively playing political games with central government for funding. Kent County Council's success in attracting funding in the 1980s and 1990s reflected this. KCC paid a great deal of attention to such relation-building effort with central government. This was aided by Kent's geographical proximity to Whitehall, which meant face-to-face contact was facilitated more often than in Lancashire or the West Midlands and social networks were more likely to exist amongst local

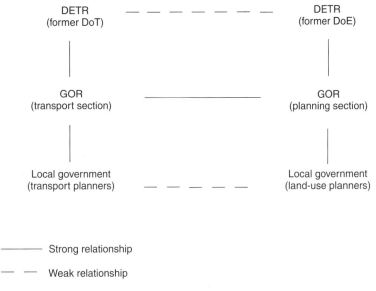

Figure 6.2   Intergovernmental relations in transport planning

government officials and central government civil servants. Bringing civil servants and ministers to the locality was thought to be an excellent way of getting messages across. A number of innovative funding packages were secured through the adept playing of strategies such as these.

Similar policy communities are replicated to greater or lesser degrees around the UK and were observable in our other two localities. The uniting bond here was often a shared professional one, although the tight control central government retains over transport funding arguably makes such relationships a necessity. However, this close linkage had the effect of excluding other influences and preventing other voices from being heard. This exclusion in part explains policy continuity in the transport field in the postwar period and the difficulty other agendas, such as the environmental one, have had in gaining influence over transport policy at national and local levels.

The relatively closed nature of these transport planning policy communities not only prevented other discourses from getting leverage but also helped to mystify the processes of transport planning for other stakeholders. Attention to relations within the policy communities had often isolated local transport planners from their colleagues in their own local authorities. Frequently, actors told us that they felt transport planners 'work as they've always worked, as if they're living on a different planet' (Lancashire land use planner). This fundamental fracture between the frames of reference and the working practices of different professionals within local authorities had significant effects upon policy development and interpretation. In the long run this insularity left transport planning somewhat behind dominant pressures for change amongst other stakeholder groups. There were signs by the late 1990s that this insular culture was changing, with the integration of transport and planning in government regional offices and in the DETR, and from the sorts of pressures coming from within localities, as illustrated in the West Midlands case.

The only area where the vertical relational emphases were not as dominant was the West Midlands. Here the relics of the West Midlands County Council, such as the co-ordinating committees that still exist, notably the Chief Engineers and Planning Officers Group (CEPOG) and the continued existence of the Passenger Transport Authority, all provided a challenge to the professional policy network. Perhaps because PTA officers had similar backgrounds and ways of thinking to local authority transport planners, they succeeded in promoting a public transport view where one may not have existed 'inside' local authorities. As a result, local councils were developing long-term public transport strategies as a reaction against 'one-off solutions to things' (West Midlands transport planner). Indeed, this greater relational capital in the conurbation enabled the West Midlands to develop and pursue innovative approaches and change central government's own agenda. The first 'package bid', for example, was unsolicited from central government.

Tendencies towards greater integration at subnational levels were in evidence, however. The regional level in Lancashire and the West Midlands became an important institutional place for transport issues to be discussed. In both cases transport corridor principles were very much to the fore, although the interpretation of corridors was very different in each case. The perceived need for major new strategic infrastructure such as the Birmingham Northern Relief Road, trans-Pennine infrastructure options, the western orbital motorway proposal and the West Coast Main-Line rail upgrade, all gave impetus to efforts at alliance building. In Kent, there was less of a regional approach in evidence, despite the importance of the infrastructure, extant and proposed, for the county, for the south east region and indeed the rest of the UK.

Inter-local authority conflicts were evident in all our areas. County–district tensions were very apparent in both two-tier areas. The understandable desire on the part of many local authorities to capture transport investment meant that county councils often found themselves in a difficult brokerage position in being the recipients of the demands of lower-tier authorities.

In general terms, the level of dialogue between departments within local authorities was variable. In Kent, chief officers encouraged cross-departmental co-operation. This was evident in the outputs of the authority, such as the Structure Plan. As a result, the ways of working ingrained in KCC's transport planning department had partly led to the lessening of one of the critical fractures in policy development found in our Lancashire and West Midlands cases, that which separated the planning department from their engineering colleagues.

Beyond the public sector: non-governmental alliance partners

Outside the public sector, two forms of alliance were most significant. Alliances of (mainly) business interests allied to local economic growth agendas and environmental coalitions often formed in response to a specific project, but also sometimes to campaign about more strategic issues.

Environmental groups such as the Council for the Protection of Rural England, Friends of the Earth, wildlife trusts, cycling groups, local action networks and statutory bodies such as the regional offices of the Countryside Commission and English Nature, were all present in transport debates in our case study areas. Where they formed alliances, typically these coalitions were loose-knit, aimed at sharing resources and lobbying together over certain issues. Much of this work was a response to individual schemes and policy documentation, but significant strategic lobbying was also a feature. The groups came together over certain issues but also remained separate at times, as some groups preferred not to associate with emotive argumentation and to rely more on reasoned 'scientific' approaches. The groups often sought to produce a common line on particular policy issues. In Lancashire, road-building proposals were a great mobilising force for such alliance building. The alliance considered that they had some success with their attempts at lobbying, as some schemes were dropped in the Structure Plan preparation process. This success was felt by members of the alliance to be tempered by the large number of road projects that remained in the plan. Similarly, the Channel Tunnel Rail Link proposal in Kent mobilised a number of environmental groups to join forces to influence route choice and develop environmental mitigation measures. Initially, central government and Union Rail were very hostile, but after initial work a useful dialogue was maintained and most participants were pleased with the way this alliance developed. In other areas campaigners had an influence over policy, but it depended very much on one or two key individuals. Their influence was dependent on the openness of key public sector individuals to their point of view and whether or not they were subsequently admitted to the policy community.

Networks primarily focused on giving business a voice in spatial strategy making, such as the North West Partnership, the North West Business Leadership Team and the West Midlands Regional Economic Consortium, featured transport highly in their debates. The key players in these networks also cropped up in other arenas where transport and land use planning tended to be discussed. Business interests were more prominent in Lancashire and the West Midlands than in Kent, although active network building by KCC economic development officers was going some way to tackling this absence. Enterprise Plc (formerly LEL) had a privileged 'insider' relationship in policy making in Lancashire owing to the closeness of LEL's relationship with the elite in the ruling Labour Party. Chambers of commerce were not generally very active in the key transport policy arenas, except in the West Midlands case. The structured nature of business privilege, however, was important rather than the exertion of a direct influence through lobbying. Business was privileged with regard to transport policy because of the objectives of economic competitiveness it shared with local authorities (Saunders, 1979).

In relation to central government, business and the roads lobby were no longer getting the same level of insider status with civil servants and ministers that they had in the 1980s (Holliday, 1993). They were being told to 'get into public arenas like everyone else' (government regional office civil servant). The roads lobby itself has never been well represented in local politics (Hamer, 1987) and our research confirms this. This loss of influence at national level and shifting policy agendas therefore implies something of a crisis for the lobby.

Discussions of spatial strategy and strategic transport policy rarely seem to involve service providers despite the continued importance of partnerships in service provision, the implementation of 'park and ride' and ticketing co-ordination. Here local authorities were using limited regulatory and financial levers relating to park and ride, town centre environmental improvements and provision of bus lanes to bargain with bus operators into renewing fleets and contributing to these wider improvements. These alliances were often made more formal through 'quality partnership' arrangements, but engagement in strategic issues was the exception rather than the rule. Although there were some benefits, public transport privatisation and deregulation were unanimously thought to make service co-ordination more difficult. The numbers of stakeholders involved made co-ordination a problem, while restructuring within public transport operating companies had also undermined such opportunities. Within such firms, network planners had been laid off and fleet managers and schedulers were forced into fulfilling this role with, typically, less awareness of strategic transport issues.

As in other issue areas, the increasing importance of the EU, especially in terms of providing finance for transport projects, was affecting the way local authority transport planners worked. All our areas had offices in Brussels, with regular visits by transport officers. KCC deliberately brought Neil Kinnock, EU Transport Commissioner, to look around Kent and discuss cross-border transport issues. The continued decline in national money for transport projects through the 1990s made courting Brussels for finance all the more important.

Re-integrating transport issues and the planning system

This account shows clearly that the dominant discourses surrounding transport policy making were in a transition phase. At national level a rhetorical shift from 'predict and provide' to demand management was virtually complete even before the change in national government in 1997. Policy change was prompted in part by the new generation of road protests and a growing concern over the effects of private vehicle use on the environment, as well as cuts in government spending. A growing dissatisfaction with the usefulness of traditional transport planning techniques and the 'predict and provide' approach was also important (Goodwin, 1997). The full scale of this shift has taken time to filter through and both locally and nationally many institutional, cultural and political barriers linger on (Owens, 1995; Richardson and

Heywood, 1996; Vigar *et al.*, 2000). This can result in differences between local authorities' land use policies and the implementation of transport planning strategies. This differentiation resulted partly from the existence of separate policy communities for transport and land use planning and the degree of isolation of one from the other.

By the end of the 1990s, however, the local transport and land use planning policy communities were engaging in more dialogue with each other and with other stakeholders. Land use planning and transport departments were becoming more closely tied together in all three localities. The environmental agenda was the key driver behind this integration, although shifting signals from central government (themselves in part a product of the environmental agenda) and changes in the places from which transport planners get projects financed (that is, the reduction in the importance of transport funding per se and the increasing importance of the Single Regeneration Budget and European Regional Development Fund monies) have also forced greater horizontal networking. In terms of the arenas for policy discussion, transport issues became more prominent in regional policy debates and in discussions amongst environmental and business communities. For both communities this increasing prominence was driven by more pervasive congestion problems and by a deepening understanding of the environmental consequences of transport choices.

Transport policy communities always thought of themselves as being sensitive to environmental concerns and believed that these issues were well integrated in transport policy and decision making. However, this view reflected a narrow perception of the 'environment'. Until recently, the 'environment' for transport policy communities involved planting trees beside motorways and tackling the more tangible effects of transport (noise, visual intrusion and so on). A new conceptualisation of the environment was reframing the transport policy discourse. As ecological issues began to gain weight in transport planning discussions, policy had to change significantly to accommodate such concerns.

This rise in the prominence of an environmental discourse was not to the total exclusion of other discourses. An economic competitiveness discourse, 'roads for prosperity', while not as dominant at central government level as it was, still appeared at local levels as a lobby for specific links. The dominance of the economic competitiveness agenda in local politics was evident in Lancashire and Birmingham in the late 1980s/early 1990s where the 'predict and provide' ethos was simultaneously being magnified by the wider polity in these two areas. In

Lancashire in particular, a core group of politicians were vital in determining a policy emphasis which favoured private car travel over other modes in the belief that roads were essential for economic competitiveness. This led to a level of road building in the structure plan that went contrary to both the advice of planning officers and the strategic direction of the plan. The closeness of the local authority's economic development arm to the locus of power in the county council was in part responsible for this view. Similarly, in Birmingham, the dominant view in the development department and the elites of the local authority in the late 1980s was that roads were essential to maintain the city's competitiveness. This view became allied with the dominant paradigm of the engineers in a powerful coalition for road construction, despite many opposing voices in the conurbation.

Social issues in transport planning have traditionally crystallised into debates over 'accessibility' and 'mobility'. These concerns were still present, especially in relation to access for the disabled, but social issues get less attention than environmental and economic agendas. Transport planners and their local authority departments had limited control over tackling social issues in an era of market provision. Such issues were often ghettoised within transport planning departments and the social agenda had narrowed (Vigar, 1999). Disabled access was a prominent issue and in rural areas concern remains over maintaining a basic level of public transport service provision. However, transport's very obvious role in relation to wider debates over social exclusion, for example, was rarely raised as an issue. This lack of policy attention is compounded by an emphasis amongst the transport policy communities on large-scale capital projects (resulting partly from central government regulation and financing), as such issues are rarely amenable to such technical fixes.

The key institutional arenas for the discussion of transport issues were typically closed to all but the chief transport officers in local government, although in the West Midlands the CEPOG, the arena of chief engineers and chief planners, produced real integration across the two policy sectors. The planning system should in theory provide the framework within which transport policy sits and schemes are considered. In some cases, transport issues did provide some of the impetus for the strategic direction of plans. The focus on transport corridors in Lancashire and the West Midlands is only partly about transport issues per se, but proved to be an important device for integrating transport and land use planning. The development plan, however, was not a key driver of transport policy in any of the localities examined. Plans provided arenas for the discussion and development of transport policy and an opportunity for stakeholders from beyond the transport policy community to have a say over transport policy direction. Without the formal arenas of the public inquiries and the opportunities for comments prior to this, there would be no formal channels for many stakeholders to express their views and perhaps to have influence. However, as suggested earlier, decisions tended to arise elsewhere and enter the legitimising arena of the development plan with considerable advocacy from local government officers and/or members. The lack of usefulness of land use planning policy arenas is partly explained by the dominance of the professional transport policy network and its separation from these arenas.

By the turn of the century, the 'new realist' view had assumed dominance in UK transport planning. This shift was principally driven by the search for alternatives to road building. Locally, its penetration was highly dependent on the degree to which congestion was experienced in particular localities (Pemberton and Vigar, 1998). So environmental discourses were not institutionalised and they still came up against the project-focused ways of thinking inherent in the working practices of the highway engineer. Different approaches were often difficult to communicate across professional cultures: 'It has not been easy telling highway engineers that they needed to give up highway space for buses' (West Midlands transport planner). Policies were frequently conditioned more by capital schemes, by budget heads determined in Whitehall and by shorter-term political and project-based considerations. This situation was also changing by the end of the 1990s. It may be that greater local autonomy will flow from local authorities gaining extra revenue-raising powers with respect to parking and congestion charging (DETR, 1998c) and this will prompt more public discussion of transport priorities and investment. In more general terms, local authority officers were opening up to the views of other stakeholders, but this was a slow process and did not often fit with the culture of the engineer:

> At the beginning of my career I was in mains drainage, [it was] absolutely wonderful, all you have to do is produce a plan, if you don't do this, this area will flood, agreed, go away and do it, no-one ever looks down your trench and says they're the wrong coloured pipes, but in transport everyone is a transport planner, everyone drives a car, uses the train. (County council transport planner)

Development plan making could provide a vital role in the integration of transport and land use planning. However, Local Agenda 21 and Local Transport Plan preparation processes are also now competing for this role. The relationship between these arenas is unclear. Transport is deeply integrated with the key regional concerns of all stakeholders; environmental sustainability, quality of life and regional competitiveness. However, in the recent past transport has often been divorced from such debates, confined to discussion amongst its narrow policy communities.

7 Managing Waste: an Emerging Discourse in the Planning System

Changing approaches to waste management

Every year in the UK over 400 million tonnes of waste is produced (DoE, 1995b), about half of which is 'controlled waste' comprising 'household, industrial and commercial waste' (HMSO, 1990b, p.83). By far the greatest proportion of this, including 83 per cent of household waste, goes to landfill (DETR, 1998g). Disposal of waste in landfill sites has become contentious for a number of environmental and amenity reasons. However, unlike other policy issues covered in the previous three chapters, the discussion on management of waste is a relatively new issue for the UK land use planning system. That said, various developments in the 1990s, both within and outside the planning system, have begun to move waste management issues and the allocation of sites for waste facilities to the forefront of national and local planning policy agendas.

This chapter focuses on the role of the planning system in regulating the provision of sites for waste facilities and its relation with waste disposal and regulatory policies and practices. The sites in question are primarily for the disposal of municipal solid waste through landfill or incineration. Drawing on the three case studies, this chapter provides an account of the remarkable discursive shifts that have taken place in waste management issues during the 1990s. It also focuses on the rapidly changing institutional landscape within which policy agendas and discourses were situated.

Waste reduction versus waste disposal: a discursive conflict

The early municipal solution to handling waste, particularly in large cities, was to burn it in incinerator plants, some of which produced electricity. Later, the rising amount and the changing nature of the waste stream created a rationale for centralised sorting and recycling of waste, but only as a marginal activity associated with the operational efficiency of incinerators. However, by the early 1930s, the use of incineration began to decline sharply as the cheaper method of tipping waste proved to be a more economical option.

'Landfill' assumed a dominant position in the disposal of waste. However, the energy crisis of the 1970s and the predicted shortage of raw materials led to a renewed interest in recycling, with a focus on energy recovery from waste. A green paper, *War on Waste*, promoted 'local salvage schemes' and urged people to 'learn, or relearn, the habit of regarding waste material as potentially valuable resources' (HMSO, 1974, p.2). This was accompanied by statutory provisions in the Control of Pollution Act of 1974 which, for the first time, required local authorities to examine ways of promoting recycling. Despite these provisions, the increasing labour costs of kerbside collection and the effects of economic slowdown in the 1970s in waste material markets resulted in the collapse of many established recycling schemes (Gandy, 1994). Moreover, cuts in local authority expenditure reduced the ability of the public sector to maintain such activities. By the mid-1970s, therefore, the issue of recycling slipped down the public policy agenda. At the same time, the costs of incineration, coupled with criticism of its associated air pollution, reduced its use in the UK to one of the lowest levels amongst developed countries. The disposal of waste through landfill continued, almost unchallenged, to dominate waste management policy and practices throughout the UK. The introduction of market mechanisms into local authorities' arrangements for collection and disposal of waste in the 1980s further bolstered the dominance of landfill as a waste disposal solution, with economic efficiency becoming the dominant criterion in determining policy. The existence of an active minerals industry and the availability of geologically suitable sites meant that landfill remained the most economically viable option.

Since the late 1980s, however, the potential of recycling has found a new salience as part of the wider environmental sustainability agenda. Prompted in particular by the European Union's increased attention to the promotion of sustainable waste management (CEC, 1989), notably the requirements of the EC Framework Directive on Waste (75/442/EEC as amended by 91/156/EEC and 91/962/EEC), the British government adopted a waste strategy based on a hierarchy of options (see Figure 7.1). This urged local authorities to focus their attention on the top of

Reduction

Re-use

Recovery*

Disposal

*Material recovery (recycling and composting) and energy recovery (incineration)

Figure 7.1 The waste hierarchy

the waste hierarchy (DoE, 1992d, 1995b). The strategy also introduced two new interconnected spatial organising concepts by promoting the principles of regional *self-sufficiency* and *proximity*: the management of waste as close as possible to the place of production.

By the late 1990s, the concept of the 'waste hierarchy' had found its way onto the waste policy agenda. In many areas of the UK the difficulties of finding suitable large landfill sites focused attention on the use of incineration with energy recovery. However, tensions were increasingly manifest in the polarisation of debate on recycling versus incineration. At one end of the spectrum, many stakeholders favoured a moratorium on new incinerators (for example, LPAC, 1997) in order to get recycling activities established. At the other end, the influential packaging industry lobby and a fast-growing private sector waste management industry promoted the highly profitable, capital-intensive option of incineration with energy recovery (*New Scientist*, 1998; *Green Futures*, 1998). Despite such tensions, the concept of the waste hierarchy put energy recovery through incineration on a par with material recovery through recycling, on the grounds that both options reduce the amount of waste being landfilled. How the concept of the waste hierarchy was adopted and operationalised was therefore highly amenable to the interpretation of different stakeholders, as illustrated by our case studies documented below. Those involved not only had to shift their frame of reference from a discourse focused on landfill in the name of economic efficiency, but were also confronted by conflicting interpretations of the new discourse of the waste hierarchy, underpinned as it was by environmental values. Moreover, the new approach regarded waste policy making as a series of simple descending steps down the ladder of the waste hierarchy. In practice, however, there were fundamental barriers in adopting the options at the top of the ladder in a market-dominated economy, as well as tensions between the various options, such as the impact of incineration on the level of recycling and vice versa. These tensions were compounded by other issues, not the least of which were local authorities' long-term contractual commitments to waste disposal companies and the lack of alternatives at reasonable cost in many areas. Two central government policy documents, *Planning Policy Guidance Note 10* and *Less Waste More Value*, produced by separate divisions within the new DETR, caused further confusion by giving contradictory advice to local authorities. While the former stated that 'no automatic preference should be given to any options within the recovery category' (DETR, 1998f, para.12), the latter suggested that 'incineration with energy recovery should not be undertaken without consideration first being given to the possibility of composting and material recycling' (DETR, 1998e, p.10). How these tensions were resolved in practice is discussed below.

A complex web of regulatory systems

The shifting waste management discourses and practices in the 1990s took place against a background of constant change in institutional contexts characterised by the continuing process of privatisation, the formation of new regulatory mechanisms, increasing confusion over roles, responsibilities and relationships, the rise and fall of established arenas and networks, the increasing profile of landuse planners' roles, and more recently emerging regional mechanisms.

In England, responsibilities for managing waste lie with different tiers and departments of the local authorities. In general, district authorities are responsible for the collection and recycling of waste as well as preparation of waste-recycling plans, while county councils are responsible for arranging the disposal of waste through contracts with private sector operators, the preparation of waste local plans and the determination of waste planning applications. (The unitary authorities combine the responsibilities of districts and counties.) Until the creation of the Environment Agency (EA) in 1996, such authorities also prepared waste management plans and regulated the recovery and disposal of waste. Additional complexity results from the division of regulatory responsibilities between land use planning and pollution control systems, each operating under different legislative frameworks. The environmental impacts of landfill sites are regulated largely through the licensing system introduced by the 1974 Control of Pollution Act (consolidated in the Environmental Protection Act 1990 and the Environment Act 1995) and carried out by the EA in consultation with other regulatory bodies. The planning system plays a marginal role focused mainly on safeguarding local amenities, while the pollution control system focuses on waste-related environmental pollution. A cornerstone of this system was the concept of *best practicable means* (BPM) later widened to *best practicable environmental option* (BPEO) (RCEP, 1988). This latter concept focuses on the means by which desirable standards for dealing with pollution might be met within what costs it is reasonable for the polluter to bear. The result has been 'a system of comfortable negotiation between government technicians and industry' (Cullingworth and Nadin, 1994, p.138). This informal and relatively secretive system relied through the 1980s and 1990s on voluntary compliance, within a narrow and closed policy community, dominated by the regulators and the industry. Environmental groups played a marginal reactive role (McCormick, 1991). These arrangements resulted in extremely low standards in many waste disposal authorities (HCEC, 1989) where 'the cheapest tolerable option was too often deployed instead of the best practicable environmental option' (HMSO, 1990b, pt II). Thus the combination of a dominant economic imperative and a negotiated regulatory system resulted in a growing number of landfill sites operating with low environmental standards.

Meanwhile, the location of waste disposal sites was determined by the planning system, largely in the context of a national policy vacuum. Until 1994, when the first national planning policy guidance on waste (PPG 23) was issued (DoE, 1994b), the legislation had solely concentrated on waste licensing and pollution regulation. The role of the planning system in the management of waste was largely neglected. A revised PPG23 (DoE, 1996d) was criticised by the industry and local authorities for its lack of clarity and effectiveness (Adams, 1996). The Labour administration abandoned the revision and instead published a draft PPG10 (DETR, 1998f) which reiterated the waste hierarchy and proposed a regional co-ordinating mechanism. However, despite the lack of consistent national policy, for planners the siting of landfill was a relatively easy task because sites were often available through the process of mineral working. The 'holes in the ground' created by quarrying were often used as tipping sites. Thus waste disposal activities were regarded by both the regulators and the regulated as temporary, logical and even useful extensions to mineral development.

This seemingly beneficial association of mineral extraction and waste disposal, coupled with the general availability of 'technically' suitable sites for landfill, made land allocation through the planning process relatively unproblematic through the 1980s and into the 1990s. The strongly-held and persistent discourse of 'filling holes in the ground' pre-empted the planning system from searching for other spatial ordering concepts and limited its task to formulating a series of often standard site-specific regulatory criteria. Planning policies for waste, often no more than two or three policies tacked on at the back of the development plan, were primarily confined to a set of 'bad neighbour impacts' criteria to be drawn upon where and when development control decisions on specific sites were to be made.

The 1990s, however, witnessed a major change both in the planning system and in the approach to environmental and subsequently waste management issues. Government legislation made the preparation of specific development plans for waste mandatory. These were to complement the waste disposal plans which, prior to the formation of the EA, were produced by the waste disposal department of local authorities under the pollution control system. Thus, on the one hand, the process of plan making itself introduced the potential for long-term strategic planning for waste, and began tentatively to challenge the site-specific approach. On the other hand, the plans found, in theory, an enhanced status in the decision-making processes (see Chapter 1).

The result was a higher profile for waste issues within the planning community. What had traditionally been a marginal activity for planners became an increasingly significant area of local authority planning policy. The arenas of the planning system increased the number of stakeholders involved in framing waste management policy. This happened at a time when the previously relatively unproblematic task of landfill site allocation in former mineral workings became increasingly contentious. First, stricter regulatory criteria, particularly for protection of groundwater, began to challenge the suitability of 'holes in the ground'. Second, public pressure against landfilling increased, especially amongst those people who had put up with years of mineral extraction previously.

Therefore, for a planning system which was relatively new to the challenges of waste management at a strategic level, the allocation of sites for waste disposal became not only an environmental challenge but also a political nightmare. Opposition to the siting of waste facilities, often maliciously labelled as 'NIMBYism', was reflected in the large number of objections to waste local plans (Petts, 1995). In cases where public reactions had been particularly vociferous, some local authorities cut short the debate by avoiding site identification in development plans. The resultant inconsistencies in the regulatory criteria for site allocation throughout the country and the uncertainty this created for the waste disposal operators mobilised the industry to lobby the government for a change in what they called 'the planning gridlock' (Waste Planning, 1996).

One role for the EA was to ensure effective co-ordination between all the key waste regulatory functions (DoE, 1995b). Although the introduction of the EA contributed to the co-ordination of regulatory functions through combining three major regulatory bodies under one roof, it weakened the links between waste licensing and the land use planning system. The two functions which used to be carried out by a single local authority, although in different departments, were now split between two organisations: one accountable to its local constituency, the other to central government. The legislative division between the planning and pollution control systems was complemented by the organisational split, adding a new layer to the existing complex web of regulatory networks and to the confusion over 'who does what'. Despite government guidance which urged local authorities to avoid duplication of regulatory controls, in practice there were several grey areas where the boundaries of the planning and pollution regimes overlapped. Moreover, the removal of the regulatory functions from local democratic arenas potentially increased rather than diminished such duplications. Having lost their licensing controls, the local authorities further stretched their planning powers to ensure that local political and environmental concerns were not overlooked. The siting of waste facilities, with their associated environmental implications, was a contentious political process, one which locally elected politicians were not keen to leave unchecked in the hands of a centrally-appointed and technically minded quango whose agendas as well as administrative boundaries differed from those of local authorities.

The formation of the EA also led to a reconfiguration of institutional relationships by breaking up the networks of local authority waste regulation officers which had been established either on a statutory or a voluntary basis. The disruption of these regional advisory mechanisms not only led to the collapse of waste planning co-ordination among the local authorities but also broke the existing, albeit ad hoc, links between regulatory and planning functions. Despite various link-making initiatives by the EA, effective co-operation and integration with the local authorities proved difficult, inhibited as it was by differences in the mentalities and discourses of the two organisations and their different constituencies and policy agendas.

Selecting options from the waste hierarchy: policy agendas and discourses

In this rapidly changing context, planners began to interpret the government's 'sustainable waste strategy' in different ways, depending on local circumstances. Each of our case studies took a different development path as they shifted from an emphasis on 'filling holes in the ground' towards adopting the principle of 'the waste hierarchy'.

Urban-rural conflict in the West Midlands

In the West Midlands region there was a long standing consensus that, given the highly urbanised nature of the West Midlands conurbation, and hence the scarcity of suitable land, a proportion of the conurbation's waste should be accommodated in the surrounding shire counties. The implementation of this principle was helped by the existence of void space for the disposal of waste following mineral extraction. In turn, the conurbation provided facilities for the treatment of special waste in the region which, although small in quantity, requires specialised disposal facilities and techniques. Thus a 'comfortable consensus' built up between the conurbation and the shires which remained unproblematic for many decades. Articulated as the discourse of 'interdependency', it dominated the debate on waste in the Regional Planning Guidance (RPG) Conference of 1993 when, for the first time, waste management issues found their way onto regional planning agendas. In this debate both elements of the discourse began to break down, allowing a new discourse to slowly penetrate into the discussion. Indeed, as part of a sustainable development agenda, ideas on the need for waste reduction had already been 'flowing around at officer levels, trying to get political support' (metropolitan district planner). On one side of the debate were some of the county councils and the environmental groups who were trying to steer the discussion away from disposal (Saunders, 1993, p.71). On the other side were the waste producers and the waste industry who continued to emphasise disposal and the role of the market in developing disposal options. Meanwhile, the conurbation districts emphasised that 'there would be a continuing demand for disposal facilities in the shires' (Saunders 1993, p.74). Despite the general acceptance of regional '*interdependency*', it was recognised that continuing with past trends could lead to local political problems in the shire counties as capacity in existing mineral extraction sites began to be used up. Getting waste disposal through local political processes for locally produced waste was difficult; it was even harder if much of the need for such sites was generated in distant parts of the region.

By this time the new concept of the waste hierarchy was penetrating the regional debate, appearing in the draft *Regional Planning Guidance* (GOWM 1994). The final version of the guidance fully reflected the discourse of the waste hierarchy (GOWM, 1995), which by then had received official central government recognition. However, it did so in one page of broad-brush statements which reiterated the waste hierarchy principle and neglected the real issues of the growing conflicts between the shires and the conurbation on the disposal of waste.

However, the regional Waste Regulation Joint Advisory Committee's report brought these tensions to the surface by quantifying the availability and usage of landfill capacity in the region (JAC, 1995). This made councillors and officers aware of the issues. The report also provided a robust foundation for the shires' objections to the conurbation districts' waste policies. Thus, by the mid-1990s, the consensus on interdependency began to lose credibility. The one-way flow of waste from the conurbation lost part of its underpinning justification, which was the availability of 'holes' in the shires. This breakdown of a long-term practice and the formation of a new frame of reference took place as a result of a series of 'external' pressures intertwined with locally specific 'internal' circumstances. The external forces came in the form of the EC's regulations adopted in the UK's 'new' waste strategy, which provided the concepts for the local-level debate. The principle of regional self-sufficiency was reinterpreted as county-level self-sufficiency by the shires to legitimise their arguments against the import of waste. Along with these external structuring forces, the region was experiencing increasing local political and environmental problems associated with the disposal of waste. The 1980s and 1990s witnessed a significant rise in the amount of waste produced, particularly in the conurbation, and the level of exported waste into the adjacent shires continued to grow. The conurbation's four incinerator plants treated only a fraction of the total waste arising in the region. While the region had sufficient landfill capacity in the short term (until 2000), this lay almost entirely in Warwickshire and Staffordshire.

By the mid-1990s, it had become evident that a waste management policy based on a continuing and unchecked flow of the waste stream from the conurbation to the shires was no longer sustainable. The uneven cross-boundary flows of waste and its land use implications thus added a new layer of interregional conflict to the traditional ones surrounding housing and economic development sites (see Chapters 4 and 5). Using the rhetoric of the 'new' waste strategy, the shires objected to being assigned the contentious task of site identification for waste produced outside their administrative boundaries. The principle of self-sufficiency gave the shires ammunition to legitimise their argument. The metropolitan authorities, however, resisted any change to the traditional approach, although most of the region's waste arose in the conurbation. Their passive approach was reflected in their unitary development plans. The Birmingham UDP, for example, did not include a single policy on waste treatment location. This led to objections at the public inquiry (MacBryde, 1992). Birmingham City Council's reply to these objections was that 'although waste disposal is certainly a matter which may be considered in a development plan, it is not considered necessary to include specific policies or land allocations in the UDP' (ibid., p.67).

This situation illustrates that the evolution of thinking in waste management had remained profoundly remote from the plan-making arenas. This resulted partly from the allocation of waste planning responsibilities to one metropolitan authority (Walsall MBC) following the abolition of the West Midlands County Council and partly from the limited influence of environmental agendas in all the conurbation's UDPs. This limited influence was itself a product of the strength of the urban regeneration agenda and also of the time of UDP preparation in the late 1980s, predating the mainstreaming in planning practice of the sustainability debate which is evidenced in the rhetoric of the Kent and Lancashire structure plans (see Chapter 3).

In the surrounding shires, however, a more complex situation existed. While they were looking more closely at the environment, albeit from an amenity standpoint, they adopted different policy approaches to dealing with waste. Counties such as Shropshire, had a less pressing need for extra landfill capacity within the time span of their plans, and so had little immediate incentive to get engaged in the complexity of the new discourse. Waste policies in such plans were merely concerned with policy criteria rather than site allocation. By contrast, waste was a 'big issue' in those shires which were at the receiving end of the exported waste. For these authorities, particularly Warwickshire and Staffordshire, the new discourse provided a new frame of reference to challenge the inflows of waste. In their emerging waste local plans, they utilised the discourses of 'proximity' and 'self-sufficiency', reinterpreted as county-based rather than region-based self-sufficiency, to provide the policy legitimisation for resisting their role as the unchallenged recipient of the conurbation's waste.

The breaking of the long-standing consensus between the conurbation and its periphery reached its decisive point when the new wave of waste management plans and waste local plans began to emerge in 1996. These plans faced strong objections from their neighbouring authorities. As discussed below, the plan-making arenas became a battleground for the interplay of the persisting traditional discourse and the emerging ways of thinking. The conurbation's Draft Waste Management Plan of 1996 had to be lodged with the national government to resolve the objections received from Staffordshire and Warwickshire. Objectors claimed that the plan failed to produce policies to reduce the continuing demand for landfill capacity outside the conurbation for the disposal of waste produced within it. Subsequently, the conurbation authorities objected to the waste plans produced by the shires, on the grounds that they failed to provide for the conurbation's waste (Waste Planning, 1996). In response to the pressure from the shires, the metropolitan authorities upgraded the capacity of their incinerators, often to include energy recovery. This provided them with a 'technical fix' solution to their household waste problem as well as allowing them to conform with the principles of the waste hierarchy. However, this process was not unproblematic either. Firstly, the new and upgraded incinerators with increased capacity potentially led to the import into the region of waste from elsewhere, as well as affecting the policies for waste reduction and recycling. Secondly, one upgraded incinerator in Tyseley (in Birmingham District) generated considerable local objection. Thirdly, a lot of industrial and commercial waste would still leave the conurbation for disposal, mainly in Warwickshire.

These discussions reflected a general shift away from the traditional discourse towards a new frame of reference for identifying waste disposal and recycling locations. The discursive shift was most visible in waste local plans in those shires where the disposal of imported waste was more contentious. Thus, whilst the rhetoric of the waste hierarchy was almost universally accepted and deployed by all players, by the end of the 1990s the adoption of alternative management options in the West Midlands was contested and largely influenced by local political issues and the availability of disposal facilities.

Replacing landfill with incineration in Kent

The intensity of minerals extraction in north and east Kent led to a concentration of waste disposal activity in these areas. In 1993, almost half of Kent's landfill capacity for non-inert waste was in the north, and one quarter in the east of the county (KCC, 1993b, p.28). This historical pattern continued to dominate the county council's waste disposal strategy in the 1990s, so that the majority of newly proposed waste facilities were also in north Kent and particularly around the Medway towns.

Until the early 1990s, landfill, particularly in quarries, remained Kent's dominant waste management policy (KCC, 1993b, p.33). This was reflected in the 1990 Kent Structure Plan where the historical association of minerals extraction and waste disposal activity was reflected in the grouping of waste disposal and minerals policies together in the penultimate section of the plan. The plan states that 'the usual, and normally most economic, method of providing disposal facilities is by controlled landfill, either into former mineral workings or by land raising' (KCC 1990, pp.132–3). The plan reflects a strong 'presumption in favour of proposals for waste disposal' subject to a few technical and operational criteria (ibid., p.132). While the plan confirms that 'suitable disposal sites are becoming hard to find in Kent', it emphasises that other options are 'regarded by the industry as unacceptably high cost alternatives to landfill' (ibid., p.133).

However, by the early 1990s, the absolute reliance on landfill began to lose its dominance in waste policy agendas. The long-term strategy shifted to a 'mix of waste management methods' (KCC, 1993b, p.51). Various policy documents which were produced in the early/mid-1990s reflected this shift. For example, the 1993 Structure plan incorporated the new policy discourse both at a symbolic level, manifested in the organisation of the chapters and the style and language of the text, and at a substantive level, manifested in the policy content of the plan. The discursive shift is echoed in the Plan's strategy which stated that, 'the County Council will seek to encourage and maximise, in the following order, clean production; waste minimisation; reclamation and re-use of waste; and recycling' (KCC, 1993a, p.58).

Various interconnected factors, ranging from the more tangible local pressures on the use of land and changing European and national regulatory standards to more intangible pressures stemming from changing environmental attitudes and discourses, were responsible for this change. The local pressures came from having to dispose of 4.5 million tonnes of waste per annum, of which one million was imported from London (KCC, 1993b, pp.48–9). A rising level of waste had led to an acute shortage of suitable landfill sites. By the early 1990s, existing landfill capacity, particularly for non-inert waste and especially in west Kent, was anticipated to come to an end by the year 1999. At the same time, the likelihood of identifying new sites became increasingly slim owing to stricter environmental standards, particularly from the Environment Agency (EA). Historically, minerals extraction and in particular chalk excavation for cement manufacturing in the Dartford and Medway Valley areas had played a major part in providing potential 'holes' for landfilling of waste. However, areas rich in chalk are among the major sources of potable groundwater which provide 85 per cent of Kent's water supplies. Therefore these areas were strictly protected by the EA from potential pollution caused by waste disposal.

Competition for scarce land resources and the difficulties of getting planning permission for waste disposal sites pushed up land values for suitable sites in Kent more substantially than in other case study areas. Therefore, even prior to the introduction of the landfill tax in 1996, 'cost was already pushing the county council in the direction of moving away from landfilling unprocessed waste' (county council waste disposal officer). The rise in land value in turn provided the incentive for the waste industry, first, to take over smaller disposal companies to enhance their land assets and, second, to look into alternative waste management techniques. The flow of planning inquiries/applications for development of facilities such as recycling and incineration plants signalled an emerging market in these areas.

So the county council had already come to terms with the necessity of moving away from landfill prior to the emergence of such discourses at national level. This is clearly echoed in the Structure Plan polices which 'consider favourably proposals for minimising, re-using and recycling, so as to reduce the volume of waste to be disposed of within the County' (KCC, 1993a, p.59). However, when it came to prioritising the available options listed above, the various pressures were pushing the waste strategy in two distinct directions. One was based on a long-term view in which priority was given to the options at the top of the waste hierarchy, the other was driven by the need for a short term 'technical fix' solution for reducing the volume of waste going to the diminishing reserves of landfill sites. The origins of both approaches are clearly traceable in the waste policies of the Waste Management Plan (KCC, 1993b) and the Review of the Structure Plan (KCC, 1993a).

However, neither the limited and aborted consultation process for the former, nor the topic-based, selective nature of the examination-in-public (EIP) for the latter, provided the much needed arena for deliberations and discussions of the emerging waste policy discourses in Kent. The seven issues identified for discussion at the EIP focused mainly on economic development sites and housing, excluding waste issues and the waste industry's representatives (KCC, 1994a). Thus the formal planning policy arenas remained entirely remote from the discussion on waste and alien to the waste policy community. In the absence of active stakeholders in the EIP, the broad brush waste policies of the Structure Plan swept through the adoption process without any articulated discussions, leaving the conflict of interests to emerge at the public inquiry into the Waste Local Plan (WLP).

The main aims of the WLP (KCC, 1994b) were 'to husband land resources' through, firstly, increasing the working life of existing landfill sites by 'reducing the amount going there' and, secondly, 'by seeking to locate new waste management operations on existing or committed development land' (KCC, 1995, p.1). Within this general context, the plan did not identify any new landfill sites and instead gave 'priority to identifying land for … [a] waste to energy plant' (ibid., p.29). The latter was 'seen as an effective way of achieving substantial reductions in the total amount of land needed for the disposal of waste' (ibid., p.10). Four locations were identified as potentially suitable for the development of waste to energy incinerators.

Subsequently, the plan's overall strategy as well as its twin aims became entangled by strong objections, causing a prolonged public inquiry and delay in its final adoption. The first element of the strategy, moving away from landfill, upset the waste disposal industry. The industry objected to the whole approach of the plan, considering the strategy 'to be both unrealistic and unachievable' (ibid., p.4). The industry's general view was that 'the Plan should make specific provision for landfill/landraising' (ibid.). The environmental groups objected to incineration on the grounds of 'pollution risk, particularly from emissions', and considered that such policies provided a 'disincentive to future waste segregation and recycling schemes' (ibid., p.10). The second strategic element, the proposed locations of incinerators, attracted 'a very large number of objections' (ibid.) from affected local communities. Those voices which had not been given the opportunity to be heard in previous arenas were finally raised in the inquiry. Of over

3000 objections, the majority focused on proposed sites for incinerators in and around the Medway towns.

Such proposals might be seen as contrary to other policy initiatives in the Thames Gateway which were aimed at improving the area's image. This reflected a lack of integration between waste planning discussions and area regeneration strategies. The proposals were considered by the objectors, mainly local action groups and residents, 'to be a discouragement to new investment' as well as having 'adverse impact on the local area' (KCC, 1995, p.10). The inquiry ended without easing the conflicts around some of the plan's most contested policies and proposals, not least because of the approach of the inquiry inspector:

> [There was] tremendous upset locally [because of] an appalling cop-out by the inquiry inspector. He basically did not make a decision on [the incinerator proposal] and said, 'Well, peculiarly we need to leave this for a detailed planning application', which is frankly no good to man nor beast really. (District planner)

Thus the emerging waste strategy was crowded out of planning arenas by other priorities and was therefore left unchallenged until it arrived at the formal arenas of the EIP and public inquiry. Lacking the relational and knowledge resources to relieve the built-up tensions, the potential arbitrators in these arenas postponed the debate, to be unfolded again in adversarial planning application and appeal processes.

So local environmental and land use pressures, an acute shortage of suitable landfill sites, coupled with the ambiguities of the waste hierarchy (particularly the undifferentiated weight given to 'recovery' options), directed KCC towards the adoption of energy from waste incineration as its main policy. Public opposition to this strategy, however, showed that the county council approach failed to address the tensions embedded in the recycling versus incineration debate, and people's perception of risk associated with incineration. County planners knew this, but felt powerless in the face of market forces which were rapidly moving in favour of energy from waste incineration. This was evident from the flow of planning applications for such development. For example, in Halling, Blue Circle Industries and the county council were promoting an incinerator as part of a proposed cement works and were hoping that job creation opportunities at the latter would 'divert attention from' the former (county council officer). The result at the end of the 1990s was something of an impasse.

Emergent self-sufficiency principles in coping with waste in Lancashire

Waste policy discourses in Lancashire resembled those in the West Midlands, with a similar focus on the intra-regional flow of waste and substantial export from the metropolitan areas of Manchester and Merseyside to shire counties such as Lancashire. However, in the 1990s, discussions on waste remained marginal to regional and county-level strategy discussions, despite the fact that 'the North West probably generates more waste than any other UK region' (NWRA, 1995, p.18).

However, as in other cases, the 1990s marked a discursive shift in the management of waste in Lancashire. This was manifest in two areas: one was the move away from unchallenged acceptance of landfill as the 'best' option, towards a gradual reduction of landfill sites and an intention to increase recycling activities; the other was the move away from importing waste from the conurbation to achieving self-sufficiency at the county level. As in the other areas, both of these new discourses were resisted by the waste disposal industry and the metropolitan districts. They were contested from their initial conception during Structure Plan preparation to their inclusion in the final draft of the Lancashire Minerals and Waste Local Plan (LMWLP). In the end, the county council's waste strategy, the outcome of multilayered negotiations and compromises, continued to be highly dependent on landfill during the life span of the plan. Extra landfill capacity in fact was identified in the plan. This became the subject of public opposition and the suspension of the public inquiry by the inspector.

Until the mid-1990s, economic efficiency considerations were prioritised in Lancashire's waste disposal policy (LCC, 1993, p.119). Given the availability of 'holes in the ground' through mineral workings as well as opportunities for coastal landraising sites, landfilling and landraising continued to be LCC's dominant waste management policy. Thus, in the 1990s, around 3.9 million tonnes of solid 'controlled' waste were disposed of in Lancashire every year, of which more than 95 per cent was landfilled or went to landraise. However, the capacity of existing sites was rapidly being used up and alternative sites were unlikely to be available in the medium term. Given these constraints and incoming regulations from the EU, a new waste management discourse began to gain momentum. The EU-promoted language of the waste hierarchy was articulated in the review of the new

Structure Plan to justify its policies on reducing the amount of untreated waste going to landfill sites, and to focus on provision for waste generated within the county rather than the wider region. The plan's waste policies, which later proved to be some of the most controversial policies at the examination-in-public (EIP), aimed to reduce the amount of waste disposed of by landfill by limiting the number of sites. The policies also aimed, for ease of site regulation, to move towards a smaller number of strategic sites which were mainly operated by the county council-owned waste disposal company. Prompted by different motivations and interests, a whole host of stakeholders reacted to these policies, on the grounds that 'reduction in landfilling capacity will prevent Lancashire meeting regional waste disposal needs ... and increase disposal costs' (LCC, 1993, p.384). The focus on waste generated within the county rather than the wider region also came in for criticism.

LCC's response to these concerns reflected the articulation of the new environmental vocabulary among the county planners. Under pressure to handle the increasing amount of waste in the context of diminishing landfill capacities, they drew partly on the county council's 'green' agenda (see Chapter 3) and partly on new EU regulations, to emphasise that 'the environmental capacity of Lancashire to accommodate new landfills is strictly limited and there is European legislation in place which is intended to reduce the quantities of waste needing disposal' (LCC, 1994b, p.385). LCC criticised the metropolitan districts for seeing 'waste disposal as synonymous with landfilling, and landfilling as the only feasible disposal route' (ibid.). In referring to regional waste issues, LCC's response reflected the lack of effective regional strategy and mechanisms for discussions on waste, stating that, although 'the draft RPG advice suggests that sub-regional movements of wastes should be minimised wherever possible, no detailed agreement has been reached at regional level, and Lancashire Structure Plan is not the right place for unilateral action.' (ibid., p.379).

LCC's waste policies were subject to further discussion in 1995 in the arena of the EIP, yet, owing to continuing lack of a formal regional agreement on waste disposal policy (LCC, 1996, p.130), reaching any form of compromise proved to be difficult. The adjacent local authorities and the National Association of Waste Disposal Companies objected to the failure of the plan to address the problems of waste arising in the nearby conurbation. LCC insisted on opposing the continuation of past trends (LCC 1996). However, the EIP panel recommended that the policies should be modified to 'include waste arising in proximity to the County ... and ... that a network of waste disposal installations ... be established' (ibid., pp.132–3). Based on the objections by the waste disposal industry who considered the reduction in landfill as 'premature until alternative solutions are available' (ibid., p.134), the panel also recommended another modification to reflect the fact that 'the proportion of waste disposed of by landfill will be progressively reduced' (ibid., p.136).

Prior to the EIP, the preparation of the LMWLP was well under way. Although the preliminary consultation on the LMWLP coincided with the publication of the Structure Plan deposit draft, the tensions which were about to arise in the EIP had not yet hit local plan preparation arenas. In September 1994, LCC attempted to involve a wide range of stakeholders in four focus groups in order to open up lines of communication between key actors, explain plan preparation procedures and obtain views of a wider range of stakeholders on different policy options. One of the primary aims of the exercise was 'to identify need, amount and location of sites for treatment/disposal of waste' (LCC, 1994c, p.5). While the key issues raised were similar to the concerns expressed during the Structure Plan preparation, they did not create the same amount of heat as they later did in the arena of the EIP. Planners commented that the lack of confrontation was due to the fact that many stakeholders either did not take such informal arenas and broad-brush discussions seriously or were not willing to share information with other players: 'they are there with commercial rivals, some just listen, keep cards close to their chest' (county council planner). Thus, whilst LCC's initiative to set up these new forums helped develop relational resources in the waste policy community, it did not succeed in achieving concrete agreements on key issues.

The subsequent consultation draft of the MWLP examined four alternative strategies:

1. radical reduction in landfill through recycling and incineration;
2. progressive reduction of landfill capacity at fewer strategic sites and gradual replacement by other modes of disposal;
3. maintenance of the status quo, that is continued reliance on landfill; and
4. replacement of landfill with two or three medium-sized incinerators (LCC, 1995b).

The diminishing number of landfill sites coupled with the political need to incorporate the waste hierarchy and the EU regulations meant that LCC could not adopt the status quo option, neither could they develop the radical reduction option which was far too ambitious given the local authority's limited power and resources. The last option was equally problematic since it was not only highly technical and capital-intensive, it was also politically contentious. The timing of such considerations alongside a local election made it an extremely difficult option to garner support for, as no local politician could support it and hope to get elected. Thus the planners did not rule out the possibility of inserting the incineration option at the modification stage, after the local elections. The progressive reduction option was therefore adopted. This served LCC's vested interests as the owner of some strategic sites. Moreover, despite LCC's intention to gradually move away from landfill, the outcome of the EIP and mounting pressures from the conurbation and the industry pushed the LMWLP to identify sites for landfilling of waste generated both within and outside the county (LCC, 1995, pp.72–6).

LCC planners were in a difficult political position. The waste local plan was prepared at the time when national waste policies were constantly changing. The regional and local policy contexts were also frequently renegotiated and so local planners had to prepare the plan 'against a rapidly moving background'. They inserted the waste hierarchy in the plan even prior to its emergence in national guidance, but failed in attempts to maintain the self-sufficiency principle at a county level.

LCC's waste strategy was further diluted as the LMWLP was placed on deposit in 1997. This time, the exact level of demand, calculated by the newly published Waste Disposal Plan, was also incorporated. The Plan's commitment was to provide 'for the disposal by landfilling of 42 million tonnes of waste produced in, or in proximity to, Lancashire between 1995 and 2006' (LCC, 1997c, p.117). After taking into account an ambitious 25 per cent target for recycling, LCC was left to identify 8 million cubic metres of landfill space. Of the five sites identified in the consultation draft, two had already received planning permission for major extensions, therefore three sites were proposed to meet the need for the extra landfill capacity (ibid., p.120). One was to serve north Lancashire, the other two were close to the Manchester conurbation. In addition, the plan safeguarded further land for future waste disposal and adopted a positive approach to landfilling of waste at extensions to existing sites. It is therefore clear that, despite the proposed 'landfill-reduction strategy', the plan became loaded with various policies relating to provision for future landfill capacity. These crowded out the plan's tentative attempts to promote and encourage other more environmentally sustainable methods of waste management.

Parallel to the approach adopted in its 'minerals' section, the plan meticulously followed the 'predict and provide' route to the release of landfill sites based on crude calculations of future demand forecast prepared by the waste regulation officers. This purely technical exercise masked the planners' intention to implement a reduction in landfilling and overlooked the political and public tensions which subsequently arose from the technical approach. LCC waste planners felt powerless in the face of market forces and the national and regional pressures for accommodating the waste from the nearby conurbation:

> it doesn't seem to me to be sensible public policy that Lancashire will be pursuing a high cost waste management strategy whilst still under pressure from the metropolitan [districts] to provide landfill facilities to deal with their waste. Landfilling is being foisted upon us from adjacent areas ... [because the] conurbation districts are simply chasing the market. (County council waste planner).

In Lancashire, therefore, the new concept of regional self-sufficiency was perceived as a step backward since it obliged the county council to provide landfill capacity for waste generated outside the county, an action contrary to its initial aspiration of achieving self-sufficiency at county level and gradually reducing the number of landfill sites. Had they been able to follow that route they probably would not have had to identify new capacity, at least in the plan period, and hence would have avoided the subsequent public opposition. Such a delay might also have allowed LCC's preferred recycling strategy to 'bite' in a meaningful way.

Complexity, fragmentation and reconfiguration: institutional relationships

By the 1990s, waste management had become a highly contentious area of public policy with increasing tensions between the industry and the regulators and between citizens and the state over regulatory policy. This took place at a time when institutional relationships were subject to major transitions. The highly fragmented mechanisms of the past were further unsettled by changing institutional roles and responsibilities, making it extremely difficult for stakeholders to address emerging tensions in a coherent way. Nevertheless, a significant shift in policy discourse was achieved in waste management policy. The following accounts summarise how this shift was handled by the actors and networks in each locality.

Overcoming institutional fragmentation in the West Midlands

The discursive conflict between county councils and metropolitan districts took place in the context of parallel and profound changes in the landscape of institutional relationships in the region. Since the mid-1980s, these relationships had been subject to constant change. The abolition of the West Midlands Metropolitan County Council in 1986 divided the waste disposal responsibilities in conurbations into seven separate authorities. Subsequently, these functions were co-ordinated through a Joint Waste Disposal Sub-Committee, with Walsall MBC given the task of coordinating waste policies. At the regional level, a new network of local authorities began to take shape in 1990 when, following the government's guidance, the West Midlands Waste Regulation Joint Advisory Committee (JAC) was formed. This committee was the main mechanism for developing regional action, producing information on the amounts and flows of waste and providing a basis for co-ordination of waste disposal and planning at the regional level. Its actions were in turn dependent on the production of waste disposal plans by individual local authorities. The preparation of these plans, however, was disrupted by the formation of the Environment Agency, as was the embryonic regional co-ordinating mechanism set up by the JAC.

Prior to these disruptions, the JAC achieved a major step forward in building up links with the regional planning arenas as well as incorporating the discussion on waste in the agenda of the Regional Planning Guidance Conference in 1993. Previously, neither the reactivation of the West Midlands Regional Forum nor the process of preparing regional strategic planning guidance in 1988 had provided sufficient impetus for widening out the waste policy community and linking the discussions on waste to mainstream planning debates. The conference provided the opportunity for waste issues to appear for the first time on the regional planning agenda. This was a temporary arena which pulled in those who had a stake in waste issues and had often been either reluctant or unable to engage in dialogue previously. However, the participants in the debate highlighted the fact that the waste policy community remained relatively narrow in its composition. This narrowness was subsequently reflected in the nature of the argumentation (Saunders, 1993). Since then, these relationships have been subject to continuous redefinition and reshaping with the planners, the industry and environmental groups playing an increasingly important role.

Although the JAC was dominated by the local authorities and had no representation from the waste industry or other groups, it had provided an opportunity to achieve a degree of co-ordination, particularly with regard to technical issues and the provision of data on waste production and disposal. However, the emergence of the EA halted most of these activities and reconfigured the institutional networks. When the RPG Advice was published in 1993, the forthcoming changes had already been announced. So, given the uncertainty, the Advice urged local authorities to 'formulate a regional waste strategy which can be developed further by the EA' (WMRF, 1993, p.31). This, however, did not take place. In fact, the formation of the EA displaced the waste regulation officers, restructured them in a new organisation under a new set of rules and relationships and shifted their agenda from developing a regional strategy to collating data. Therefore, at the time when co-ordination and strategic thinking on waste management were most needed in the region, a new layer of organisation was introduced which not only lacked established relations with other players but it also found it difficult to put its own house in order: 'The EA has become a very complex organisation ... Planning authorities might have found it confusing and that partly is because of the EA itself, pulling in different groups from different organisations under one umbrella ... There is a question of who does what in the EA' (water company officer). The fragmentation of responsibilities was confusing for both regulators and the public: 'They don't know who to turn to, where to influence to make changes' (EA officer). Meanwhile, the GOWM failed to provide a linking mechanism with the EA, at least at the time of transition.

Further, the limited opportunities for public consultation in the EA's licensing procedures forced the conflicts over facility siting into local planning arenas. The local authorities drew on plan-making and development control arenas to influence strategic decisions on waste management and hence to compensate for their loss of regulatory power and retrieve some local political accountability. The EA's focus on the sites which they regulate rather than on more strategic issues, as well as the lack of clear-cut responsibilities between the planning and the pollution control systems, made it easier for the local authorities to exercise such influence. Meanwhile, the abolition of the JAC, the ambiguities of the EA's roles and responsibilities and its relationship with the local authorities, as well as the rising conflicts between county councils and metropolitan districts, worked as a catalyst for regional level co-ordination through the WMRF.

Kent: changing intergovernmental relations

In Kent, a greater degree of institutional stability in waste management existed through the 1990s. Prior to 1998 local government reorganisation, the county council had been the waste disposal and waste planning authority for the whole of the county area since the 1970s. The stability at the county level, however, did not necessarily reflect the situation elsewhere in the south east region where institutional fragmentation in London, in particular, had caused major difficulties for managing waste at the regional level. Discussions over the massive flow of waste from the capital to the rest of the region had traditionally given a high profile to discussions of waste in regional planning arenas. Therefore, unlike the case of the West Midlands where waste was a newcomer to regional planning forums, in the south east, waste planning had a particularly strong regional dimension.

For a number of years, SERPLAN had sought to deal with some challenging regional issues, such as the significant disparities in local landfill capacity across the region, London's export of waste and, most importantly, the region's predicted exhaustion of its landfill capacity (Greenhaigh and Turner, 1997, p.3). Another significant feature of waste planning in this region was the availability of comprehensive data on waste which was periodically collected and published by the former South East Waste Regulation Advisory Committee (WRAC). Unlike the situation in the West Midlands, where such information never found its way into free standing planning guidance, SERPLAN had continued to provide regional waste planning advice (for example, SERPLAN, 1997). Therefore, despite some criticisms about the usefulness of this guidance which tended, it was suggested, to 'just parrot the national strategy' (EA officer), waste had a higher priority in mainstream planning arenas as compared with the West Midlands and the north west. Contrary to the active role played by the SERPLAN forum, GOSE took a marginal role in waste planning discussions in the region. The WRAC provided the main networking channel on waste issues between Kent and SERPLAN. As in the West Midlands, its role in setting up Kent's waste strategy and articulating EU and central government's policy on waste had been central. The formation of the EA, however, unsettled these relationships. Establishing links between the local authority and the agency was particularly problematic at the beginning.

There were two further problems faced by the EA during its early years. The first was the lack of sufficient data and clear national guidance on how to replace the outdated information in the waste management plans which were still the only available contextual frameworks for the preparation of waste local plans. The second problem was the EA's limited technical regulatory role, which hindered its capacity to engage in a meaningful dialogue with other stakeholders and, in particular, local authority planners who were increasingly moving to the forefront of waste planning debates.

The relationship between KCC and its constituent districts was particularly delicate and highly politicised when it came to the geographical distribution of waste facilities throughout Kent. In the past any such conflicts of interests were played out at the site-specific level through the development control process. Even the process of reviewing the Structure Plan did not stimulate a debate on waste issues. These remained detached from the discussions which were taking place among the county's waste regulatory officers in parallel with, but outside of, the mainstream structure plan forums. The reasons were twofold. First, waste planning was considered marginal and hence was crowded out by other pressing issues even in places with a long history of filling mineral holes with large volumes of imported waste: 'In Dartford, waste is quite a sensitive issue, but it is not nearly as fundamental or strategic an issue as the housing one' (district planner).

Second, the main forum for discussions on waste had no established links with those planning forums which included district planning officers, such as the area working parties. In addition, the broad-brush nature of structure plan policies did not alert the districts to any forthcoming conflict of interests over site identification. Such discussions were drawn into the plan-making arenas only when the preparation of the county-wide waste local plan was under way. Even then, the scope and the effectiveness of such debates were constrained, for two reasons.

Firstly, the poor relationships between the districts and the county planners postponed any such debates to the adversarial arena of the waste local plan public inquiry. This is best illustrated by Dartford Borough Council's objection to the plan's identification of a site for a waste facility in an area designated for the development of a highly prestigious and economically significant science park. The county council accepted the objection and withdrew the proposal. The fact that such conflicting land use proposals had not been picked up prior to the inquiry reveals poor integration between different planning issues, lack of interaction between different planning arenas and limited communications among different layers of planning authorities and planning officers.

Secondly, KCC waste planners, concerned with 'best technical solutions', were wary of involving district planners because of their limited expertise in waste planning and the impetus for the districts to get involved being parochial and immediate. This was reflected in the variation of the districts' responses to the waste local plan proposals. Those districts which exported their waste and whose areas had not been identified as a potential location for waste facilities were reluctant to develop a more active role in the strategic debates. Their approach could be interpreted as opportunistic. For example, in Thanet, 'waste has not tended to be a major issue. Most waste disposal takes place outside of Thanet District ... so Thanet has not had to look at waste in too great a detail' (district planner); in Maidstone, 'waste, frankly is not a key issue. It all goes outside to landfill. Kent's waste local plan revolves around three key incinerators, the nearest one is Halling, which we think is wonderful because it is not in our patch' (district planner).

In areas where waste facilities were proposed, the plan caused strong public opposition. The respective local authorities did not themselves object strongly. Their carefully calculated responses to the county's new waste strategy was a form of political expediency. It was easier to let the county council carry responsibility for these difficult siting decisions: 'districts may find it comforting that the county council is the planning authority; it means they can object to something but, if it's permitted, they can say, "It wasn't us"' (county council planner).

However some district planners realised that the attitude to strategic waste management would have to change if the proximity principle came to underpin the policy framework. This principle demanded better intraregional co-operation and co-ordination than the 1990s fragmentation of responsibilities allowed. Within the South East region, the shire counties had historically been the administrative tier for waste management and were generally seen to be the most appropriate level for applying the principle of self-sufficiency. However, the application of this principle at the county level was undermined by two processes, the export of London's waste to the neighbouring counties and the formation of unitary authorities within the counties. The latter added a new layer of institutional arrangements to the confusion, complexity and fragmentation.

Building up relational resources in Lancashire

Lancashire County Council's efforts to shift the discourse of waste management towards 'landfill reduction' took place in the context of a national and regional policy vacuum, as well as a highly fragmented and changing institutional landscape. As in our other cases, the latter made it difficult to communicate the new strategies effectively with all the stakeholders. Although they were discussed in a number of planning forums, they swept through these without sufficient time and depth being given to their land use implications. The formal arenas such as the structure plan examination-in-public (EIP) and the waste local plan public inquiry became adversarial, making agreement extremely difficult. Attempts at building agreements through informal forums also failed owing to the inflexibility of commercial stakeholders in the informal arenas, such as the focus group seminars (see above). Therefore LCC's attempt to use the planning process to articulate the new strategy proved more difficult than envisaged. The constant changing of the policy background and the fragmented nature of the relational resources made it hard for the key actors outside the county council to reflect on the new strategy in a coherent and consistent way in order to reach a degree of consensus. This was reflected in what the EIP Panel called 'the apparent lack of a co-ordinated approach to treatment and disposal of waste' which was seen to be 'partly due to the division of responsibilities ... and partly due to the absence of any firm national and regional guidance' (LCC, 1996, p.138).

The dispersal of responsibilities was manifest at various levels and with respect to several policy agendas. For example, influencing the contractors' disposal methods to incorporate the pre-treatment of waste, which is a major step towards any reduction of waste going to landfill sites, was the responsibility of the county council's waste disposal authority. However, given the reluctance of the industry and LCC's emphasis on cost effectiveness in awarding tenders, such initiatives were held back (ibid., p.135). This caused interdepartmental policy conflicts because the waste strategies developed through the planning system had little chance of being implemented through the waste disposal contracts. Another layer of fragmentation lay in the collection and recycling of waste. At the time of the EIP, LCC had not received reassurance from the district authorities with regard to their ability to meet recycling targets (ibid., p.131). However, the districts felt that LCC had underestimated the potential of recycling. Reaching agreements was undermined by poor communications: 'we offered to talk to them ... but they haven't taken us up, you can read into that what you will...[we] suspect they decided [there were] more [political] miles as far as County [Council] bashing is concerned' (county council planner).

At the regional level, the discussion on waste remained patchy and incoherent: 'there was no regional forum dealing with disposal as there was for minerals; although officers for the authorities met informally, it was difficult to reach a consensus view on provision of waste facilities' (LCC, 1996, p.131).

An informal grouping of waste regulation officers, the North West Voluntary Regional Committee on Waste Regulation, made recommendations to the NWRA. Their terms of reference were similar to those of their West Midlands counterparts. The membership of the officers group was dominated by waste regulation officers and issues. Therefore, when the regulatory responsibility of the county council was transferred to the EA, the group lost both the majority of its officers (down from 25–30 to four or five) and its *raison d'être*. Although there were some linkages between the group and the NWRA, these were not as systematic as other policy areas. The tensions between the exporting areas of Manchester and Merseyside and the LCC's search for self-sufficiency limited the evolution of a co-ordinated approach.

Similarly, the work of other subregional networks, notably the Lancashire Environment Forum, remained largely unaffected by the discussions on waste. The low profile of discussions on waste in the regional and subregional groupings at the time of our interviews mirrored the situation in most parts of the country. The formation of the EA was seen by the EIP panel as the solution to all these co-ordination problems (ibid., p.138).

Later events showed that none of these expectations were fulfilled. Indeed, as in the other case studies, the formation of the EA added yet another institutional layer and further disrupted established, albeit poorly co-ordinated, relationships. However, rising interregional tensions, pressures on available landfill sites and the need to adopt the self-sufficiency principle pushed waste issues and the formation of a regional co-ordinating group high on the north west regional planning agenda. This gave the officer group a new lease of life. Its remaining members, particularly the waste planners of Cheshire, a shire county which had suffered most as a result of large-scale movement of waste from the conurbations, re-established the group under the Waste Management Working Group of NWRA. The officer group consisted of representatives from the waste planning and disposal authorities, waste recycling officers, waste industry (mainly landfill operators) and the EA.

Subsequent work in the south of the region (NWRA, 1997) highlighted the problems in implementing a waste strategy based on recycling, composting and incineration. Chief among these were the lack of executive power, a shortage of resources, the poor quality of support from local politicians who were reluctant to attend meetings, strong public and political oppositions to incineration, and a conflict of policy agendas between waste disposal and waste collection authorities.

In 1998, this model was proposed by the draft PPG10, as an appropriate regional mechanism to 'provide specialist and expert advice on options and strategies for dealing with the waste' (DETR 1998f, para. 36). The Regional Technical Advisory Bodies (RTAB) would report their 'technical findings and options' to the Regional Planning Conferences who would 'identify a preferred regional strategy' (ibid. para. B4). The structure and remit of the RTAB resembled the mechanism which has been in place for aggregates planning since the 1970s. This response to the conflicts in waste planning had aimed to depoliticise a highly political process by emphasising a technical remit and by narrowing the range of participants to a small group of regulators and regulated. Although the RTAB proposal enhanced the role of the planners and the waste industry in waste management, it did little to incorporate other stakeholders, notably the environmental groups and the local communities, a major shortcoming of the NWRA approach.

The Planning system and waste management

The case studies provide an account of the remarkable discursive shifts, and the rapidly changing institutional relationships, in the management of waste in the 1990s. They illustrate the acute tensions over the development of waste management options and the allocation of sites for waste facilities. The European Union's emerging waste policies in the late 1980s generated a wave of change which in a relatively short period of time reached all areas of waste management debates in the UK, unsettling the established policy and practices and bringing to the fore hidden political and environmental tensions. The evolution of the waste policy discourse, manifested in a move away from 'filling the holes in the ground' towards adopting the 'waste hierarchy', took different development paths in different localities. The intention to move away from landfill was universal in all cases, yet the selection of alternatives was diverse, reflecting the influences derived from locally specific factors.

In Kent, the immediate demand for waste disposal in the context of an acute shortage of landfill sites and the difficulties of identifying sites capable of meeting regulatory standards, plus the visible signs of market interest in alternative waste management technologies, led to a policy of energy from waste incineration. In Lancashire, where the existing landfill capacity was sufficient for the county's waste but not to take a significant share of the adjacent conurbation's, a genuine, though modest, attempt by the planners to move away from the 'cheaper-the-better' discourse to a 'landfill reduction' strategy was successfully challenged by the conurbation and the industry. The regional self-sufficiency principle was used to structure arguments against the county council's policy intention of limiting the landfill provision for disposal of the county's own waste. The outcome was a landfill-dominated waste local plan which got entangled in a public inquiry enveloped by vociferous public opposition. In the West Midlands, the concept of self-sufficiency was picked up by the county councils and interpreted as 'county-level self-sufficiency', rather than regional self sufficiency. This then broke the traditional 'comfortable consensus' based on the 'interdependency' between metropolitan districts and surrounding shire counties. The self-sufficiency principle was used, in a similar way to that proposed by Lancashire County Council, as a legitimation tool to challenge their long tolerated role as the recipient of the unchecked flow of waste from their neighbouring conurbation.

The discursive shifts took place at a time when the institutional land-scape surrounding waste management was also undergoing major transitions. This impeded the development of coherent approaches among key stakeholders and the dissemination of the new discourse around the relevant policy communities. In all the cases, the new EU waste strategy was initially disseminated by the waste regulation officers, who were the first group in local authorities to be informed of the new regulations through the pollution control system. Within this context, local waste strategies were developed in waste management plans and then 'lifted into' the emerging development plans. By 1993, therefore, the Kent and Lancashire structure plans were reiterating the EU's vocabulary for the management of waste. This suggests that the local authority planners were ahead of the national *planning* guidelines in promoting some of the principles of the waste hierarchy. This was most visible in Lancashire, where the planners attempted to use plan-making processes as key resources for articulating the new discourse prior to the national strategy in order to reduce landfilling of waste. Lifting the policies from the waste management plans which were subject to little consultation meant that tensions often remained concealed until they reached the arenas of the planning system. With few national and regional guidelines on how to adopt the new discourses, the local planners had to take the strain. But, as illustrated by the case studies, the land use planning system had little influence on the implementation of the waste hierarchy given, firstly, the fragmentation of waste management responsibilities among various local authorities' tiers and departments and the Environment Agency, and, secondly, the tensions between the high-cost options at the top of the hierarchy and the waste disposal authorities' prime concerns with the economic costs of privatised disposal contracts.

It is therefore ironic that, whilst the planning system had little leverage in pursuing the new waste discourse, the planners were pushed to the forefront of an increasingly contentious debate (Davoudi, 1999). In all cases, the planning policy arenas became the battlegrounds for the interplay of the conflicting interests. While the consultation processes embedded in the system widened the traditionally closed waste policy community to include a more diverse range of stakeholders, this has taken place at the end of policy development processes where adversarial and polarised debate is difficult to avoid.

However, given the absence of public participation mechanisms in other areas of waste policy making and the removal of the regulatory function from locally accountable authorities, the potential role of the planning system in providing inclusionary arenas capable of levering in local political and environmental concerns should not be underestimated. Such potentials would have increased substantially had the system been capable of linking the economic, environmental and social aspects of waste policies. However, as illustrated by the Dartford case in Kent, where a waste local plan identified a site for waste facilities in a location where another local plan had proposed a prestigious science park, development of such 'joined-up' thinking in the planning system still had a long way to go.

In the past, discussions on waste were dominated by engineering and technical issues and notions of economic efficiency in waste disposal practices. While the latter still prevails, environmental concerns were gaining increasing voice in policy debates by the mid-1990s, although often without having much influence over actual policies. The sectoral nature of the British planning system and the marginal attention given to the discussion on waste in mainstream planning forums hindered the development of a place-based integrated approach to waste planning. The traditional practice of filling holes in the ground pre-empted the planning system from pursuing other spatial-ordering concepts. The location of quarries often dictated the location of landfill sites. The pressure to move away from landfill began to change this, particularly after the adoption of EU regulations (COM (97)105) and the principles of proximity and self-sufficiency. However, the adoption of these new concepts does not necessarily mean that there will be a positive concern for the quality of those places where the waste facility sites are to be located. Further, Planning Policy Guidance Note 10's proposed apportionment processes, carried out in the technical arena of the proposed RTAB and based on the patterns of the past, are most likely, firstly, to confine the regional discussions on waste to a 'numbers game', similar to the much contested, prescriptive and 'top-down' practice in housing land allocation (see Chapter 4) and minerals planning (Davoudi, 1997) and, secondly, to exclude quality-of-place considerations from the debate. However, as illustrated by our case studies, the local political and environmental tensions will not go away: they will be heightened and eventually played out in local political arenas and increasingly during the consultation processes of the planning system.

Part III

THE DISCOURSES AND INSTITUTIONAL RELATIONS OF THE PLANNING SYSTEM

8 Planning Discourses in Transition

Introduction

The previous four chapters have shown how four different sets of issues were argued about and translated into the arenas of the planning system. In each issue area, ideas were continually evolving, in the face of internal contradictions and external challenges. What is striking, however, is that each had its own dynamics, with limited and variable links with other issue areas. In this and the following chapter, we explore these differences, and what they tell us about the nature of spatial strategy making in England in the 1990s. In this chapter, we focus on the dimension of policy content, the policy agendas that were evolving and the policy discourses that underlay them. In the next chapter, we examine the social relations of policy development and dissemination, through an assessment of the evolving policy networks, communities and arenas identified in Part II. In both, we seek to explore the extent to which the evolutions generate a potential for a more territorial focus in spatial strategy development. We are also interested in what kinds of linkages are made among policy sectors and how far there are signs of real involvement by a wide range of business interests and citizen groups in these governance processes. In Chapter 10, we draw our analysis together to consider the implications for the future role and practices of the planning system.

The focus on policy discourses serves to identify policy purposes. What do participants seek to achieve by getting involved in strategic planning activity? How are issues conceptualised and translated into specific analyses, policy ideas and particular policy actions? What is the relation between exercises in framing strategies and the ongoing flow of decisions about investment projects and regulatory permits? Examining such questions involves exploring the 'conversation' of strategic planning practices. This is evident in the explanations, justifications and descriptions provided in policy texts and debates, and in the more private reflections of participants. Analysing such material does not merely require consideration of the surface rhetoric of a policy discourse. It also involves examining the ambiguities and interest conflicts that may be masked by the rhetoric. In this chapter, we first set the scene by locating current policy developments in a broad historical trajectory. We then develop our analysis to help summarise the policy discourses evident in each of the four policy fields discussed in Part II. This provides the basis for a consolidated account of the discourses competing for dominance in contemporary British planning policy. We show that there was much evidence of shifts in policy discourse, with changes in both specific policies and in their framing conceptions. However, there was little indication by the mid-1990s of a greater territorial focus, or of integration between policy areas or more inclusive modes of policy development and legitimation.

Spatial ordering concepts in British planning

One of the qualities identified in all the policy areas discussed in Part II was the limited explicit attention to spatial dynamics. Some very general and long-standing spatial conceptions were deployed in all our areas. Notions of free-standing settlements surrounded by green belts were evident in the deeper frames of reference in all our cases. Other conceptions were also gaining influence. In the West Midlands, tension between the conurbation and its hinterland (the 'shires') continued, fuelled as it was by issues which dissected administrative boundaries, with debate framed by the policy of protecting the green belt. Here and in Lancashire, policies of strategic corridors were used partly to draw elements of a region together around a common strategy. Particularly in the West Midlands, the attempt to reframe spatial conceptions with 'corridor' concepts had difficulty getting leverage because of the strength of the notion of the conurbation contained by its green belt. In Kent, the division of the county into distinct areas of north/east and mid/west provided a strong steer for policy development. Such divisions were largely taken for granted, and were rarely questioned. Otherwise, strategy development focused on policies about amounts and criteria, or the characteristics of particular sites. Only in Kent was there a strong focus on place qualities, and this centred on the areas of major development.

The lack of vigorous debate on strategic spatial ordering concepts in the 1980s and 1990s contrasts with the immediate post war era. Then the physical form and functional spatial order of cities was a major pre-occupation of regional and urban planning strategies. This shifted in the 1960s to conceptions of the functionally integrated dynamic space economy of regions, to be understood using the tools of regional geographical analysis, with policies articulated through rational planning processes (Ward, 1994; Hall, 1988; McLoughlin, 1969). The first conception shaped the development plans of the 1950s and the second the structure plans of the 1970s. Both conceptions had clear spatial ordering ideas, of a city region focused around a city centre, with land uses hierarchically ordered in relation to land value, the highest being in the city centre. Settlements were expected to be contained within green belts and village envelopes. Within the city, urban areas were to be organised as reasonably self-contained neighbourhoods, with local facilities and transport routes to higher-order facilities in city centres. This model came under increasing strain from the 1960s, as inner city problems once again became evident while decentralisation proceeded apace. The emphasis on implementation in the 1970s, and on area transformation and market-led development promotion in the 1980s, turned attention away from strategic viewpoints on spatial organisation.

By this time there were multiple conceptions of the planning task to be found in planning practice (Underwood, 1980; Healey and Underwood, 1978; Brindley *et al.*, 1989; Thomas and Healey, 1991). All these studies highlight competing and co-existing framing ideas that combine in different ways a concern with planning policies (the 'substance' of planning interventions) and a consideration of the procedures planning should work through (the 'process' of planning intervention). By the 1980s, the emphasis was increasingly on the planning system's role in 'balancing' competing interests in land along with enabling market processes. This did not encourage attention to the evolution of territorial sociospatial relations. Nevertheless, the elements of the spatial strategies articulated by the town designers of the 1940s and 1950s, continued in the 1960s and early 1970s, and survived in agendas of projects pursued in subsequent decades, particularly the definition of green belts, hierarchies of centres and road-building programmes. Notions of the integrated regional space economy also persisted into the 1990s in the routinely accepted assumptions of much structure plan analysis and language (Graham and Healey, 1999).

As the chapters in Part II illustrate, these old ideas of spatial organisation survived, embedded in practice routines, in local politics and in deeper cultural assumptions. New ideas reframe policy rhetoric, as with the new environmentalism of the 1990s (Owens, 1994; Healey and Shaw, 1994), generating pressures for change in strategic concepts. However, when these are translated into specific polices and practices, they are often merely wrapped around old agendas and projects. The result can be politically unstable, leading to contestation which creates openings for the new framing ideas to lead to significant changes in policy practices over time. The accounts in Part II show that strategic plan making in the 1990s in England reflected a policy landscape of multiple discursive struggles, between old ideas and new ones, and between different strands of new ideas. In some cases, as in the transport field and in waste management, these struggles are obvious. They were played out in different arenas, the outcome of which significantly affected where investment took place and which business interests and localities gained and lost. In others, as in the treatment of economic development sites, new discourses evolved less publicly, and had problems disseminating from one arena to another. In some situations, the articulation of new ways of thinking occurred largely outside the arenas of the planning system, as in the case of transport and waste. In the case of housing and economic development, ideas developed elsewhere in a general way, such as 'competitiveness' and 'sustainable development', were given specific meanings when developed in the planning context. These different trajectories then jostled with each other in plan-making arenas and planning inquiries, unsettling the discursive continuity of planning strategies.

Analysing policy discourses

This complex evolution of policy agendas and underlying discourses demands some attention to the forms of expression of 'policy' and the institutional work which policy discourses perform. There is increasing recognition in the policy analysis literature that policies are not just statements of intent, to be taken at face value, but complex performative acts, created in institutional settings and presented on stages where audiences have multiple and often conflicting demands and expectations (Edelman, 1977; Majone, 1989; Schon, and Rein, 1994; Yanow, 1996; Muller, and Surel, 1998). In these performances metaphor and myth help to give 'sense' to what is said (Yanow, 1996). A policy discourse is thus more than the 'policy agendas' which have been discussed in the policy analysis literature for many years (Parsons, 1995). It refers to the frames of reference through which specific policy agendas are constructed (Schon and Rein, 1994). It involves sets of concepts, many often hidden from view, as well as an array of arguments, metaphors and phrases. Policy discourses are produced, borrowed and adapted by policy communities in policy networks, for specific audiences. Any analysis therefore needs to uncover the specific producers, consumers and their relations and purposes. Policy discourses provide a language of representation – of space and place, of local environments, of sociospatial arrangements and policy processes – which can provide powerful images with a capacity to convince, to disseminate widely and become key 'referents' in subsequent policy debate (Lefebvre, 1991; Motte, 1997; Peizerat, 1997; Muller and Surel, 1998). In this way, new policy ideas may become widely diffused, framing ways of thinking about an issue across a wide array of policy communities and arenas. In the context of British urban governance in the 1990s, where power was distributed among diverse agencies and loci of legitimacy, the ability to persuade became a key quality of effective urban and regional policies.

The persuasive work of policy performance has two dimensions. Firstly, policies must be shown to be legitimate. Both planners' skills in careful analysis and argument, and the procedures of consultation and inquiry in the British planning system, may be considered as routines designed to persuade different audiences that particular policies are justified. But in the contested world of local environmental policy, the invocation of science and techniques, logic and correct procedure may not be enough to convince a critical 'public', supported by media which these days act almost like a Greek 'chorus' (Nussbaum, 1986), sustaining a continual commentary on planning issues. This 'chorus' both expresses and shapes public concerns about local environments and the qualities of places. In this context, persuasive rhetoric may use metaphors and myths which seem to elide potentially conflicting concerns into a consensual image. A powerful myth in a conflictual context is one which can hold the 'incommensurable' in creative tension (Yanow, 1996). The rhetorical strength of the metaphor of the 'green belt' carries this power in Britain. In recent years, the concept of 'sustainable development' has been used in the hope that it has a similar capacity (Owens, 1994; Mazza and Rydin, 1997). The metaphor of 'employment land', which focuses on generating jobs for local needs, but also legitimates landtake for industrial enterprises, performed such legitimating persuasive work in the past. As Yanow argues (1996, p.206), the policy process is as much about the 'allocation and validation of symbols of status', about values and identity, as it is about the allocation of tangible resources and instrumental behaviour. Policies which are metaphorically aligned with the existing symbol structure, the referents, in the minds of legitimating audiences, the 'chorus' for public policy, are likely to have a stronger chance of being accepted than those which are not (see also Tarrow, 1994). The difficulties of moving away from an emphasis on road schemes, and the attractiveness of the new environmental arguments for reducing landtake for greenfield development, provide illustrations of this point.

The requirements of legitimacy are not the only audience for policy rhetoric. If policies are to have material effects, those who control the rules and resources to produce these effects must be persuaded to act in line with the policies, and to co-ordinate with each other. The second dimension of the persuasive work of policy performance is therefore its role in translating policies from statements to material effects, to actions. This issue has long been discussed in the literature on policy implementation (Barrett and Fudge, 1981). Policy discourse analysis focuses on the persuasive power of the systems of meaning or frames of reference within which a particular policy is situated. Hajer (1995) distinguishes two stages of transformation in policy discourses: first, there is the structuring of a new discourse and its acceptance by key policy communities; second, the discourse has to be institutionalised, embedded in the routines of the various arenas for action. This involves processes of translation and enrolment of networks and groups in the new policy frame (Callon, 1986; Latour, 1987). Only if both processes are accomplished will a new discourse have real material consequences as well as symbolic effects.

A policy discourse, therefore, is not just a particular policy, but a frame of reference within which specific policies are articulated and specific 'interests' are both identified and positioned. Policy analysis which merely evaluates what a policy actually says will miss the complex meanings it carries. The task of a discourse-based policy analysis is to locate policies in the social relations of their production and consumption, and to 'deconstruct' them to identify their meanings, power and potential consequences in these contexts (Edelman, 1977; Tarrow, 1994; Schon and Rein, 1994; Hajer, 1995). This task of deconstruction or, following Foucault, of social archaeology (Rabinow, 1984) does not focus primarily at the level of the linguistic analysis of the subtle vocabulary of the 'policy text' (Fairclough, 1995), although such analysis can be very suggestive (for example, Myerson and Rydin, 1996). Instead, it emphasises the systems of meaning and references within which policies 'make sense' (Peizerat 1997). But 'sense making' happens in our minds at several levels, only some of which become visible, even to those who articulate policies. Schon and Rein (1994) suggest that policies are framed at three levels, that of the explicit policy approach or policy theory (for example, arguments over site allocations, or over the prioritising of bypass schemes); that of the primary institutional context (for example, the policy community, as in the housing 'numbers game', or the 'predict and provide' approach in transport planning, or 'filling holes in the ground' in waste planning); and that of the broad cultural context which tends to get taken for granted in policy discourse (for example, the broad acceptance that the countryside should be protected from 'urban sprawl', that settlements large and small should therefore be 'contained'). Some policy conflicts are confined to the first level and can be seen as contentions within a discourse. The problem in situations of institutional change is that conflicts are likely at the second level, leading to confrontations between discourses, as in the case of both the transport and waste management debates. These problems become even greater where conflicts open up deeper tensions which challenge patterns of social behaviour or economic organisation. In such situations, the overall parameters within which discourses are generated may be in contention. The problem for the new ideas in the transport debate is that they demand very considerable shifts in people's behaviour and lifestyles. Similarly, the new 'waste hierarchy' debate set one type of firm (landfill waste companies) against another (waste recycling enterprises). Such tensions made politicians nervous of taking the measures needed to force change, through tougher taxation and regulation, for example, for fear that too many people would object. Thus the connection between the new discourse and the social formation may be too weak to allow the new discourse to displace the old and become embedded in policy practices and politics.

The analysis of policy discourses thus aims not merely to 'deconstruct' discourses, but to examine the dynamics of discourse development, consolidation and change. Policy discourses evolve through continual reinterpretation and invention among policy communities.

The chapters in Part II illustrate the way the idea of 'environmental sustainability' has rapidly permeated planning discourses, though with variable effects (Owens, 1994, 1997; Healey and Shaw, 1994; Blowers and Evans, 1997; Mazza and Rydin, 1997; Rydin, 1998). Some metaphors generated within the planning community have had enormous durability. The notion of 'green belt' is itself perhaps the most powerful metaphor ever invented by the British planning community. As every marketing expert knows, language, whether verbal, visual or numerical, has enormous capacity to travel, but its use and interpretation is difficult to control. Spatial and design images are particularly valuable in this regard in the planning field (Healey *et al.*, 1997b; Neuman, 1996; Faludi, 1996). A sign of the weakness of territorial focus in British planning discourses in the 1980s and 1990s was the lack of a powerful spatial imagery.

When policy discourses are fragmented and unsettled, or when old discourses are under intense pressure because the 'chorus' no longer believes in them, some explicit work of discourse structuring is needed. The 1993 Regional Conference in the West Midlands is seen as an attempt at such a discursive restructuring. But institutionalising the new agenda proved difficult, as many competing forces pulled in other directions. In contrast, the mid-century ideal of the contained city with its green belts was adopted enthusiastically in the context of a politics objecting to the first signs of car-based urban sprawl, at a time when rebuilding the city and quality of life for citizens were key political priorities. How discourses are structured and institutionalised is thus highly contingent on time and place, as Hajer (1995) shows in his analysis of the acid rain controversy in Britain in the 1980s.

In our accounts in Part II, we have shown how new policy discourses have been created, transmitted and translated across the institutional landscape of strategic policy making. We have also emphasised the institutional work they perform. In these dissemination processes, new discourses may transform the old, or they may be absorbed into them. The metaphors and myths of a policy frame articulated in one institutional arena might become detached in another, and take on different meanings. Both their rhetorical power and their capacity to organise action may be lost as a result. Part II provides many examples of old ideas being rhetorically wrapped in a new language, giving the impression of change to the legitimating 'chorus', but masking the continuation of 'business as usual'. For the institutionalisation of a new discourse to take place, while old metaphors may remain, they need to be attached to new meanings, to be mobilised for new actions. The new policy frames need to penetrate below the level of the explicit policy theory, to change the frame of reference of the relevant policy community, or communities, in a widening institutional landscape. If the new frames demand broader changes in economic organisation and social life, or if new frames of reference are emerging within the contextual dynamics, the discursive changes may need to find new positions and referents if they are to gain legitimacy and mobilising power in relation to these broader social and cultural movements. In the next section, we examine the kinds of shifts which emerged in the policy discourses identified in Part II, the nature and scale of these shifts and 'who is enrolling whom' as they evolve.

The contents of planning policy discourses

In Part II, we examined four different policy areas. In the West Midlands, economic competitiveness concerns pervaded most issues and linked discourses about transport with those for site allocation for economic development. In Kent, the locations of major housing and economic development sites were increasingly linked to area development strategies In Lancashire, sustainable development principles were beginning to influence many policy areas. Despite these linkages, the discourses through which the issues were framed had largely evolved in a self-contained way, within separate and distinctive policy communities. Sectoral, functional organisation prevailed over place integration. The arenas of the planning system were by no means the primary institutional location for the articulation of spatial strategy. While they served this purpose with respect to housing development and the location of large sites for economic development, the discourses about the location of transport routes and waste disposal sites were shaped by broader developments in these policy areas. These were then translated into, or merely 'lifted into', the arenas of the planning system. This limited the power of the planning arenas to make strategic linkages between them. By the late 1990s however, the evolution of popular concern with environmental quality and sustainability, the recognition of the connections between the policy agenda of economic health and competitiveness and that of social and environmental quality, among policy elites and some business groups at least, created pressures by the late 1990s, for more consideration of linkages between policy issues, encapsulated in the New Labour rhetoric of 'joined-up thinking'.

The 'housing numbers game'

In the context of the British planning system, the housing discourse had long been dominated by a frame of reference which sought to balance development demand with strong landscape conservation strategies. The policy outcome was a major restriction on development locations. The well-established result was to maintain high land values on 'greenfield' sites allocated for development, to restrict housing choice and to sustain an increasingly oligopolistic residential development industry (Hall *et al.*, 1973; Bartlett *et al.*, 1996; Healey, 1998c). Since the 1970s, housing land policy was framed in close relation to policies on green belt and landscape conservation. Spatially, the images of contained towns surrounded by green belts lived on from Abercrombie's day into the 1990s, in a politics of the defence of open landscapes from development incursions (Hall, 1988; Ward, 1994). The 1960s notions of urban 'containment' were buttressed by the priority of urban 'regeneration' in the 1970s (justified by concern for inner city social conditions). In the 1990s, the imagery of the 'compact city' (Breheny, 1992; Jenks *et al.*, 1996) and the championing of 'brownfield' site development over greenfield sites gave this approach continued support (justified this time by concern for energy conservation and pollution reduction).

In this highly politicised context, the discursive solution promoted by the major national level stakeholders was to turn to technical calculation. Demand was calculated on the basis of demographic projections, disaggregated to the regional and subregional level using trends in past regional growth. Regional projections were then assessed in relation to estimates of stock availability and location to arrive at a number of dwelling units needed in particular subregions in specific time periods. These amounts were then located according to assessments of land availability and environmental constraints. Site location criteria, in these calculations, had traditionally reflected planners' considerations of land suitability and servicing costs, as well as environmental conservation criteria. Behind these apparently technical considerations, there also lurked in many areas an acute awareness of local politics, which encouraged the allocation of large sites in less contentious areas. The residential developers, for whom the large site allocations were reasonably attractive, nevertheless recognised that the most attractive sites commercially were often those which were most politically contentious.

Faced with conflicts of growing intensity, the technical discourse of the 'housing numbers game' was elaborated through the 1980s, with the housebuilders encouraged by national policy to get involved in deciding locations and introducing 'market criteria' as a location principle. In parallel, the environmental interest was articulated at national level, most vigorously by the Council for the Protection of Rural England, whose political weight served to balance the influence of the housebuilders. This negotiative practice, as realised in the 'numbers game', dominated the housing discourse in all our case study areas. Struggles over numbers were reflected in such metaphors as the calculation of 'windfall sites', meaning those which came forward unexpectedly during the plan period. Struggles over locations used metaphors of land qualities ('brownfield/greenfield') to highlight the discourse of containing development within landscape constraints. Chapter 4 shows that the numbers game evolved slightly differently in each locality, reflecting local histories and geographies (for example, the impact of SERPLAN discussions in structuring the housing debates in the south east, and the fine-grain consciousness of local landscapes in the Kent housing debates). Nevertheless, national policy statements (DoE, 1992c) did not merely structure the policy positions in each locality, they provided the dominant discursive frame of reference for the policy community. Drawing on the language of the transport debate, by 1997 the New Labour administration found it convenient to call this a 'predict and provide' approach (DETR, 1998h).

In a situation of enormous potential conflict over sites and, in many areas, an active politics of contestation, the dominant technical discourse provided a stable frame of reference at the level of the policy community. By the mid-1990s, this had become an introverted practice, conducted by a policy community consisting of national civil servants, local planners and the House Builders Federation, actively monitored by a critical 'chorus' orchestrated by the Council for the Protection of Rural England which drew on a deep well of popular concern. It made use of the intellectual capital of demography, information about available sites and a local awareness of site allocation politics. At this first level of policy discourse, to use Schon and Rein's approach, conflict is expected and the technical language is used to provide a conflict resolution mechanism (how many new dwellings to allow for, where, when). The consensus is to be found at the second level, with national civil servants and ministers, the housebuilders and the nationally organised environmental pressure groups continually playing out their roles in the numbers game. Below this, and largely unarticulated in policy developments and conflicts, lie the deeper cultural referents, old culturally valued planning ideas, which form Schon and Rein's third layer of policy discourse. These relate to the form which housing development should take (houses with gardens, except in denser urban areas), what housing means to people (a home and an investment) and the space organisation of urban regions (settlements contained within green belts and village 'envelopes'). This deeper level acts as a major 'demand management' tool. It is only at this level, and at the level of debates on specific sites, that the role of housing in establishing the qualities of places gets consciously articulated.

The strength and continuity of the 'numbers game' lies in its mechanism for resolving conflicts over what are the most substantial allocations of land for new development in any urban region. However, during the 1990s, a number of forces increasingly undermined its justificatory logic. The two principal forces were, first, changes in housing demand which indicated a much more differentiated and consumer-sensitive housing market (Maclennan *et al.*, 1997). The second was the increasing pressure to resist further greenfield site development and concentrate development on brownfield sites, in cities or near transport nodes. These changes challenged the consensus within the policy community and raised questions about the implicit conceptions of landscape and lifestyle. These forces came to a head in the debate on where to locate a predicted increase in households of 4.4 million between 1991 and 2016 (DoE, 1996e; Breheny and Hall, 1996; DETR, 1998h). There was increasing pressure to recast the debate, making links to arguments about environmental capacity constraints and to the qualities of urban areas and their capacities to absorb household growth. Finally, the housing discourse was being dragged into wider debates, with attempts to develop a regionally differentiated discourse of 'demand management' focused on brownfield site targets (DETR, 1998h) and, potentially, greenfield site taxes to pay for brownfield site clearance (DETR, 1998a), and with more concern for the qualities of places (CPRE, 1999). However, the 'numbers game' remained so deeply embedded among the key policy communities that it was difficult to articulate an alternative although the metaphor of 'monitor and manage' was mobilised with some success to challenge the determinism of 'predict and provide'. In Hajer's terms, restructuring of the policy discourse had hardly begun in this policy field by the end of the 1990s.

'Employment land', economic competitiveness and area transformation

In contrast to the housing land issue, the policy discourses on the location of large sites for economic development purposes were much less deliberately structured in national level planning policy. As a result, older approaches were less firmly embedded. The new discourse, though well-developed in regional economic development activity, was less coherently addressed in planning arenas. A version of a demand-led numbers game structured the planning discourse until the 1980s in all our three areas, reflecting a widely shared frame of reference articulated in the early postwar period. The planning task in this discourse was to redistribute the jobs which a robust economy produced, to locate them in areas of higher unemployment, that is, of 'job need', and then to provide space for the factories which would create the jobs within locational constraints defined by infrastructure provision and landscape policies. 'Employment land', a term used in many plans of the 1970s, provides an example of Yanow's consensus-maintaining metaphor, eliding the interests of employers and workers. In this way, the needs of the economy could be cast in the cloak of a social policy of job provision, justifying landtake against environmental arguments.

However, this discourse was undermined by the evident weakness in many local economies from the late 1970s. Company restructuring generated redundant sites and demanded new plants. It became evident that a simple equation could not be made between jobs and sites. The economic development sections of local authorities and regional business development alliances shifted towards an approach more focused on companies and competitiveness. Jobs were not going to arrive by themselves: they had to be actively created and maintained by deliberate action in building up regional and local economies. Facilitated by a national policy of encouraging business development, two of our localities embraced an 'economic competitiveness' agenda, focused on providing a stock of sites to serve different types of business demand. Drawing on research on regional economies and inward investment opportunities, a 'portfolio' approach was developed in the West Midlands which highlighted the arguments for allowing significant land release of greenfield sites. These ideas filtered through into the north west, where a similar approach was adopted a few years later.

In this discourse, a region or subregion was positioned in a European economic space, competing to attract inward investment (and, less explicitly, EU subsidy). Economic imperatives arising from the toughness of this competition were then used to justify the allocation of sites which 'broke' environmental criteria. As with housing site allocation, the discussion of sites proceeded without much reference to 'place', beyond the immediate qualities of the site (good infrastructure links, greenfield and so on.). The same spatial conceptions underpinned the selection of sites as with respect to housing. In both Lancashire and the West Midlands, the location of development had long been constrained by the containment philosophy. Gradually, in both areas, the new environmental arguments tightened the noose of containment, already very tight in the development politics of the West Midlands. In this context, the metaphors of 'premium sites', 'major investment sites' and 'flagship sites' were used to continue to legitimate the priority given to economic development to a 'chorus' of concerned local politicians, pressure groups and constituents. There was a difference, however, from the old 'employment land' discourse. In this new 'economic competitiveness' discourse, only some sites, the large, strategic locations, needed to have priority. By the 1990s, economic competitiveness could less easily be used as a blanket 'override' of environmental policy than had been possible in the 1970s and 1980s.

In Kent, the 'employment land' discourse continued into the structure plans of the 1990s, justified by careful analyses of job needs. Here local opposition to further land for development was very strong, articulate and influential. The 'employment land' discourse had value in such a context, as it provided a local justification for policies which facilitated the interests of businesses. The planning strategy sought both to attract new firms into the area and in some instances to encourage them to go to the currently less attractive areas. This 'persuasive discourse', as articulated in the Kent structure plans, was part of a process of producing sites alongside area transformation projects. The qualities of places, both in their defence against development and in their transformation, were much more significant in the Kent economic development discourses than in our other two areas. Integrated place making, drawing on the skills of specialist consultants, provided a justificatory vocabulary which embedded sites in social and environmental logics as well as economic ones. But rather then transforming the discourse in the primary planning arenas to reflect these new area development logics and translate them into a broader subregional spatial strategy, the discursive evolution among the county planners in Kent was towards the 'economic competitiveness' discourse already well developed in the West Midlands and Lancashire, bolstered by a strong engagement with EU and national government initiatives.

The discursive evolution with respect to sites for economic development may thus be generalised as one from a 'needs provision'/growth accommodation' agenda to an 'economic competitiveness' one. A weaker discourse of area transformation was maintained by the high priority given in national policy to the Thames Gateway project and its funding. This latter discursive shift gained its strength from deep changes in perceptions of the nature of the economy and its vulnerability. It was also still constrained by long-established spatial organisation principles, that is, the 'Abercrombie' landscape. But it sat uneasily with the new environmental discourse of demand management. Where the two encountered each other, policy proponents argued for an economic 'override' principle. This was given blanket encouragement by a generalised pro-business national policy in the 1980s, and was reiterated with respect to major 'inward investment' sites by the New Labour administration (DETR, 1998a, Annex).

Challenging 'predict and provide'

In the transport field the struggle between competing discourses was very obvious. Here the dominant policy of the postwar era, that of attempting to meet ever-increasing demand through continued road construction, was overturned. Such a shift resulted from the efforts of stakeholders who sought to defend the countryside, challenge the energy consumption and pollution effects of the car, and attack the congestion and loss of public space generated by strategies aimed at providing for private vehicles. It took the environmental movement's identification of invisible air pollution generated by the car and the recognition of the escalating costs of continued provision for an apparently insatiable demand for road space to move their campaigns onto the national policy agenda. The first shifted the attention of the public 'chorus' for transport issues from improving the convenience of car travel to the adverse consequences of car use. The second arose from operational considerations and the recognition that providing more road space generated new demand as well as easing travel conditions for existing users (SACTRA, 1994), with the result that congestion seems insoluble through road-building strategies. The 'new realism' promoted in the 1990s (Goodwin *et al.*, 1991) emphasised demand management, in contrast to previous strategies for accommodating the car. It also promoted integrated policies for all modes of travel, as opposed to separate consideration for public and private transport. It emphasised the need for strategic links between investments in the transport network and key planning decisions on the location of development, largely neglected since the 1970s. By the end of the 1990s, the new policy discourse was well structured and widely recognised, infusing national policy statements on transport (DETR, 1998c). However, its diffusion across the governance landscape was uneven, especially where the economic competitiveness discourse encouraged the metaphor of 'roads for prosperity'.

Our case studies illustrate this uneven development and diffusion. The new discourse had not merely to displace and reconstruct long-established practices in core arenas. It had also to make new linkages, drawing transport into the heart of other policy arenas. There it encountered the dynamics of other policy discourses moving in different directions. Local discourse institutionalisation was much more problematic than the national-level rhetorical transformation. In Lancashire, the old discourse lived on in the Surveyors' Department with their lists of schemes for funding, in the politicians' championship of bypass schemes for their constituents, and the local communities' continuing concern to get through-traffic out of their towns and villages.

The West Midlands pioneered new policy ideas in the transport field, introducing the 'package approach' for their investment bids to national government and developing the intellectual capital for a demand management approach through 'integrated transport studies'. But these transformations did not come easily. A significant policy moment was needed before the 'predict and provide' agenda in Birmingham City Council's transport section could be displaced by a 'demand management' approach.

There were also continuing tensions between 'demand management' strategies and the concerns of the economic development policy community which viewed the quality of the regional road network as a regional competitive asset. The tension between economic development and quality of urban life issues raised the question of whose interests should take precedence in mediating conflicts between economic competitiveness agendas and demand management strategies. Business, residents and environmental groups might all support improving urban public transport in principle, but many groups found it difficult to connect demand management principles with their experiences of traffic conditions on the ground. This can be seen in continuing battles over existing roadspace, perhaps the archetypal example being over the outcomes of pedestrianisation for local retail trade. Such contestation was certainly evident in Kent, where, although the shift to demand management strategies received powerful support from local electorates' adverse experiences of road building in the 1980s, this local discourse restructuring encountered difficulties when translated into the detail of strategies and investment programmes.

Although our cases show that the new discourse unevenly permeated the local institutional landscape, significant changes happened at the level of the policy community. Powerful highways/transport departments were 'enrolled' in the new discourse, which was repositioned in relation to broader policy agendas about the location of development. But there remained problems in translating the new discourse into specific actions and policy positions on specific issues. To assist in this new integration of transport and development, spatial metaphors were revived, with conceptions of 'corridors', as alternatives to the expanding metropolis, with its radials and rings of the Abercrombie era. But, as discussed above, these ideas challenged deeply embedded implicit conceptions of spatial organisation. By the end of the century, they had achieved only limited influence over policy debates. The dissemination and institutionalisation of the new transport 'realism' was thus held back, both by the resistance of parts of the established policy community to new agendas which undermined their power and practices, and by the lack of strategic integrated conceptions of urban and regional space across related policy communities. Without the reconstitution of this deeper cultural frame, the fundamental shifts in the behaviour of residents and firms, currently structured by the prioritising of road travel and travel time savings, will be very difficult to achieve. Nor will it be possible to resolve the substantial conflicts between the economic competitiveness and quality of urban life agendas which currently uneasily co-exist.

However, although the 'new realism' was unevenly developed in our three cases, the powers and practices of national government significantly accelerated the scale and speed of the change. National government signalled a new approach in a white paper (DETR, 1998c), in its approval of transport investment projects and plans, and in its planning regulation criteria. It also organised two rounds of 'national debate' on the transport issue, which helped to broadcast new awareness and policy ideas among a wide range of both old and new stakeholders in the transport field. However, national measures to promote the rationing of roadspace, and tough taxation on car use, were limited by ministers' anxiety about the political consequences. Cultural resistance to restrictions on car use remains strong.

Re-structuring waste management practices

The location of waste management facilities typically generates intense local political conflicts, as a type example of a LULU, a locally unwanted land use. In the UK, the potential for conflict was increased in the 1990s by the impact of environmental arguments, encapsulated in EU legislation. This required localities to search for ways of reducing the waste they produced and treating more of it within the locality. As a result, the location problem could no longer easily be 'exported' from places with a well-developed politics of opposition to sites to more accommodating places. Tensions between waste exporters and importers grew, the latter harnessing arguments of 'self-sufficiency' to buttress their case. Meanwhile, the volume of waste generated continued to increase and the supply of 'holes in the ground' to accommodate it diminished. The pressure to change the established 'landfill' policy discourse thus came both from supranational policy and from local politics. But structuring and disseminating a new discourse proved difficult, and took place within a limited policy community. The 'chorus' of media and pressure group concern, so evident in relation to housing and transport issues, was largely absent from the waste issue, except in relation to individual proposals for disposal sites. Nor did national planning policy promote the need for change as strongly as in the transport field. Local practices and national planning policy in effect co-evolved, in response to the new political landscape encouraged by EU policy and the creation of the Environment Agency. This was done largely in isolation from all the other policy issues addressed in planning arenas.

The discursive shift which took place was, as with transport, at the level of the policy frame, Schon and Rein's level two. In each of our three areas, the practice of predicting demand and finding supply in available sites generated by the aggregates and mineral extraction industries was challenged by the concept of the 'waste hierarchy'. This encouraged the move away from landfill as the only waste management option, but provided an unstable grounding for the evolution of alternative strategies, as different lobbies promoted different positions in the hierarchy. This was particularly evident in the case of the 'recovery' option, where recycling was put on a par with energy recovery through incineration. The 'new' waste strategy also introduced two interconnected concepts, the principles of 'proximity' (to the source of waste production) and 'regional self-sufficiency'. In the West Midlands, the self-sufficiency arguments helped the shire counties resist further exporting of waste from metropolitan areas. In Lancashire, the same argument was used rhetorically to resist further imports from the Greater Manchester and Merseyside conurbations. However, conurbation interests, the commercial pressures from the waste disposal industry and the county council's own interests as an owner of landfill sites meant that the new discourse struggled to influence waste planning policy. It was in Kent that the discursive shift was most evident. Here the levels of waste exported from London, the lack of sites, the high costs of land and the potential for groundwater pollution in the delicate chalk geology all challenged the continuation of the landfill policy. The commercial power swung behind waste incineration, where new market opportunities were emerging.

Technical solutions such as waste incineration were, however, challenged by those arguing for reducing the amounts of waste generated. Thus the agenda of options moved from technical to cultural solutions and from general principles to behavioural changes at the fine grain of the design of products and everyday practices. This pushed the required discursive shift down into a deeper layer of cultural assumptions embodied in daily behaviour. In contrast to the transport field, where environmental pressure groups and finally national government itself forced wide-ranging discussion about the need for a cultural shift in attitudes to the car and behavioural shifts in its use, there was no 'great debate' orchestrated by national government about waste management. All the national government offered by the end of the 1990s was to take the issue out of political contestation and to confine the debate within the proposed regional technical advisory bodies, developing a form of the numbers game (DETR, 1998e). This seemed unlikely to reduce the level of conflict. It also encouraged an aspatial approach to waste management, focused on waste production and management options, with little consideration of how these related to other dimensions of social life and the business environment in localities, or the qualities of the

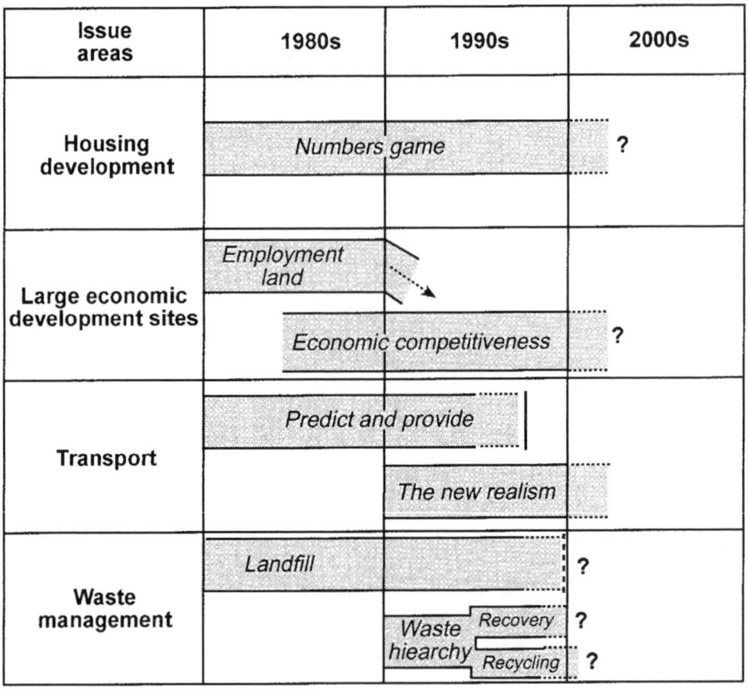

Issue areas	1980s	1990s	2000s
Housing development	Numbers game		?
Large economic development sites	Employment land	Economic competitiveness	?
Transport	Predict and provide	The new realism	
Waste management	Landfill	Waste hiearchy — Recovery / Recycling	? ? ?

Figure 8.1   The evolution of policy discourses in four issue areas

places where the location of waste facilities was suggested. All these factors limited the articulation and dissemination of new waste management discourses, both locally and nationally.

Framing conceptions in planning policy discourses

At the level of policy frames, our four policy areas evolved in largely separate ways, although techniques (the 'numbers game' and the 'sequential test') and metaphors ('predict and provide') from one area sometimes slipped over into another (see Figure 8.1). This reflected the power of the functional/sectoral organisation of policy communities in the British context. The result, given the strong role of national government in shaping policy agendas and the increasingly fragmented institutional landscape, was a multiplicity of policy discourses, in uneasy co-existence and competition. Nevertheless, there were significant shifts in strategic spatial discourses in the 1990s, and some of these were promoted by common factors, notably the struggle to recast policy agendas in the light of new environmental conceptions. The pressures for these shifts, though greatly encouraged by the stance taken by national government through the Planning Policy Guidance Notes (PPGs), were nevertheless significantly affected by local politics and by the internal contradictions of established discourses.

Thus external pressures, such as EU policy shifts and global economic conditions, had an impact on a co-evolving agenda of local and national policy discourses concerning spatial strategies and planning issues. The power of British government centralism therefore worked only in part to structure policy frames. It is perhaps better understood as both a negative force, limiting, challenging and undermining the emergence of alternative locally articulated frames (in waste management, in housing), and as a positive force, providing resources for local discourse development (in housing and in transport). During the 1990s, its negative force made intersectoral co-ordination and territorially focused policy discourse difficult (the topic basis of the PPGs). Its positive resources mixed the rhetoric of new agendas (sustainability) with new techniques which tended to reinforce old ones (the numbers game and the sequential test). One result was that the spatial strategies produced both without and within planning arenas tended to have narrow agendas, with little effective integration between different policy areas as they affected the quality of places. Development plans were in effect collections of policies derived from diverse policy discourses developed often by different policy communities in separate policy arenas (see Figure 8.2).

Yet at a deeper level, below the conscious rhetorics of the various policy communities, there were commonalties across the four policy areas. Three powerful discourses underlay policy development and policy debate in the 1990s with respect to spatial strategy (see Figure 8.3):

1. *Accommodating demand*, in the context of locational limits set by landscape conservation policies. This is an old discourse for the planning system. Strategic planning involves, in this discourse, predicting trends in various activities, and finding principles for locating the resultant demand across regional and local space, constrained by policies for the protection of landscape and amenities. This demand accommodation approach was

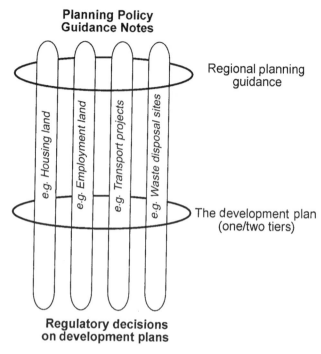

Figure 8.2   Sectoral emphases within the planning system

given the 'predict and provide' label in the transport field, a term which had migrated to other policy areas by the end of the 1990s. This discourse largely grew up within planning arenas, shaped by deeply embedded conceptions of contained urban settlements and by national policies which ebbed and flowed in their support for environmental restrictions on greenfield development. The main developments in the 1990s buttressed the 'provide' part of the equation with technical calculation to give an appearance of objectivity in the context of intense local contestation.

2. *Developing the competitive assets of urban regions,* as a contribution to regional and national economic performance. This is a more proactive version of the previous discourse, realigned to an argument for prioritising particular sites and schemes over all other considerations, for economic reasons. This discourse had powerful support from local politicians and business groups and

the Department of Trade and Industry. It was also supported by the development of conceptions of urban regions in competition with each other across Europe (Newman and Thornley, 1996; Harding, 1997; Oatley, 1998; Hall and Hubbard, 1998; DETR, 1998d). Most of the development of this discourse occurred outside the arenas of the planning system. The frame was imported in part or wholesale into the economic development sections of development plans. Initially, this discourse gave little attention to spatiality, but increasingly the qualities of places, rather than the portfolio of sites, were emphasised.

3. *Demand management to protect environmental qualities*, particularly with respect to resource conservation and pollution reduction. This discourse developed rapidly in the 1990s at the level of rhetoric, both nationally and locally. It surrounded the planning system with an infusion of local environmental politics as well as providing a new policy language to adjust to. It produced significant shifts in thinking and practices with respect to intraurban transport, edged into interurban road transport (Goodwin, 1996) and introduced a new discourse into the waste management field. It was driven as much by the public expenditure limits on meeting predicted, unconstrained infrastructure demand as by resource conservation arguments. But these new ideas disseminated only slowly into the housing and economic development issue areas. In the rhetoric of national planning policy, environmentally informed ideas were supposed to coexist with the other two frames under the metaphor of 'environmental sustainability'. This metaphor became increasingly stretched and undermined during the 1990s, as the demand management discourse clashed with both of the other discourses in public inquiry contexts. This created pressures for more integrated and 'holistic' approaches to spatial strategy making.

Traces of two other discourses were to be found in our analyses, 'leftovers' from an early period, but crowded out by the policy evolutions of the 1980s and 1990s:

4. *Providing for needs*, the dominant social policy discourse of the early postwar era. Echoes of this were found in arguments and statements in the 1980s, but by then it had largely become absorbed in the 'demand accommodation' discourse. By the

1990s, it was barely articulated in general policy rhetoric. This discourse was largely imported into planning arenas from the broad welfare state discourse, when town and country planning was expected to play an important role in providing good-quality living environments for all. It lived on in our cases in concerns for housing needs, and in a few attempts to extract 'community benefits' for local groups (Healey, Purdue and Ennis, 1995). But these residual traces provided very little basis for the concerns with quality of life and social exclusion which began to emerge with the New Labour government in 1997.

5. *Shaping the qualities of places.* This again was a strong strand of planning policy thinking in mid-century, and was the core contribution of the field of planning to wider public debate at that time. The emphasis on place quality was progressively displaced from the strategic to the neighbourhood level during the 1960s and 1970s, and was largely linked to urban regeneration area transformation projects and new settlement schemes in the 1980s and 1990s. It was at this level that it was manifest in our cases, and was only of strategic significance in the Kent context. Nevertheless, the inheritance of the mid-century strategic spatial conceptions lived on, particularly in the politics and imagery of the green belt. The power of this metaphor served to inhibit the emergence of alternatives such as transport corridors and concentrated decentralisation, and encouraged images which carried old ideas forward, notably the 'compact city'. By the late 1990s, concern with the qualities of places was returning to public policy with greater vigour, backed by concerns for promoting the quality and 'liveability' of urban areas.

Overall, our analysis confirms that significant transformations in planning policy discourses occurred in the 1990s, though unevenly developed with respect to both discourse structuration and institutionalisation. These developments in the planning field were widely shared elsewhere in Europe (Newman and Thornley, 1996; Healey *et al.*, 1997b). But the penetration of the new discourses of 'economic competitiveness' and 'demand management' met many points of resistance as old frames of reference lived on and new ones were poorly understood or in conflict. It cannot be said of England in the 1990s, as Faludi and van der Walk (1994) argue for the Netherlands, that a coherent and pervasive discourse or 'planning doctrine' existed which united and co-

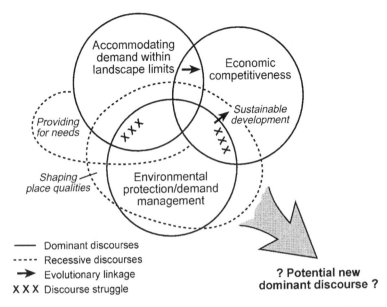

Figure 8.3   The changing discourses of the planning system

ordinated the key actors in the spatial planning field. Although the metaphor of 'sustainability' was often used as a unifying rallying cry (Owens, 1997; Blowers and Evans, 1997), the tensions within it, and between it and the economic competitiveness discourse, opened up further dimensions of conflict, as people argued over its interpretation, both generally and in specific instances. By the end of the decade, the new metaphors in much of the environmental, economic development and quality of life initiatives of the New Labour administration were 'integration' and 'holistic' approaches. But what was to be linked through integration, and the range and linkages to underpin holistic conceptions, were barely specified (Healey, 1998d). Nevertheless, these efforts constituted a tentative form of place-focused or territorial integration.

The dominant deeper-level policy discourses identified above provide only limited intellectual resources for such an endeavour. New models of urban region dynamics have so far had only a limited impact on planning policy discourse, though there are signs of new ideas beginning to filter into the planning field (Graham and Healey, 1999). The most significant sources of new models are in the European regional economic development literature, and in ideas about holistic systems models of environmental sustainability. These dominant discourses pay little attention to the interconnections of activities in places, although the 'Demand Management' discourse has some potential for this. Despite attempts to activate debates about strategic spatial conceptions, as in discussions about 'transport corridors' in the West Midlands, these had very little leverage even at the level of policy rhetoric. As a result, old ideas of 'contained settlements' live on subliminally and actively in the thinking of both planning policy communities and the wider and often very articulate 'chorus'.

This leads to two general conclusions about the planning system. Firstly, the system's arenas made a limited contribution to innovating place-based 'visions' and strategies in the 1990s. Secondly, to the extent that such conceptions were promoted, it was through old agendas living on, rather than new ones being articulated. In effect, the system was being pushed and pulled by conflicting forces, with little proactive capacity to articulate integrated and coherent place-based 'visions' and strategies. How far was this the result of a failure in developing ideas (a weakness of intellectual capital) and how far the result of the structure and practices of governance (a weakness of social and political capital, and/or evidence of the power of structuring constraints)? To shed further light on this question, in the next chapter we explore the evolution of the policy communities and policy arenas through which these policy discourses were developed, disseminated and institutionalised, and how they served to constrain and promote strategic spatial policy discourses.

9 The Policy Communities of Spatial Strategy-Making: The Future Emergence of a Regional Corporatism?

Analysing policy communities

We now turn from a discussion of policy agendas and discourses to the institutional relations of policy making. As the previous chapter highlighted, policy discourses do not flow evenly through localities. Their adoption and dissemination are critically related to the existing institutional landscape, both in terms of formal organisations and the relations between stakeholders. This chapter assesses the impact of such institutional dynamics for spatial strategy making and the penetration of policy discourses.

How might we examine such impacts? Chapter 2 highlighted a number of ways to approach the analysis of the institutional relations of policy making. It concluded by advocating a sociological variant of the new 'institutionalist' approaches (Hall and Taylor, 1996). As developed in the planning field (Healey, 1997; Healey *et al.*, 1997b), this uses the concepts of policy communities and policy arenas to organise accounts of the practice of governance. Policy communities are conceived as clusters of stakeholders who share common frames of reference and substantive issues of concern. Policy arenas are the places where issues of concern are discussed. As such, they constitute the institutional sites which act as nodal points for stakeholders, or provide a locus for the activities of policy communities in developing and disseminating policy. These concepts are discussed further below.

Institutionalist analyses look beyond the immediate organisations responsible for governance, as do regime and regulation theories (see

Chapter 2). Sociological institutionalism goes further, arguing that there is no sharp division between state and society (Hall and Taylor, 1996). This emphasises not only that 'governance' involves more than merely the activities of government agencies (Rhodes, 1996; Stoker, 1999); it also emphasises the importance of the various social relations within which individuals in organisations are embedded, as well as the specific responsibilities arising from their role in a particular organisation. The concepts of policy community and policy arena provide tools with which to approach an analysis of these relations.

Through the lens provided by these concepts, we return to the three themes addressed in this book: the extent to which governance arrangements are being transformed, the extent to which economic, environmental and social policies are being integrated, and the breadth and nature of participation in spatial strategy making. We are particularly concerned with the implications of the relations between stakeholders in our three localities for the operation of the land use planning system and its impacts, as well as with what this has to say for the evolution of subnational governance processes more generally. It is well recognised that policy making in the UK tends to take place in distinct, often professionalised, policy networks with strong connections vertically, that is, between national and local government (Marsh and Rhodes, 1992). This chapter examines how such networks contribute or inhibit attempts at integration across policy sectors. We therefore explore how cross-sectoral issues affect the current composition of policy networks and how such issues were dealt with by the existing policy communities in our localities.

Policy communities are characterised by a particular set of dominant relations and frames of reference. Given the trends towards centralisation and sectoralisation in UK governance outlined in Chapter 1, we might expect vertical relations between central and local government to dominate. However, the land use planning system provides the opportunity for horizontal links with other stakeholders from diverse institutional positions (Thornley, 1991). The tension between horizontal and vertical linkages in our localities was a recurrent theme in Part II. Nevertheless, in line with the expectations outlined in Chapter 1, the practices illustrated in Part II show the continuing power of the vertical relations, combined with a narrowing of the remit of the planning system, thus reducing the pressure to develop rich horizontal linkages. The increasing control of central government over local government finance and the inertia present in Whitehall's continued sectoralism reinforced segregated, vertical policy communities. The integration of policy through a territorial focus was not encouraged in such an institutional context.

Despite these trends, our examples show that local-level actors retained a capacity to develop strategy and make horizontal linkages. In this chapter we examine how localities utilised this capacity to deal with contemporary governance pressures. In doing so, we examine how far the attempt to build horizontal, place-focused policy communities widens the membership of such communities, as opposed to re-establishing more control over policy agendas by local policy elites, to build a form of territorial corporatism. We also assess the innovation capacity of such territorial policy communities.

This chapter first expands on the meaning of policy communities and policy arenas. It then examines the different policy communities which were active in our four issue areas and the arenas which drew community members together. It goes on to explore the extent to which new communities and arenas were formed to challenge the established policy communities and the extent to which policy communities with a more territorial focus were emerging. The chapter concludes by commenting on the role of planning policy communities and arenas in these processes.

Stakeholders, policy communities and spatial strategy making

The policy community concept focuses on the 'who' of policy relations. It is recognised colloquially when we refer to 'the highway people', 'the planners' and 'the people at the county [council]'. Such terms refer to groups of people who seem to think and act in similar ways, drawing upon a pool of common resources and language. The notion of policy communities is well-established in the policy analysis and political science literatures, though with different definitions and usages. It emerged in the 1970s particularly from the work of Heclo (for example, Heclo and Wildavsky, 1974) and was consolidated through the writings of others (for example, Richardson and Jordan, 1979). In these instances it was used to convey the existence of small numbers of stakeholders, centred on particular national government departments, who carried a great deal of power with regard to public policy and decision making. Such communities were characterised as being 'corporatist' and closed to varying degrees to outside influence. Their insularity was seen to nurture a shared set of views which framed the ways of thinking and the practices of those involved, and which was passed on to new entrants through education and in-work acculturation. Marsh and Rhodes (1992) located the phenomenon of a policy community in a typology of 'policy networks'. They proposed a spectrum from cohesive 'policy communities' to more disparate issue-specific networks, each defined in relation to a central government department. Others have looked for a more micro-level and fluid view of policy communities, as relatively small groups of participants in policy processes that emerge to deal with an identifiable class of problems (Agranoff, 1990; Cole and John, 1995; Grant and McNamara, 1995). Our approach focuses on two levels. On the one hand, there are 'work groups' who share common assumptions and practices and see themselves as having some distinguishable coherence in relation to other work groups with whom members interact. At a wider level, there are 'communities of reference', through which common traditions, experiences and values are shaped and interpreted. The professional infrastructure available to planners and civil engineers provides one example, as do the vertical relationships built up through the implementation of areas of government policy.

This second definition moves the focus beyond the construction of elite policy groups, the focus of attention in urban regime theory. Participants in policy communities have experience of face-to-face interaction in various 'communities of association'. These wider communities provide a store of knowledge resources (or 'intellectual capital') and social contacts (relational resources or 'social capital') for workgroup members (Innes *et al.*, 1994; Healey, 1998b). The experiences of the workgroup in turn help to develop and consolidate the knowledge resources and social capital available to the wider community membership.

Policy communities can form around sectors and subsectors of government policy (Marsh and Rhodes, 1992; Cole and John, 1995; Rhodes, 1997). For example, the land use planning policy community is distinctive in its formal organisation, reinforced by a professional body (Rydin, 1998), but under the umbrella of this identification co-exist groupings which may have greater affinity with non-planners than with, say, those working on the regulation of development. There are in effect a large number of different subsectoral clusters. In Part II, we noted clusters of actors in the context of land for housing. Their frame of reference focused on national policy and the arenas where this was expressed, but they were also regularly interacting with policy groups at local and regional level. Further clusters were evident in relation to economic development, linked in this case to a broader economic development nexus, and also in relation to transport and waste management issues. This suggests that a strength of the policy communities loosely aligned under the 'planning umbrella' was their fluidity and capacity to link with each other and to clusters which emerge around new territorial issues. Spatial planners in the constitution of their work practices were continually renegotiating the tensions between sectoral and territorial divisions in policy organisation, and hence their own identities.

Policy communities are thus more than just collections of individual actors or sets of networks, although identifying the key actors and the networks in which they are located is an important dimension of the analysis of policy communities in practice. Actors draw on and interpret the knowledge resources available to them, and mobilise the resources of the policy community to act in particular ways. But any actor in governance arenas may be a member of more than one policy community and is certainly involved in several social networks at once. Thus networks of social relations provide strong channels through which ideas can be diffused and actions pursued. This enriches the resources of knowledge and social trust they have access to, but may also generate tensions and contradictions in understanding and obligations. Such tensions may lead to innovation and change, to developing new knowledge resources, building new relational resources and reconfiguring policy communities. But tensions may also lead policy community members to defensive entrenchment and conservative behaviour, seeking to resist threats to their institutional territory and competencies (Marsh and Rhodes, 1992). The findings of Chapter 6 in relation to transport policy making provide an example of the latter behaviour.

Policy communities are typically surrounded by other parties who have some kind of relation to them. Only some of these will be aware of the key players in the policy communities or have access to networks which would give them links to the policy-making core. We use the concept of 'stakeholder' to define this universe of potentially concerned parties. This term originated in the business literature (Eden, 1996), but has been usefully widened in relation to public policy to include, 'any person, group, or organisation that is affected by the causes or consequences of an issue' (Bryson and Crosby, 1992, p.65). Some stakeholders have no idea they are affected. A key question for the analysis of policy communities is therefore the composition of the policy community relative to the stakeholder universe and the way the policy community relates to that universe.

The focus on policy communities, actors in networks and stakeholders directs analytic attention to the evolving institutional landscape of 'groupings' and relational webs which enact governance in specific times and places. The development of enduring features of policy communities may be the result of struggles over membership and definition, and over the content of shared understandings. So it is important to identify the dynamics of change in policy communities and their constituent actors and networks, and the power relations and driving forces behind these. Following structuration theory (see Chapter 2), these driving forces may be traced in the rules which are acknowledged, the resources which are used and the frames of reference which shape accepted ways of thinking and acting.

In relation to our concern in this book with the extent of transition and transformation in strategic planning practices, we would expect to find evidence of change dynamics not merely in the internal evolution of specific policy communities, but in the extent to which new policy communities were being created. We might see territorial alliances challenging the traditional functional/sectoral organisation of British government. If new forms of trans-sectoral integration were being sought, we would expect to find attempts to enlarge or reconfigure policy communities and build new networks to connect previously separated policy communities. If this reconfiguration was merely regrouping the members of existing policy community elites then we would conclude that changes under way are corporatist in form. However, if new communities are wider, including stakeholders not involved previously in governance processes, we can conclude that more inclusionary and participative processes may be emerging.

Policy arenas and spatial strategy making

The policy arena concept emphasises the 'where' of policy, the institutional sites and nodal parts of networks where members of one or more policy communities come together to develop ways of thinking about issues and mobilise the capacity to act. These institutional sites could be fixed in time and space, as in a public inquiry, or they could occur as a flow of debate, conflict and decision in several locations and over time, as in the definition and selection of major industrial sites in the West Midlands (see Chapter 5). Such arenas may be created by formal law or government action such as a public inquiry, or they may emerge informally, as in the West Midlands example above.

As issues of concern emerge they tend to flow through various stages, from broad discussion to more formal deliberation, debate and conflict resolution (Bryson and Crosby, 1992). This process converts the discussion into a piece of 'abstract structure', a 'black box' of soft technology, which then shapes subsequent actions, though continually subject to reinterpretation and challenge. Bryson and Crosby (1992) argue that different kinds of arenas are used at different stages: 'forums' for the broad discussion, 'arenas' for more formal delibera-tion and 'courts' for formal arbitration should it prove necessary. The former tend to be more informal, diffuse and ad hoc, the second more formal creations, typically by a public sector institution, and the latter arise from the judicial system. This sequence relates closely to the British planning system, where informal discussion may lead to more formalised debates over development plan preparation or development applications, with specific proposals eventually tested in the formal public inquiry and, in a few cases, the courts.

One important aspect of this flow of policy issues through different arenas is that different policy communities and associated networks cluster around different arenas. Some power is needed to shift issue agendas from one arena to another. The power of procedure may do this in formal processes, though there has to be some force to generate the momentum to proceed. Where the arenas are informal, some mobil-isation activity is needed to shift the agenda along (Tarrow, 1994). That such movement occurs is evidence of the power of those in the prior arena to influence the agendas of those in other arenas. But this influence may be achieved by a consolidation or packaging of the policy issues such that many nuances of understanding and meaning are lost. To disseminate well, a policy idea needs to be located in a well-understood frame of reference and 'translated' in terms which can be understood by different policy communities. Again this process can be related to Latour's (1987) idea of a 'black box' whereby the produc-tion and diffusion of different ideas gets fixed into a single form when carried forward to the next stage of the dissemination process.

Although formal policy systems may specify how an issue is supposed to progress through various policy arenas, as in British development plan making, there is always potential for struggle and choice over which arenas to use for which issue and at what stage in its development (for example, at what spatial level to refer to site specificity in the hierarchy of plans and policy guidance in planning systems). The selection of an arena involves choices, even if only implicitly, about who has access to the arena, how they may get access to it and how 'user friendly' its internal practices are (Healey, 1997). There is considerable potential for competition among arenas, especially where these are informal. This may happen at the early stages of issue formulation, for example between developing urban regeneration projects through development plan formulation or through the process of bidding to subsidy programmes. But it may also happen at later stages, for example where there are overlapping responsibilities between different regulatory systems, as currently happens between the planning system and the Environment Agency. Arenas are thus likely to vary not only in the policy communities which cluster around them but in the rules and resources which can be mobilised through them.

We could expect to find evidence of transformation and transition in governance processes in the reconfiguration of arenas and in the way existing arenas are used. We would anticipate that this would bring problems in dissemination and translation, as the different arenas might be reconfiguring at different speeds. If a territorial emphasis was developing, we would expect to see the creation of new arenas with a territorial focus, which would challenge sectoral/functional forms. If more emphasis were being given to specific economic, environmental or social issue dimensions, we would expect this to be evident in concerns to shift the criteria used to develop and judge proposals. If there were real attempts to involve new stakeholders in governance processes, we would expect to see attention to facilitating such involvement in policy arenas.

Reconfiguring policy communities and policy arenas

This section reviews the main 'communities of association' evident in Part II. These were of three types. The most obvious were issue-based, where stakeholders from different institutional positions came together to structure ways of dealing with an issue. The second were focused on place and territory, seeking to interrelate issue agendas as they related to the development of that territory. The third significant type were interest-based communities, focused on the objectives of firms in particular business sectors, or particular environmental groups, for example.

Issue-based policy communities

In the housing issue area the principal actors were local authority planners, the House Builders Federation, central government through its regional offices and through the Department of Environment, Transport and the Regions (DETR) and some environmental groups, notably the Council for the Protection of Rural England. The same groups of participants were found at national and local levels. National-level discussions framed subsequent activities in localities. The lower-level negotiations were played out through a technocorporatist set of bargaining processes at regional and subregional levels. Centralisation tendencies were therefore strong, with the DETR retaining a tight hold on technical calculation and policy development. Stakeholders in lower-level policy communities were trapped in a game, the rules of which were determined at national level. Their ability to modify central government intentions were largely limited to determining the location of housing 'numbers' allocated to them.

This situation was widely acknowledged across the UK in the 1990s. Key players in the policy community knew the rules. Only at the level of plan inquiries and contestation about specific planning issues were other stakeholders allowed a say, and by this point in the hierarchical process they could make little impression on rules. But they could influence location decisions, and it was here that intense conflict took place (Hull and Vigar, 1998; Murdoch *et al.*, 1999). So, whilst local-level arenas were heavily constrained by the actions of the national arena, it was still worth getting involved at this level. As a result, the pattern which at first appears highly vertical and centralised is much more nuanced and locally varied. Since 1997, this potential for localising the nexus has been encouraged by central government's moves to devolve some authority to subnational levels and break with the 'predict and provide' approach (DETR, 1999a). If this impetus continues, subnational, and particularly regional, arenas are thus likely to take on a renewed significance and new groupings of actors may start to reconfigure the issue agenda in this previously stable policy community

In the employment land issue, new arenas relating to economic development, mostly at regional level, were generating new policy discourses in both Lancashire and the West Midlands. Participation in the alliances creating these new visions was quite wide compared with previous eras, with business interests such as chambers of commerce, inward investment agencies and training and enterprise councils noticeably more prominent. The extent of the real influence of these agencies was variable, as shown in other research (Peck, 1993; Peck and Emmerich, 1994), but ideas were being shared and understanding amongst participants was being generated through debate in a way not present previously. The employment land issue differs from that of housing land in that central government played a quite different and fragmented role. Connections between local government and the DETR over site allocation through regulatory practices were of less significance in this case, in contrast to the relations through which national government and EU subsidies for economic development were distributed.

As a result, local policy communities had more room to manoeuvre and took on a greater significance. Local authority economic development officers had a great deal of influence in such discussions, working within local economic development policy communities which linked economic development agencies, land use planners and business interests. Planners were still involved in the allocation of land in plans but this function was a relatively small one in the context of overall economic development policy agendas. Planning discourses were significantly shaped by the debates conducted in these wider arenas.

One consequence was a tension between land use planning policy arenas and those where economic development policies were articulated. In Lancashire, the process of locating strategic employment sites involved a range of agencies. However, the decision-making process was complex and there was some confusion over policy objectives. Whilst a number of stakeholders in the economic development world were involved, the district planners who had to locate the site in their plans and deal with the detailed development impacts were not. This resulted in difficulties in 'fitting' the strategic policy to local implementation practices. The failure of the regional and county economic policy community in Lancashire to reach out to the local-level land use planning policy community thus almost led to the loss of the strategic objective, as resistance built up to a little understood proposal. In the West Midlands, no such difficulties were encountered as issues were shared amongst a wider policy community which included district authority representatives from the land use planning policy community.

Thus, in a context less heavily structured by vertical relations than in the housing field, conflicts between levels and arenas of subnational governance could break out. The land use planners preparing development plans were largely marginal to economic development communities. Their role was to legitimise allocations. But the planning arena gave access to the voices of environmental groups and the critique of economic development policies. The resultant tensions in our cases prefigure those emerging across England in the late 1990s, in the relations between the regional development agencies and the strengthened role of regional planning guidance (DETR, 1999a).

The waste and transport issue areas represent examples of policy communities which had evolved as separate groupings from either the main land use planning communities or the economic development arenas. They were both strongly linked to the technical expertise of the civil engineering profession. In both cases, they were under pressure from environmental agendas. As a result, they were having to reconfigure their own agendas, draw in different expertise, involve new stakeholders and develop new policy relations.

Transport in particular had evolved a classic 'functional form' as a professional policy network (Marsh and Rhodes, 1992) with internal cohesion and a strong power base in national and local government. At the national level, the engineering ethos meshed with the policy orientation of civil servants who controlled the allocation of investment resources. These linkages created strong relationships between central and local government stakeholders (see Figure 6.2.)

These close-knit sets of relationships were further accentuated by a traditional division in transport planning activity based on modes of transport. Within local authorities and the DETR, officers still tended to work to agendas associated with a particular mode. This modal emphasis had real implications for shifting policy in local transport policy communities, as 'highway engineers' had an inherent tendency to channel resources for highways. This partly explains the slowness of policy change through the 1990s and the continuing policy inertia within the sector (Vigar, 2000; Vigar *et al.*, 2000). Power relations in this sector thus flowed through vertical channels. The national government exercised control over local transport policy communities principally through control over funding processes. By the end of the 1990s, there were small signs of a shift, with opportunities given to local authorities to raise funds locally through congestion and parking charges (DETR, 1998c, 1998k). This was complemented by the expanding role of regional planning guidance in determining regional investment priorities and policies for transport (DETR, 1999a). As in the economic development field, the regional level was emphasised as the means of integrating regulatory and investment strategies, and of accommodating the pressures for more horizontal policy integration.

The waste regulation field experienced a great deal of institutional change through the 1990s, with responsibilities shifted away from local authorities, and increasing national government intervention. Waste regulation became the responsibility of the Environment Agency, with waste disposal merely one of many tendering processes local authorities retained. In two-tier local authority areas a core of waste planners were divided into waste disposal authority officers and waste planners working on waste local plans. Dialogue between the two elements was limited. In metropolitan areas, following abolition of the metropolitan county councils, responsibility for waste issues across conurbations was typically taken by one metropolitan district authority. This left land use planners in the remaining authorities with very little knowledge regarding waste policies and how they might interact with other issues. In metropolitan areas, therefore, waste planning tended to become a technical 'backroom' exercise, largely disconnected from unitary development plans preparation. A resultant policy vacuum led to decisions in individual authorities, for example, over waste incineration plants, which were taken in isolation from wider plans for waste disposal.

In this situation, the planning system played a conflict resolution role at the site level rather than providing a mechanism for strategic discussions. However, this closure of the waste planning policy relations around technical issues led to objections from environmental groups and others, who used the arenas of the planning system as an avenue for objection. The recognition that political contestation could not be avoided on waste issues was clearly evident in the tensions between the 'importing' and 'exporting' authorities. While local efforts at establishing self-sufficiency principles were beginning to bite, this principle was often used by importing authorities for political reasons rather than those arising from environmental criteria. As in our other policy fields, the regional level was emerging as an important arena for resolving these tensions, although with a continuing emphasis on technical processes.

Thus, in the cases of both waste and transport, policy relations were unstable, with new arenas being developed and new stakeholders drawn in. In both fields, the regional level was being asked to carry more weight in policy development and conflict resolution. There were also more muted pressures to widen policy relationships at the local level, and to link policy development here to debates about the qualities of locales. These shifts had the potential to increase implementation capacity for the new agendas and to develop more legitimacy for new directions. However, for both of these policy communities, the opening up process was difficult and did not fit well with established cultures, grounded in technocratic competencies.

Territorial alliances

Our four issue areas all illustrate the continuing power of sectoral government, and its focus on the delivery of specific policy 'functions'. By the end of the 1990s, this kind of thinking was challenged as representing self-contained 'silos', or 'tunnel vision'. The metaphor used to challenge this approach, deeply embedded in both national and local government, was 'joined-up thinking' and 'integration'. A key meaning of such integration was that policies affecting particularly territories and locales should be interrelated and driven by common and coherent strategies (DETR, 1999a; Social Exclusion Unit, 1998). Our accounts in Part II show some evidence of the prefiguring of such place-focused integration.

The most obvious of these evolutions were at the regional level. In part, the push to the regional level was still oriented around policy sectors with merely a decentralisation of the policy development emphasis. But even here this was accompanied by a widening of stakeholder involvement, which encouraged more territorially focused strategy, particularly in the relation between economic development, planning policy and transport (Vigar *et al.*, 2000). As the new regional development agencies were getting established, and the relations between their economic development strategies and the strengthened regional planning guidance were evolving, there were signs in some regions of the emergence of coalitions of interest within which territorially focused policy communities could develop. The West Midlands provided the best example of this prefiguring of new institutional relations.

A significant indicator of the emergence of a territorial focus was the development of new spatial organising ideas. The most notable example in our cases was the concept of 'transport corridors'. Although around for a long time in planning arenas in both the north west and the West Midlands (although in quite different forms), the corridor idea crystallised in the 1990s through the preparation of regional planning guidance. In the West Midlands, discussion of the potential of the corridor idea brought together land use planners, through chief planning officers groups, transport professionals, and other stakeholder representatives, notably the House Builders Federation and the Council for the Protection of Rural England. The concept provides a rare example of an idea which originated and developed within a land use planning policy community. Despite this, there were a number of concerns in the West Midlands, not least regarding the relationship of corridor strategies to statutory planning processes, as the corridors idea developed outside formal planning processes and after development plans had been adopted.

At the level of locales, the most striking examples were in the Kent area development partnerships. The Kent Thames-side partnership was particularly successful in developing a strategic place-focused vision which integrated economic, environmental and social concerns. Partly as a consequence, the initiative was able to lever funds from a variety of sources, particularly central government, to support preparatory work. It capitalised on strong links to politicians and civil servants to shape the activities of the existing issue-based policy communities present in Kent and had the support of central government and a major landowner. Even so, it proved difficult to get all local stakeholders to agree to the strategy. This provides a telling example of the way established sectoralised institutional relations fracture attempts at building horizontal place-focused alliances, even where these have strong central government political and official backing.

The third institutional locus for place-focused thinking was the arenas of the planning system itself. This was significant because most projects generated in other policy communities had to 'pass through' the legitimating arenas of the system. This requirement was reinforced by the legal and policy assertion of the significance of the development plan through 'section 54a' (see Chapter 1). In addition to the formal arenas of plan consultation and inquiry, and the review of development impacts in the regulatory permitting process, there were informal arenas within which policy issues were discussed and strategic ideas developed. These arenas were typically focused on chief planning officers groups (CPOGs) or, as in the West Midlands case, a Chief Engineers and Planning Officers Group (CEPOG). Considerable work in the production of regional guidance, development plans and other strategy passed through such arenas. Much of the contact with central government and the negotiations and horse trading about issues such as housing land allocations and transport infrastructure proposals were done at this level. Similar groups to the CPOGs existed amongst local politicians and officials lower in the local authority hierarchy, where officers often take up the technical mobilisation of ideas passed down from CPOGs. These informal groupings played important roles in brokering relations between districts and regional/national-level discussions and in framing policy agendas (see Kitchen, 1997, for a further example).

These chief officer groups and the constellation of stakeholders who interact with the players in these arenas had become a key locus of power at the local authority level. However, this did not necessarily mean that they had innovative potential, or were capable of integrating sectoral policy agendas around place qualities. Social relations built up over many years were important here. In places such as Kent, many built environment professionals remain in the county throughout their working lives while occupying different positions in different organisations. This insularity and the subsequent development of relational resources provided an added sense of a planning policy community in such an area. Various stakeholders attributed a great deal of importance to such relations, 'chief [planning] officers are people I play tennis with' (pressure group director and former county council employee). Thus a professional interest becomes tied into social networks which contribute to the construction and maintenance of social capital. The effects of this tight-knit community on strategy making were double-edged. On the positive side, such relations provided a rich set of common understandings that did not need to be rehearsed amongst the key individuals, and continued contact built trust amongst community members. However, on the negative side, a resultant lack of outside knowledge in the policy community could lead to difficulties in absorbing fresh ideas and new policy agendas.

The role of land use planning arenas should not therefore be overstated. The activities of local authorities in bidding for monies, and the associated processes of networking between officers and members and with partner organisations occurred mainly beyond plan-making arenas, with any relevant outputs 'lifted into' the planning system when the need arose. The functional divisions within local authorities exacerbated this, with local plans sections responsible for plan preparation while implementation and other non-statutory functions take place elsewhere. There may be good administrative reasons for these divisions, but they distanced the work of policy formulation from that of implementation.

Interest-based policy communities and networks

Two types of alliance were drawn into, or proactively positioned themselves in, the issue fields discussed in Part II: groupings of business interests, and alliances formed around environmental concerns. Environmental networks were in evidence in all of our areas, some prompted by local authorities, others developed from the grassroots. Such alliances were formed either to lobby for a higher profile for environmental issues in the agendas of business and government or to contribute directly to environmental improvement in particular areas.

The most interesting examples of such groupings formed around environmental issues were found in Lancashire. First, at a local level, a collection of groups in Lancaster were part of a culture of grassroots environmental action in the town. A similar clustering of groups also centred on the village of Wye in Kent. The influence of both clusters on public policy was limited, however. Second, in Lancashire, at county level, a great deal of networking took place amongst public, quasi-public and voluntary groups who shared resources and lobbied together for common goals. Groups would also campaign together and separately, as the demands of groups' respective memberships and public profiles and reputations demanded different approaches. The influence of such alliances varied greatly, as did the openness of the main policy communities towards them. Some groups sought to gain 'voice' in the main policy communities. Nevertheless, they tended to be outside the core policy communities where planning and policy processes were actively constructed and shaped. This outsider status is often assumed out of choice, as some groups wished to be seen to maintain a distance between themselves and those with authority. This had implications for policy communities and their ability to generate strategic commitment across a broad range of stakeholders. The one environmental group which actively sought to be, and consistently was, admitted to the policy communities was the Council for the Protection of Rural England. In housing debates, it became used in the 1980s and 1990s as a counterpoint to the producer group, the House Builders Federation (see Chapter 4). What was striking in our cases, however, was the lack of linkage between the arenas where environmental groups could get access to influence and the arenas to which the business lobbies obtained access. Even in the planning arenas, to which environmental groups obtained most access, there was only limited filtration of the ideas generated through Local Agenda 21 initiatives into the four issue agendas examined in Part II, despite the great relevance they all have to local environmental quality.

Business interests have a long history of constructing lobby groups to influence government. The West Midlands was widely thought to be awash with such groupings. The West Midlands Regional Economic Consortium (WMREC) was a particularly active network in the development of spatial strategy, bringing public and private sectors together in the process of major employment site allocation, for example (see Chapter 5). In all areas, business groups met through associations such as chambers of commerce, but these tended to have limited involvement and interest in spatial strategy making except in specific debates such as transport. A striking example of a private sector grouping attempting to plug a perceived gap in spatial strategy occurred in north west England where the North West Business Leadership Team (NWBLT) played a central role in developing spatial strategy through the funding of a regional economic strategy (Pieda, 1993). The arenas of the NWBLT and the WMREC were increasingly used by the public sector to demonstrate that stakeholder involvement in policy making was broadening. The well-organised environmental lobbies also sought to get the attention of these arenas. This provides evidence of an increasing blurring of the boundaries of private, public and voluntary sectors in governance processes, especially in highly contentious areas such as transport policy, where there were real efforts to draw groups together to pool resources to address issues of common concern.

Our accounts thus illustrate the complexity of the institutional tendencies under way. As Imrie and Raco (1999) argue, there is no simple unilinear transformation in subnational governance in progress. Instead, while there are clearly some general tendencies, these were progressing at different speeds in different issue areas and localities, and with different configurations. Many long-established relations retained a powerful capacity to maintain their position, notably the strength of vertical central–local relations, the sectoral organisation of policy fields, the professional cultures of government officials and the well-organised lobby groups. Nevertheless, some significant shifts were emerging, which are summarised in Table 9.1. In the next section, we review their significance.

Table 9.1 Tendencies in policy communities in the issue areas

Issue area	Vertical relationships (central/local)	Horizontal relationships	Territorial emphasis	Participating interest communities
Housing Land	Nationally focused, centred on planning division in DoE/DETR. Dominated by civil servants and planners	Negotiated at regional, county and district level. Potential for intense conflict	Limited, though regional level increasingly important	HBF; CPRE Often considerable public involvement at site level
Employment Land	Limited national specification of planning policy DTI and regional offices active in the configuration of economic development investment	Fluid regional and local policy arenas, involving business representatives, economic development agencies and local authorities Dominated by economic development specialists	Regional level increasingly important; emphasis on regional strategies	Business groupings
Transport	Close relations; investment considerations structure the relationships Dominated by civil servants and engineers	Increasing linkages between transport modes, with some links to business and environmental groups	Regional level increasingly important. Some discussions beginning to link to spatial strategy (see 'corridors' ideas)	Business groups, transport industry groups and environmental groups all trying to get access
Waste	Strengthening role within Environment Agency context Dominated by engineers	Limited to the waste disposal and recycling industries	Proposals to strengthen the regional level	Industry groupings strong

Institutional innovation and the re-emergence of regional arenas

Despite the strength of the continuities identified, our accounts in Part II confirm that significant institutional innovation was under way and that pressures for further changes were building up. New relationships and arenas were being established. Existing communities were shifting their agendas. The knowledge base was changing from the domains of engineers and regulators to those of policy strategists. There were also efforts to widen policy communities, to draw together the stakeholders clustered around different modes of transport, to involve producer industries in policy debate and to link levels of government together more effectively in the discussion of policy issues. This suggested that there were potentials for the formation of new policy communities with different foci, including a territorial development perspective. There were evident trends to widen and deepen the nexus of relations with which core policy communities were connected, developing the 'thickness' of local and regional policy relations (Amin and Thrift, 1995) and expanding local institutional governance capacity (Healey, 1998b).

A major pressure for change arose from the challenge of the environmental agenda. Environmental groups were increasingly invited into consultation processes. However, the penetration of even a weak discourse of sustainability was variable between issue fields, localities and levels of governance. Rhetoric was not always translated into policies which led to practical action (Davoudi *et al.*, 1996). As others have noted, local political agendas in the 1980s were strongly oriented to rebuilding local economic strength (Gibbs *et al.*, 1996). The shift to an environmental agenda involved difficult political shifts (Marshall, 1994), but is was also clear that the penetration of environmental thinking was variable between policy communities. This represented a real problem for stakeholders who sought to promote environmental sustainability. They might succeed in getting support or in enrolling one part of the governance landscape, only to encounter powerful established policy communities with conservative outlooks. In Lancashire, for example, a transport policy community still stuck in a 'predict and provide' paradigm in the mid-1990s was aligned with an economic development nexus which believed in 'roads for prosperity'. Coupled with local political pragmatism, the two communities provided a powerful challenge to the new sustainability coalition, based principally on the policy community of land use planning. This inhibited shifts to a broader approach to transport policy and undermined the authority's declared strategic intentions (Hull *et al.*, 1996). National government exhortation thus steadily evaporated in dissemination among implementation communities.

If institutional change was uneven and in flux, it was clear that the regional level was emerging as a key locus of institution-building effort. This was nevertheless underpinned by strong local authorities and combined with the continuing strength of vertically structured central–local relations. In both the West Midlands and the north west, the regionalising impetus depended in large part on the importance given to it by key local authorities. In both Birmingham City Council and Lancashire County Council, the involvement in developing regional economic strategies could be interpreted as the exercise of 'pre-emptive power', to maintain established governance 'regimes' amidst increasingly pluralistic local governance (Stone, 1989; Stoker, 1995).

However, these regionalising impulses and the strength of some local authorities did not necessarily lead to an integrated and strategic focus on territorial qualities, still less to the integration of economic, environmental and social agendas. This reinforces the conclusions reached from the analysis of policy discourses in Chapter 8. There were strong signs that sectoralism could be replicated at the regional level. Each policy field might widen to include more stakeholders, but overlap between them was at the margins (and most evident in relation to economic development and transport). Each field had its own way of making linkages between economic, environmental and social issues. For example, in housing, social issues were structured into the discussion through demography and the long-standing agenda of social housing. The environmental agenda was carried by a lobby group (the CPRE) and economic issues were brought in by the industry lobby group (the HBF). In economic development, social issues were absorbed into business representations of labour market qualities and in the equation of providing 'sites' with creating jobs.

Overall, the regional relationships emerging in our three areas were heavily dominated by economic considerations and the competitiveness agenda. Environmental issues were largely relegated to the planning arenas of counties and districts. Thus the emerging governance relations at regional level seemed to carry forward a fragmented and segmented approach to policy fields, inhibiting the emergence of an integrated, multi-level territorial viewpoint.

It was also clear that, despite the widening of policy communities to include more stakeholders, the nexus was primarily of public sector players and a few business representatives. The only others to get involved were well-organised environmental lobby groups. A common metaphor was of the 'usual suspects', the same people, but in slightly different combinations and positions. This partly reflected the continuing strength of vertically structured central–local relations in the governance landscape.

The power of the business voice arose, however, not just through active incorporation: it was as much the result of shared objectives with the public sector and the permeation of the economic competitiveness discourse across government. However, whilst such involvement was useful to business and had an effect on policy and outcomes, the public sector remained the key instigator and focus of activity. Business needed the powers, resources and skills of local government to develop policy agendas and to establish processes for their discussion and legitimation. While the resource base of local authorities was weaker than in earlier decades, especially in relation to direct development and providing finance for initiatives, the skills and knowledge resources within the government cores of the main policy communities were of vital importance in territorial policy development. Local authorities retained their position in driving governance processes, especially through the power of the various professions to structure agendas and act as the core of policy communities. This was reinforced by the continuing centralisation, which meant that the critical relationships in policy determination were often those between civil servants and officers in local government. As a result, the participation by 'outside' stakeholders, even among business groups, tended to be on the margins rather than at the core of policy development.

The result was a form of 'corporatism' still strongly driven by public sector agendas, enlarged by a few business and other stakeholders, often with past public sector linkages. Business involvement, as found in other studies (Peck, 1995), tended to be the same faces in different arenas. This applied also to the world of partnerships in which all levels of subnational government were increasingly engaged. These were driven by public sector requirements, drawing stakeholders into processes which often stretched their commitment and interest, resulting in 'partnership fatigue'.

Overall, citizens, less well-organised environmental groups and businesses with limited appreciation of government found few opportunities for involvement in the emerging governance landscapes illustrated in our cases. Their opinions continued to be channelled either through their local politicians or through the arenas of the land use planning system. Here the most significant opportunities were in the inquiry processes, by which time policy agendas were already strongly framed. These 'open access' arenas were thus segmented off from the main nodes for policy development, many of them outside the leverage of the planning system. This not only resulted in considerable conflict in these arenas, it reduced the effectiveness of the core policy communities by cutting them off from awareness of real concerns which other groups and individuals had about the qualities of localities. More seriously, it reinforced the 'democratic deficit', the sense of distance between government and everyone else.

The role of land use planning policy communities and arenas

The planning policy community emerged, in our cases, as occupying an ambiguous position and under considerable pressure to change. In theory, its arenas provided institutional locales for articulating a new governance landscape, focused on the multi-level development of strategic ideas which could integrate economic, environmental and social dimensions of territorial development and place qualities. In practice, its ability to do this was severely constrained.

The West Midlands illustrates a situation where the arenas of the planning system were used to build strategic consensus across levels of government and with a wider array of stakeholders. But, even here, strategy development remained largely sectoralised, despite attempts to develop integrative spatial concepts, such as transport corridors. Elsewhere, sectoralism remained strong, with policies and proposals typically 'lifted in' from other arenas, to pass through the legitimating framework of the development plan process.

This legitimating process allowed some stakeholders outside the government and business nexus to express their views, but the arenas of plan consultation and inquiry were highly constrained in their form, and not readily accessible without considerable resources of knowledge and time. They tended therefore to be 'captured' by well-organised interest groups. Those 'voices' that did get to be heard then faced a policy agenda which was already well-defined, and therefore difficult to challenge except at the level of specific projects. It was also set within the narrow limits defined by the national Planning Policy Guidance Notes (see Chapter 1). This confined discussion to the 'land use' dimensions of issues, assessed in the framework of nationally developed criteria. This detached the discussion from a developmental consideration of strategic policies for managing territories and locales. The limiting effects of the 'regime of the PPGs' were compounded by the mind-sets of many in the planning community. These had become increasingly cast into a regulatory mould, implementing the criteria-driven approach to regulation which had evolved rapidly in the 1980s and 1990s (see Chapter 1). The land use planning community had difficulty reconciling its role in regulatory functions such as development control with its critical role in defending the 'public interest', and its more strategic role which frequently involved the promotion of certain schemes and policies, the 'decide and defend' approach (Selman, 1998). This raises the important question of the extent to which the logics and practices of the regulation of development are compatible with the logics of proactive strategic policy development for the management of territories and locales.

Despite these cultural tendencies and functional tensions among the planning community, the planning groups in our areas had built up a capacity to mobilise to address new issues and build new relationships as policy agendas and institutional relationships shifted. Planners were often taking initiatives, in building partnerships, making linkages between levels of government, involving new stakeholders, and so on. They were also well aware of the popular concern about environmental issues and the qualities of places which welled up in planning inquiries, in Local Agenda 21 processes and over particular development projects. Members of the planning community were thus often key 'brokers', linking the agendas of citizens concerned with local environmental qualities to local authority and regional agendas, resolving tensions between regulatory and proactive strategies, and attempting to widen sectoral agendas.

This ambiguous role of the planning policy community, both delivering a discrete function (the regulation of development) and acting as a link between levels of government and other policy communities, highlights the challenge which any attempt to build more horizontal linkages and intermediate governance arenas focused upon the qualities of places faced in the governance context of the 1990s. This context lacked well-established arenas for strategy development across a range of policy sectors. The 'multi-level' governance which existed was structured within functional/sectoral policy communities rather than around building intersectoral policy communities focused on territorial development. As a result, linking investment and regulatory decisions was difficult, and integrating economic, environmental and social issues as these were experienced by citizens and firms was problematic. The institutional space to absorb new stakeholders into policy processes was confined to the margins of governance processes. The planning system, in its formal procedures for strategic policy development and public inquiry, had an institutional equipment with the potential to open out to a different, more inclusive, strategic and place-focused governance. But this capacity was compromised by central government policy, by the power of other policy communities and by the limited horizons of many within the planning policy community.

Any effort to build a new regional and local governance capacity, more focused on territorial development and place quality, more integrative in its policy agendas and more inclusive in its policy processes, will need institutional arenas with some of the potentials of the flexible tools and competencies of the planning system. To have influence over governance in the coming decades, a critical issue for such an effort will be whether the practices of the planning system and the mind-sets of its associated policy communities can be recast to provide the institutional qualities which such an emphasis demands or whether appropriate arenas and processes will be developed elsewhere, with the planning system relegated to a marginal, regulatory function. The final chapter turns to this question.

Part IV

CONCLUSIONS: TOWARDS A POLITICS OF PLACE?

10 Spatial Regulation or Spatial Strategies: Towards a New Politics of Place

Reinventing government and the significance of the 'place' focus

In the late 1990s it was clear that the New Labour administration was initiating significant moves towards more decentralised and more integrative governance. In addition to much reference to 'integration' (Healey 1998d), the headline metaphor being used was 'joined-up thinking', to overcome the 'silo mentality' of sectoral departmentalism. This was attached to a rhetoric of stakeholder involvement, and the refocusing of government to the concerns of citizens and business, the consumer viewpoint, rather than the viewpoint of the 'producers' of government (DETR, 1998i, Social Exclusion Unit, 1998). Although there was scepticism about the degree of ministerial commitment to this agenda, by 1999 it was evident in the formal constitutional changes to government in Scotland and Wales and the creation of the regional development agencies in England. In addition, a plethora of measures affecting the way local government should work were being introduced at the turn of the century.

These initiatives were not necessarily consciously attached to a focus on territory and place, though DETR was by 1998 attaching the importance of the 'qualities of place' to the discussion of sustainable planning approaches (DETR, 1998j). It was considering introducing a statutory requirement that local authorities should promote the 'economic, social and environmental well-being of their areas' (DETR, 1998i). There was also a strong emphasis on strategy, both at the regional level (regional economic strategies and the increased significance of regional planning guidance) and within local authorities (the Community Plan). All these developments were accompanied by exhortations to involve more stakeholders in developing and implementing policy. With more power

271

passed down the government hierarchy, more attention paid to horizontal relationships and more emphasis on strategy, it will be difficult to keep issues of territorial quality and spatial organisation out of policy consciousness. As experience elsewhere shows, as more people from a locality get 'voice' in policy arenas, their direct experience of the relations between home, work, leisure, or of attracting customers and moving goods, forces more integrative place-focused perspectives.

At the regional level, the relation between transport and development agendas was already well recognised by the end of the century, and more attention was being given to housing markets, labour markets and the location of housing development. The significance of neighbourhood quality for housing markets and for the sustainability of settlements was also increasingly recognised, as were the complex patterns of movement across regional space between work, education, leisure, shopping and neighbourhood. How these interlocked with the pressure on major environmental systems, notably water and energy, and the overall richness of biological systems focused attention on the key locales of pressure and stress. At the level of locales, this interlocking becomes even more visible, as attention shifts to the micro-sites of daily life, business organisation and the fine grain of ecosystems. While, at the national level, the policy emphasis was still preoccupied with defining indicators of place qualities (DETR, 1999b), at regional and local level it will be difficult to avoid policy attention to the ways in which the forces producing place qualities interact.

But the regionalising and localising thrust is not just about developing a more integrated trans-sectoral focus to policy development and delivery, more in tune with the perspectives of citizens and business. It is also about reducing the distance between government and civil society. In this context, the concern with place quality is not just a recognition of the deep popular concerns which citizens have about the spaces they live, work and playin. It is also about the public realm of debate about the possibilities and options which stakeholders care about. As a locus of policy attention, a focus on place quality, understood in its sociospatial dimensions rather than as pieces of land use or merely physical structures, provides a rich theme for popular debate.

However, currently, in British public policy and public debate, there are limited resources available with which to structure debates about place qualities. What there are derive from traditional spatial planning debates, notably about the maintenance of clear landscape divisions between 'town' and 'country'. Or they are being pulled into discussion through the debates on the qualities of the 'competitive city', the 'sustainable city' or the 'livable city'. These are currently metaphors which have leverage primarily within particular professional communities, with only limited popular resonance. Thus the challenge of realising a place-focused politics at regional and local level demands the development of new arenas, new policy relationships and new connections between established policy communities. It requires re-equipping with an imaginative vocabulary of concepts and metaphors with which to facilitate a discussion of the issues that stakeholders are concerned about. Does the planning system have the potential to reinvigorate place-focused policy agendas?

The English planning system at the turn of the millennium

Despite the limited role the policy communities and arenas of the planning system were playing in promoting an integrated, territorially focused policy dynamic in our three areas, the evolution of the practices of the English planning system was nevertheless a significant site of institutional 'struggle' during the 1990s. The issues at stake related to content: the relative weight and meaning to be given to quality of life, environmental quality and economic priorities, and to the distributional dimensions of each of these. They also related to process: who was to have a 'voice' in determining policy agendas, how and at what stage in the policy process. Given the functional–sectoral organisation of government, the system kept in play the encounters between policy sector priorities. The system provided institutional space for multiple 'voices' to make themselves heard. But the challenges which were generated through these institutional opportunities were kept in check by the continual effort at the national level to restrict and channel policy agendas and to limit the influence of multiple 'voices'.

Our accounts of strategic spatial planning practices in three English regions illustrate the complexity of the resultant tensions. At the most obvious level, which fills local media and which surfaces regularly in the national press, are conflicts about the qualities of particular sites and the challenges presented by particular projects, for example over sites for new housing, industry, transport infrastructure and waste disposal. Local politicians, pressure groups, amenity campaigners and environmental activists struggle to shape decision processes through mobilising whatever channels of influence they can. Their activities and rhetorics feed comment and conversation on television, in the papers, in public spaces, generating a 'critical chorus' of moral discourse about the qualities of places and the capabilities of governance. This enriches general awareness about and concern for the qualities of places, as experienced by people and business in the flow of their everyday activities. Potentially, this provides a strong foundation for integrated policy agendas focused on the qualities of places.

The reality of the policy agendas and practices in and around the planning system as it evolved in the final quarter of the twentieth century did not encourage this potential. Much of the formal change to the procedures and priorities of the system was designed to contain such pressures. Activists were typically cast, in the rhetoric of national government and the language of business lobbies, as 'NIMBYs', fettering enterprise and holding up development. They were less often presented as voices from civil society, concerned to give environmental and social dimensions of issues more weight, or with viewpoints which integrate policy agendas from the perspective of everyday life. Nor were they appreciated as legitimate claims by citizens seeking to have some influence over what happens in the places they live in and care about. The potential for a territorial focus in policy agendas, for integrating functional policy programmes in terms of their impact on places and for inclusionary approaches to local environmental policy, was constrained by the way the practices of the planning system evolved.

This containment of local concern over environmental qualities was effected through the development of a national system of policy criteria, backed by the wide-ranging formal powers of central government to override local concerns. As outlined in Chapter 1, and illustrated in Part II, within planning system arenas the approach works through the specification of largely decontextualised policy principles. These detach sites and projects from their local situation. They situate them in an institutional environment, often at odds with the perspectives of stakeholders involved in the local conflicts. Instead, the approach is the product of a less overt pressure group politics which meshes political ideology and priorities as promoted by ministers with the campaigning of national lobbies such as the HBF, the CBI and professional interest groups. The evolution of the practice of planning regulation in Britain, unconstrained by much of the legal role of plans and zoning measures which prevail in most of Europe, provides the flexibility for business and political elites to pursue their particular agendas. These practices are rendered legitimate by passing through the procedures of the planning system. Although the system provides significant local arenas, – the power of the local planning authority, the preparation of a development plan – the struggle over the specification of policy criteria was waged in such a way that it was difficult for local considerations about place quality to gain influence, except where no larger stakes were in play. Local authority planners, as the system's administrators and facilitators, were further limited in what they could achieve by pressures for the speedy performance of regulatory duties. Thus the 'power-at-a-distance' exercised by central government heavily framed the playing out of local environmental conflict (Murdoch and Marsden, 1995).

The paradoxical consequence, given the antecedents of the British planning system, was that the system's practices fostered the neglect of the promotion of place quality and made little contribution to integrating policy initiatives as they affect people and firms in places. In this 'despatialised' form of planning, concern for the significance of place qualities for different groups and other environmental systems surfaces in the continual flow of conflicts about projects. It is manifest in the deeper culturally embedded attitudes to the traditional rural landscape which frame the thinking of both national elites and many local groups and politicians. But the significance of place qualities is suppressed by the regulatory regime, fragmented into arguments which can be attached to acceptable criteria. Meanwhile, attitudes to the rural landscape are largely taken as a 'given' in the British context, part of national identity and are therefore not subject to critical examination.

This nationally directed, criteria-driven regulatory regime has considerable strengths. It has for example accelerated the absorption of environmental rhetoric into planning debates by rendering the new discourse legitimate, but little has been achieved in reframing policy agendas in the more locally specific integrated forms which are essential to make places more sustainable (Selman, 1996, Haughton and Hunter, 1994). It has provided a sophisticated tool for conflict resolution, but only a few 'voices' are involved in these processes. It reduces variations in the performance of regulatory practice from one local authority to another, but has done little to promote innovation. It has provided greater certainty for developers operating on a national scale about the outcomes of their applications in different parts of the country, but it has done little to provide a more stable and risk-free environment for property developers and investors. All this has been at the cost of considerations of the qualities of places from the points of view of different groups with a stake in a place.

In this despatialised regulatory regime, the vehicle of the development plan loses its role in providing a vision of the spatial evolution of a locality. Vision statements may be made at the start of plans, but plan content is typically dominated by the translation of national policy criteria into more locally specific principles. The re-emphasis in the 1990s on plan-led planning did not mean a return of strategic thinking about spatial organisation or a significant effort in developing integrated strategies for territorial development. Instead, it reinforced the significance of local translations of national policy criteria in containing the range of issues which could be considered when planning permit decisions were made.

Despite local variations, challenges and tensions, a distinctive regulatory regime thus emerged within the structure and practices of the English planning system. The contours of this regime were clearly visible by the end of the millennium. Its form and practices articulate well with neoliberal political philosophy. It builds on the assumption that development activity is a product of private initiative, a sign of entrepreneurship which contributes to economic growth. Such growth is taken to be the overriding 'public interest' objective. The role of the planning system is to regulate this activity merely to deal with the issue of the adverse impacts of development projects, the so-called 'social costs' of welfare economics. It is set apart from any proactive investment programmes (Hall, 1997).

Rather than there being systematic formal redesign, this regime has grown within the approach defined in the 1940s. The system configured in mid-century offered much potential institutional space for local interpretation. This space has been systematically reduced by the evolution of the criteria-driven regime. National government and the lobby groups to which it listens define what are acceptable 'social costs', subject to review in semi-judicial and judicial arenas. Despite continual challenge from the more assertive local authorities (Jones, 1996; Kitchen, 1997), this regulatory 'capture' of the discourses and arenas of the British planning system and its practices is now so deeply embedded that it has acquired the status of normal routine, the hegemonic frame of reference, the only way it can be. The marginalisation of planning system arenas in the reawakening of strategic spatial planning at the turn of the century is thus only partly due to the dominance of other players and policy communities. It is also a result of the distinctive internal evolution of the system itself.

Crisis in the regulatory regime

The tensions between this regime and the new politics of place, territory and region had reached a critical juncture by the end of the 1990s. The environmental policy agendas were impossible to contain in sectoral channels, despite the creation of an Environment Agency. They were linking to the transport and economic development agendas through the search for reducing the problems of road-based transport solutions (the 'new realism' agenda) and the attempts to restrict development opportunities to already developed land (the 'brownfield/greenfield' debates). The focus on urban revitalisation highlighted the importance of the qualities of places in cities (Urban Task Force, 1999), while the social exclusion agenda emphasised the significance of interrelating the ways governance impinged on people's life circumstances (Social Exclusion Unit, 1998). The metaphor of 'joined-up thinking' both identified the problem of sectoral 'departmentalism' and challenged it. As a result, those developing economic development policy agendas were forced to recognise the potential power of environmental and place politics. Many business interests were in any case themselves interested in the promotion of place qualities as part of an agenda of place marketing and for reasons connected with their own competitiveness.

Thus, by the end of the 1990s, the nationally driven, criteria-based, regulatory regime was encountering an emerging new politics. It is as yet unclear how, and how far, these new politics will evolve. The key elements of the policy agenda of this new politics of proactive, strategic spatial development are an emphasis on place quality; integrated approaches to policy initiatives; bringing civil society into partnership with governance, alongside business; reducing the democratic deficit through reducing the distance between citizen and governance; and decentralising governance, with more initiative in localities and regions. This agenda combines a specific interest in developing the qualities of territories with the broader aim of transforming local government from a service delivery conglomerate to a strategic enabling agency, a 'community leader' in partnership with its citizens and its firms (DETR, 1998i). This policy agenda represents a significant challenge to the criteria-driven regulatory regime as developed in the planning system in the 1990s. Inserting it into the practices of the planning system partly involves changing the policy criteria and giving more weight to locally developed criteria. But this would leave the despatialised, criteria-driven regulatory regime largely in place. By the end of the century, a strong argument was developing to promote a different kind of planning (Blowers, 1997; Hague, 1997, Worpole and Greenhalgh, 1999; Urban Task Force, 1999; Hall, 1998). This involves the recovery of a proactive, strategic, place-focused capacity of the kind which dominated planning practice in the 1950s and 1960s, linked to the new ideas of collaboration and partnership which evolved in the 1990s in the practices of urban regeneration, community development and local environmental policy (Healey, 1998a).

This suggests that the planning system faces two alternative futures. In the first, it maintains the momentum of the regulatory regime evolved over the past 20 years. It exists as a regulatory regime apart from the proactive strategies adopted in other areas of regional and local development policy. It operates through policy criteria articulated for types of development, at the national level, but with some local specification. It serves as a constraint on how these strategies evolve, demanding that the impacts of development initiatives on other concerns are adequately addressed. Conflicts are addressed 'down the line' through the medium of semi-judicial inquiries and the courts. The system becomes increasingly legalised in its culture and practices. In such situations, the formal planning system and its practices are experienced either as a blockage to strategic policy development or as a necessary process, but largely apart from the strategic work, an irritating regulatory by-line rather than a significant strategic tool.

We suggest, however, that this centralised and despatialised resolution of the balance between proactive development initiatives and assessing their impacts on other policy concerns has become increasingly unstable. It generates overload at the centre, as pressure groups lobby government ministers and contest planning policy principles. It turns the processes of approving development plans and producing planning permits into complex conflict resolution arenas. It fails to address increasingly vociferous concern about the qualities of places as ecosystems, business environments, places for living and symbolic spaces. It widens the 'democratic deficit', as people feel distanced from the opportunity to have their 'voice' to make a difference.

The alternative future for the planning system is to move its processes and arenas more centrally within the emerging practices of a strategic, proactive, integrated and place-focused regional and local governance. Already the attempt to reorient regional planning guidance provides an example of such a repositioning of arenas. The target is to re-shape the proactive agendas of the regional development agencies, the investment strategies of local transport plans, the management strategies of community plans and the regulatory machinery of the planning system. However, such a shift in direction does not merely require using the tools of the system in different ways. Any transformation will also require refashioning the thought worlds and practices of the system. In effect, the system's tools, competencies and practices need to co-evolve synergetically with the initiatives in building new forms of regional and local governance if they are to play a part in this alternative future. Unless this happens, the planning system as such will have only a limited role in reinvigorating place-focused policy agendas.

Building new trajectories

To summarise our argument, we have identified hesitant steps towards new strategically driven, place-focused approaches to regional and local development agendas, both in our cases and in recent initiatives encouraged by the New Labour administration. These are still relatively narrow and fragmented in their emphasis, with a tendency to wrap old agendas in a new rhetoric and to reconfigure existing relationships around new arenas. The arenas of the planning system are uncertainly positioned in relation to these evolutions. Nevertheless, there are many forces at work which are pushing in these new directions. The governance challenge is to build new strategic place-focused policy cultures and institutional capacities in regions and localities. What does this involve?

In this book, we have illustrated the complex social processes through which policy ideas are articulated and translated into specific practices in different organisational arenas. This has served to show how broad struggles over the form and role of regional and local governance are played out through a myriad of local initiatives and accommodations. Change in policy trajectories is never easy. As Hajer (1995) shows, new policy agendas need to discredit old ones and permeate the practices through which policy work gets done. It is not just a question of adopting new agendas, or of defining who does what, or of specifying legal requirements or even of selecting appropriate personnel to perform particular tasks, the 'hard infrastructure' of a policy system (Healey, 1997). Following our institutional perspective, we emphasise that changing a trajectory involves active work in developing the 'soft infrastructure', in building new institutional capacities (Healey, 1998b).

A key dimension of such capacity building, as we introduce in Chapter 2, concerns the thought worlds, the discourses, which shape the development and dissemination of policy agendas, providing the *intellectual capital* for new approaches. Over the years, sectoral policy communities with different languages and approaches to policy argumentation have evolved around sectoral agendas. Building a discourse which focuses on strategic considerations about the qualities of places requires a different language and frame of reference.

This new discourse needs to focus on the qualities of places and the complex interactions between social life, business worlds and ecosystems. It requires a sensitivity to, and understanding of, multiple levels of interaction, from the fine-grained dimensions of specific ecosystems and neighbourhoods to the broad patterns of movement across regional space and the culturally significant identities of places at all levels. In 'multiplex' urban regions (Graham and Healey, 1999), where all kinds of relations transect a place, interacting to various degrees, the old models of functionally integrated urban regions provide little guidance. A key point to emerge in the consultation processes over the new ideas about regional planning guidance in 1998 was that there was little experience of how to conceptualise sociospatial dynamics at the level of the urban region. The store of experience of the 1960s was either lost or was inappropriate to the conditions of the late 1990s. This implies that a key investment for a place-focused strategic approach to planning will be the development and dissemination of a new language for discussing the spatiality of the dynamics of places. Experience from elsewhere in Europe, less affected by the despatialised criteria-driven approach, will provide valuable resources for this effort (CEU, 1997; Healey *et al.*, 1997b). But unless this new discourse is actively developed in such a way as to surround and rework the principles used in regulatory activity, the new trajectory will have little effect on the established discourse of land use regulation.

A second dimension of such capacity building has been very evident in the accounts in this book. A proactive, place-focused strategic planning will involve building new relationships, reconstituting 'policy communities', with different memberships and different forms of involvement. Horizontal articulation between a range of stakeholders with a concern for a place will need to at least complement, and possibly displace, the vertical relationships of the criteria-driven approach. Through these relationships, if they develop real strength and are sustained over time, a new kind of place-focused *social capital* should be generated. Already, as we have shown, there has been a steady evolution of such place-based networks and alliances during the 1990s. The demands of project funders, particularly the Single Regeneration Budget and the European Union, with their emphasis on partnership and involvement of the community, have encouraged this evolution. The new 'modern local government' agenda promotes this even further (DETR, 1998i). Nevertheless, there was ambiguity in government advice in the late 1990s. For example, on the one hand, planners were exhorted to produce plans and make planning decisions quickly, in the interests of regulatory efficiency. On the other, they were encouraged to involve more stakeholders in policy development (DETR, 1998a, 1998b, 1999a). Drawing new stakeholders into policy processes is no easy matter, as all the literature on partnership shows clearly (Hastings, 1996; Oatley, 1998; Worpole and Greenhalgh, 1999). It requires the development of commitment, understanding and trust among groups which are often mutually suspicious and divided by a history of unequal access to material and political resources. It involves moving beyond the traditional 'public participation in planning' concepts (Cullingworth and Nadin, 1994) to embrace a commitment to an interactive relationship between the state, citizen and business (Healey, 1997). How the arenas of the planning system become involved in this reconfiguration of regional and local governance will provide evidence of which of its pathways into the future becomes dominant.

Finally, local groupings and alliances will need to develop capabilities in mobilising to promote the qualities of places. Already there are signs of this emerging in many areas, as with the City Pride initiatives, the London First initiative, and the alliances described in Chapter 3. The result is the emergence of a 'voice' for place-focused policies and a demand for institutional space within which such an approach can flourish (Worpole and Greenhalgh, 1999; Urban Task Force, 1999). The proposals for mayors to govern cities in London and elsewhere are evidence of such concern. This could generate a store of *political capital* to be drawn upon to sustain place-based strategic approaches. But this place-focused politics will have to work hard to counteract the continuing pressure on national government to control the regulatory machinery of the planning system. What the outcome will be is likely to vary significantly from one region and locality to another. Subnational governance is thus entering an era of experimentation and institutional invention, in which different trajectories could emerge. How then should these be evaluated?

Evaluating evolutions in place-focused planning

As the momentum for more place-focused governance got under way at the end of the 1990s, there was increasing recognition that its contribution and impact would depend substantially on its institutional design and the practices that evolve within it. For example, the tendency towards 'partnership governance' could merely allow major business interests to dominate local agendas more effectively than they would achieve through national planning policy criteria. Will the new regional agencies develop a more coherent form of local corporatism than was emerging in the West Midlands in the 1990s? Will the environmental impetus evident in Lancashire and Kent get squeezed out? Will 'NIMBYism' prevail in some localities, resulting in social injustice and environmental strains elsewhere in territories? Will the environmental policy debate promoted so vigorously during the 1990s be sidelined because its challenge to business growth strategies will become too obvious? Will the new 'social' agenda proceed in isolation from economic and environmental concerns? Will regional and local elites constrain demands from different sections of civil society to have a say in the governance of their local environments? Will the concerns of minorities be sidelined and the potential for their oppression by majorities be exacerbated by a more localised governance? Will the chances of corrupt practice in insider dealing in land transactions and granting planning permits be increased by a more localist planning approach?

Such tendencies always exist as potentials in local and regional governance forms. If the policy objective is to promote proactive, strategic territorial development, which integrates sectoral policy concerns as they affect on places, and which encourages inclusionary governance practices, the issue for institutional design is how to limit their emergence. The task for the critical analyst is to identify what encourages and what inhibits the emergence of broadly based, integrative and inclusionary local and regional governance. The task for the policy adviser is to identify practices which encourage moves in such directions. The tools of institutionalist analysis used in this book, – policy discourses, communities and arenas – help to focus such critical attention.

Evaluating evolutions: policy discourses

It is not just at the level of specific knowledge that the discourses of strategic spatial planning need to change. What is required is shifts in underlying frames of reference. Specifically, a refocusing of attention on spatial dynamics is needed, perceived from the multiple points of view of different stakeholders. This involves developing conceptions of the ways to integrate social, economic and environmental dimensions of issues as they have an impact on the evolution of the qualities of particular places. It will involve reinterpreting, from multiple points of view, conceptions of the scale of place relations and effects. The struggle identified in Chapter 8 between the discourse of economic competitiveness and environmental protection will have to be addressed strategically, rather than being worked out on a case-by-case basis, as in the criteria-driven regulatory regime. This will reveal tensions both within each discourse and with other dimensions of place which could be brought into consideration. A critical ingredient for the development of such a strategic spatial discourse will be a deep base of formalised knowledge, rich in linkages to experiential knowledge in and about a locality, coupled with an imaginative capability to conceive of new possibilities and pathways.

The discourses around environmental sustainability and the 'sustainable city' (Jenks *et al.*, 1996; Haughton and Hunter, 1994) and about the 'wired city' in a 'virtual world' (Kelly, 1994; Castells, 1996; Graham and Marvin, 1996) already provide fruitful resources for imagining futures. The revived debate about recovering 'urbanity' and creating 'livable cities' also aims to re-imagine the futures of places (Urban Task Force, 1999, Worpole and Greenhalgh, 1999). But there are major tensions within and between these debates. The embracing concept of 'sustainable development', much used by the planning policy community by the end of the 1990s, implies that economic competitiveness can be combined with objectives of sustainable stewardship of environmental resources. This has been identified as a discourse of *ecological modernisation* (Blowers, 1997; Davoudi, 1998; Hajer, 1995). An alternative position, drawing on Beck's discussion of a *risk society* (Beck, 1992), sees the potential for fundamental conflicts between current economic modes of production and the sustainability of environmental relationships. This approach, and others like it, challenges the discourse of economic competitiveness with its assumptions of the benefits of economic growth per se. The risk society discourse displaces this principle with a concern for risk limitation. This latter discourse links to the new urban agenda, with its emphasis on quality of life. But this too can be considered in different ways. On the one hand, it can be treated in terms of place-related assets which need to be acquired or retained to provide quality of life, assessed with a technology of indicators and benchmarks. This could lead to an approach which harks back to notions of universal entitlement, and a politics of resource distribution to ensure every locale had its share of facilities. Alternatively, quality of life could be approached through the lens of both daily life patterns and diversity of lifestyles and life opportunities. In this approach, quality of life is not captured merely in assets available to people: it resides in how people feel about their 'place', their immediate living environment and their locality; it links qualities of places to identity formation, for individuals and for communities.

This opens up yet further dilemmas. Firstly, there is no guarantee that the images of 'sustainable cities' or of 'cosmopolitan urbanity' promoted by communities of professional experts and activists connect to the was different citizens value their localities and dream of futures. There is much evidence that people are suspicious of such concepts, as the products of elite policy agendas, disconnected from their own lives (Macnagthen *et al.*, 1995; Harrison and Burgess, 1994). Secondly, if more power becomes available to develop policy agendas locally, the outcomes could compromise values held by other localities, as well as EU and national policy goals. They could also oppress minority groups within a locality. The dangers of US-style 'exclusionary zoning' are well known. There is increasing realisation of the way 'environmental bads' are cleared out of wealthy localities and dumped on poorer locales (Blowers and Evans, 1997). Within Britain, there are also examples, especially in rural areas, where long-established local networks run local politics and see the planning system as a way of controlling development opportunities for themselves (Tewdwr-Jones, 1995). The result is scattered development in the countryside. Both dilemmas emphasise that the development of place-focused discourses may need formalised power to maintain a multivocal and multi-level perspective, while asserting the distinctive qualities of particular places as valued by people with significant stakes in them.

Evaluating evolutions: policy processes

A key quality of rich and multivocal policy discourses is that politicians and officials break out of the tramlines of established policy communities to recognise and respect the mobilising capacity available in civil society (Douglas and Friedmann, 1998; Hirst, 1994). Their development demands policy processes with a capacity to facilitate debates,

and translate these into strategies and policy practices, without impos-
ing too much of their own filtering conceptions (Muller and Surel,
1998; Healey, 1997). As new governance practices and local politics
evolve into the next century, it is clear that a major struggle is under
way between forces which would maintain the patterns of paternalism
and professionalism inherited from the welfare state era of mid-century,
and the new forms of local business alliance, a proto-local corporatism,
which have developed in recent years (Hull, 1998b). This is a struggle
not merely over who has power and influence, but over the processes
and style of governance. It represents a major challenge for many local
politicians, who see themselves already as 'representatives of the
people' and hence as embodying appropriate perspectives on issues. It
is also a challenge for many local authority officers, who have seen
themselves as working away 'on behalf of' local communities for many
years. If politicians and officers cannot change, it will be hard for all
the other stakeholders to locate their own specific conceptions within a
frame of reference where debates about different values and identities
can be held. Such debates also have to be open in their style, to avoid
capture by powerful interest groups lobbying behind the scenes, or
activist single-issue pressure groups who may seek to control agendas
and drown out other voices. This means, in effect, the evolution of new
kinds of citizen–state relations.

The problem for British local governance is that its traditions and
recent history inhibit the development of such relationships. Political
domination, adversarial politics, professional monopoly, corporatist
practices and pressure group politics are, in contrast, well-developed. It
will therefore be hard to develop the institutional relationships which
will allow a rich and multivocal place-focused politics to flourish. But
this difficulty should not be taken to mean that such a politics cannot be
achieved. Much of the discussion about local governance at the end of
the century is focused on overcoming the 'democratic deficit' and
bringing civil society and governance more closely together (Hutton,
1995; Mulgan, 1994; Hirst, 1994). These ideas have filtered quite
strongly into the 'modern local government' agenda (DETR, 1998i).
Developing the practices of multivocal place-focused strategy formation could provide a powerful means of innovating new relationships.
Efforts in proactive, place-focused, integrative planning should then be
evaluated according to the extent and manner in which they break away
from networks of the 'usual suspects', and open up new channels of
interaction between state, citizen and business firm.

Designing the 'hard infrastructure' to foster new discourses and processes

Given the continuing power of old sectoral policy agendas and practices, and the dangers inherent in a new 'localism', some attention is also needed to formal structures, the 'hard infrastructure' of institutional design. The regional development agencies have already been created, entrenching a sectoral mode of policy development, but responsibility for regional planning remained unclear in late 1999 (DETR, 1999a). A number of changes are desirable to the planning system itself, including the withdrawal of national government from persistent intervention in local planning decisions on plans and permits, the adoption of a more active national role in promoting research and more attention to the analysis of the dynamics of spatial change in urban regions. There also need to be changes in the resourcing and powers of local government, to provide more local and regional autonomy, particularly as regards local charges and taxes. However, some other 'hard infrastructure' changes would also be helpful to encourage local and regional governance activity to expand agendas, enlarge networks, include more stakeholders and avoid exclusionary practices.

In reviewing the formal institutional design of governance systems, more attention should be given to four issues: the nature and distribution of rights and duties, the control and distribution of resources, the specification of criteria for redeeming challenges to 'public interest' decisions, and the distribution of competencies (Healey, 1997). Some formal change is desirable in each of these areas to foster a multivocal place-focused politics. Rights to challenge decisions need to be widened to allow third parties to contest regulatory decisions about development projects. Public powers to require a strategic link between public investment decisions and regulatory decisions need to be strengthened. New criteria to challenge 'public interest' decisions need to be specified.

Perhaps the most obvious change is to limit the wide-ranging powers of national government in the planning system. In the criteria-driven regulatory process, local planning authorities are constructed as implementors of national policy. Such a conception was an increasing reality across the spectrum of local government activity in the 1980s and 1990s (King and Stoker, 1996). In continental European planning systems, in contrast, the national government tends to specify the tools available for local governments to use (as in zoning categories or development mechanisms) (CEU, 1997). In other areas of environmental regulation, national and EU legislation specifies procedures (such as environmental assessment) or standards to be achieved. A stronger local and regional government in Britain implies greater autonomy for local government. As a consequence, there should be less need for national policy on specific planning issues. The only cases where this might apply will be in relation to genuinely national or international issues which could not be dealt with regionally, such as airport capacity and development or the promotion of some aspects of trans-European transport networks. A valuable role for national government could also be in the specification of complex technical issues. Even more important is the role of national and regional government in asserting policy principles which express moral values about distributional justice and moral limits. However, if these are expressed in the language of specific targets and indicators, they will tend to drown out a multivocal place-politics. It is hard for policy groups in particular places to work out how to interrelate other people's targets with the material and symbolic realities of 'their' places. Instead, place-based policy communities should be obligated to show that they have paid attention to national principles in reasonable and fair-minded ways.

There remains an important role for national policy in encouraging effective linkages between investment and regulatory decisions. This is the point where policy ideas lever on the specification of rules and the allocation of resources. This requirement would need to be supported by rights to challenge decisions made. But whether the concern is to promote strategic, territorial integration, or specific policy objectives such as encouraging 'brownfield' development, or avoiding 'environmental injustice', the key impact of such 'hard infrastructure' changes is to affect the 'reasoning' or 'argumentation' of the policy system. This is where the administrative discretion in the institutional design of the planning system has great merit. It encourages the 'reasoned justification' of policies and permit decisions. The emphasis on 'reasoning' is not merely an appeal to logic and scientific rationality. It also draws on British legal traditions of 'reasonable judgement'. If a policy is made reasonably, both in argumentation and process, then the courts will uphold it. National policy could help to encourage strategic thinking about territorial development, pursued in a place-focused, integrative and multivocal way, by shaping local 'reasoning processes'. Local and regional authorities could be required to show, in bids for funds, in strategy documents, in funding criteria and in regulatory principles, how economic, environmental and sociocultural dimensions of localities had been examined and interrelated. They could be expected to demonstrate how a full range of stakeholders had been considered and, as far as practicable, involved in decision processes, with an emphasis on interactive involvement as opposed to passive consultation. They could also be encouraged to show how formalised knowledge and experiential knowledge had been drawn upon in the policy development process. Such an approach to national policy principles for territorial development, especially if coupled with a more equitable distribution of rights to challenge local policy decisions and an independent inquiry process, would have a substantial impact on developing a more influential, multivocal and richly reasoned local politics of place.

A new local politics of place

This book has provided accounts of efforts to evolve spatial strategies in subnational territories in Britain in the last years of the twentieth century. These efforts have proved difficult to develop and sustain, and have tended to be narrow in their policy agendas and in those who have got involved. Despite the very evident pressures for a stronger spatial focus to local and regional policy agendas, these policy arenas have been heavily constrained by national policy discourses and policy communities oriented to national politics and policy priorities. The arenas of the land use planning system have been a significant carrier of such constraints, narrowing policy agenda into channels set by national policy. Nevertheless, the 'hard infrastructure' of the design of the system includes consultation and inquiry processes which create the potential for challenges to sectoral policy agendas and allow other voices to exercise some influence. The flexibility in the system, provided by the principle of administrative discretion in the making of judgements, is also an asset, in that it has allowed the system to evolve to adjust to new circumstances. Changes are already happening in other policy communities. A wave of experimentation is going on, drawing on initiatives which managed to evolve in the 1980s and 1990s (such as Local Agenda 21, urban regeneration partnerships, village appraisals and neighbourhood planning) as well responding to the encouragement from the 'modern local government' agenda.

The challenge for the British planning system in the first decade of the new century is to shift the inherited institutional infrastructure from the trajectory into which it had been channelled by the end of the twentieth century into a richer, more place-focused, more future-oriented and more localised form. There is no doubt that this will require a deep transformative effort. But the opportunities for such an effort to succeed are much more favourable in the new millennium than they were in the 1980s and 1990s. It is not only that there are broad social and economic forces which emphasise the significance of place qualities. Such a transformation also fits well with contemporary efforts to develop a new kind of politics and a new kind of governance, in which the forces of civil society as well as those of business interest collaborate to shape what governance does, reducing the distance between government and people. Rather than the politics of paternalism, as pursued by the welfare state framework, or of titanic ideological struggle, as advocated in the twentieth-century language of class conflict, this new politics emphasises multiple opportunities, threats and struggles, played out over the qualities of life circumstances and of the values held by different people in specific places (Sandercock, 1998; Healey, 1997). Transformed into a proactive, place-focused and integrative policy system, with a rich knowledge base, a multi-vocal policy community and inclusive policy arenas, the planning system could play a major part in providing opportunities for the evolution of the practices of such a politics. Left as it is, the system not only inhibits such developments, it compromises the ability to achieve, both locally and nationally, the declared objectives of governance of our time, a sustainable and socially just combination of economic vitality, social cohesion and environmental quality.

References

Adams, D. (1994) *Urban Planning and the Development Process,* London: UCL Press.

Adams, D. Russell, L. and Taylor-Russell, C. (1994) *Land for Industrial Development,* London: E and FN Spon.

Adams, T. (1996) 'Gridlock in Waste Planning', *Waste Planning,* Vol. 18, March, pp.3–5.

Agranoff, R. (1990) 'Frameworks for Comparative Analysis of Intergovernmental Relations', School of Public and Environmental Affairs Occasional Paper 26, University of Indiana, Indiana.

Altshuler, A. (1965) *The City Planning Process: a political analysis,* Ithaca, New York: Cornell University Press

Ambrose, P. (1986) *Whatever happened to planning?,* London: Methuen

Ambrose, P. and Colenutt, B. (1973) *The Property Machine,* Harmondsworth: Penguin.

Amin, A. (ed.) (1994) *Post-Fordism: A Reader,* Oxford: Blackwell

Amin, A. and Thrift, N. (1995) 'Globalisation, "institutional thickness" and the local economy', in P. Healey *et al.* (eds), *Managing Cities,* London: John Wiley.

Amin, A. and Thrift, N. (eds), (1994) *Globalisation, Institutions and Regional Development,* Oxford: Oxford University Press.

Asheim, B. (1996) 'Industrial Districts as "learning regions": a condition for prosperity?', *European Planning Studies,* Vol. 4 (3), pp.379–400.

Ashford Borough Council (1993) 'Ashford Local Plan Second Review: Proposed Modifications', Ashford.

Atkinson, R. and Moon, G. (1994) *Urban policy in Britain: the city, the state and the market,* Macmillan: London.

Axford, N. (1994) 'Documenting recent trends in industrial property investment: the information requirements of the private sector from a practitioner perspective', in R. Ball, and A. Pratt (eds) *Industrial property: policy and economic development,* London: Routledge.

Ball, M. (1983) *Housing Policy and Economic Power,* London: Methuen.

Ball, R. and Pratt A. (eds) (1994) *Industrial property: policy and economic development,* London: Routledge.

Ball, R.M. (1995) *Local authorities and regional policy in the UK: attitudes, representations and the local economy,* London: Paul Chapman.

Barrett, S. and Fudge, C. (eds) (1981) *Policy and Action,* London: Methuen.

Bartlett, W., Bramley, G. and Lambert, C. (1996) *Planning, the market and private housebuilding,* London: UCL Press.

Bathos, W.J.S. and Mumford, D.J. (1994) *Kent Structure Plan third review, report of the Examination in Public panel, Volume 1,* Maidstone: Kent County Council.

Bauman, Z. (1992) *Intimations of postmodernity,* London: Routledge.

Beck, U. (1992) *Risk Society: Towards a New Modernity,* London: Sage.

Belussi, F. (1996) 'Local systems, industrial districts and institutional networks: towards a new evolutionary paradigm of industrial economics?', *European Planning Studies,* vol. 4 (3), pp.5–26.

Birmingham City Council (1990a) 'Draft Birmingham UDP: Public Consultation Document', Birmingham: BCC.

Birmingham City Council (1990b) 'Submission to UDP Inquiry', BCC, unpublished.

Birmingham City Council (1989) 'Birmingham UDP: Overall Direction Paper', Birmingham: BCC.

Bishop, J. (1998) 'Re-inventing Planning 3: Collaboration and Consensus', *Town and Country Planning,* vol. 67 (3), pp.111–113.

Black, A. (1990) 'The Chicago Area Transportation Study', *Journal of Planning, Education and Research,* vol. 10, (1), pp.27–38.

Blowers, A. (1997) 'Society and Sustainability: the context of change for planning', in A. Blowers and B. Evans (eds), *Town Planning into the 21st Century,* London: Routledge.

Blowers, A. and Evans, B. (eds) (1997) *Town Planning into the 21st Century,* London: Routledge.

Booth, P. (1996) *Controlling Development,* London: UCL Press.

Bourdieu, P. (1977) *Outline of a Theory of Practice,* Cambridge: Cambridge University Press.

Boyer, C. (1983) *Dreaming the Rational City,* Cambridge, Mass.: MIT Press.

Boyer, R. (1990) *The Regulation School: a critical introduction,* New York: Columbia University Press.

Bradbury, J. and Mawson, J. (1997) *British regionalism and devolution: the challenges of state reform and European integration,* London: Jessica Kingsley.

Breheny, M. (1992) 'The compact city: an introduction', *Built Environment,* vol. 18 (4), pp.241–6.

Breheny, M. and Hall, P. (1996) *The People: Where will they go?,* London: Town and Country Planning Association.

Brindley, T., Rydin, Y. and Stoker, G. (1989) *Remaking Planning: the politics of urban change in the Thatcher years,* London: Unwin Hyman.

Bruton, M. and Nicholson, D. (1987) *Local Planning in Practice,* London: Hutchinson.

Bryson, J. and Crosby, B. (1992) *Leadership in the Common Good,* San Francisco: Jossey Bass.

Callon, M. (1986) 'Some elements of a sociology of translation', in J. Law, (ed.) *Power, action and belief,* London: Routledge & Kegan Paul.

Camagni, R. (ed.) (1991) *Innovation Networks: spatial perspectives,* London: Belhaven Press.

Castells, M. (1996) *The Rise of the Network Society,* Oxford: Blackwell.

Castells, M. (1977) *The Urban Question,* London: Edward Arnold.

Champion, T. (1996) 'Migration to, from and within the United Kingdom', *Population Trends*, vol. 83, pp.3–16.

Cockburn, C. (1977) *The Local State,* London: Pluto Press.

Cole, A. and John, P. (1995) 'Models of local decision-making networks in Britain and France', *Policy and Politics*, vol. 23 (4), pp.303–12.

Coleman, J. (1988) 'Social Capital and the Creation of Human Capital', *American Journal of Sociology,* vol. 94, S95-S120.

Commission of European Communities (1989) *EC Strategy on Waste Management*, CEC (89) 934, Luxembourg: CEC.

Commission for the European Union: Regional Policy Directorate (CEU) (1997) *The EU Compendium of Spatial Planning Systems and Policies,* Brussels: European Commission.

Committee for Spatial Development (CSD) (1998) 'European Spatial Development Perspective', as presented to a meeting of ministers, Glasgow, June.

Coopers and Lybrand (1985) *Land Use Planning and the Housing Market,* London: DoE.

Council for the Protection of Rural England (CPRE) (1999) 'Plan, Monitor and Manage: Making it Work', London: CPRE.

Council for the Protection of Rural England (CPRE) (1998a) *House of Cards,* London: CPRE.

Council for the Protection of Rural England (1998b) *New Money for Old Roads*, London: CPRE.

Council for the Protection of Rural England (1997) *Waste and the Countryside*, London: CPRE.

Council for the Protection of Rural England (1996) *At the Crossroads: Investing in Sustainable Local Transport*, London: CPRE.

Cox, K. and Johnston, R. (eds) (1982) *Conflict, politics and the urban scene,* Harlow: Longman.

Critchley, P. and Smith, E. (1995) '*Lancashire Structure Plan 1991–2006',* *Examination in Public May 1995: Report of the Panel,* submitted to Lancashire County Council, Preston.

Cross, D.C. and Bristow, R. (eds) (1983) *English Structure Planning,* London: Pion.

Crozier, M. (1964) *The Bureaucratic Phenomenon,* Chicago: University of Chicago Press.

Cullingworth, J.B. (1997) 'British land-use planning: a failure to cope with change', *Urban Studies,* vol. 34 (5), pp.945–60.

Cullingworth, J.B. (1993) *The Political Culture of Planning,* London: Routledge.

Cullingworth, J.B. (1975) *Reconstruction and land use planning, 1939–1947: Environmental History Vol. 1,* London: HMSO.

Cullingworth, J.B. (1964) *Town and Country Planning in Britain,* 1st edn, London: George Allen & Unwin.

Cullingworth J.B. and Nadin, V. (1994) *Town and Country Planning in Britain,* London: Routledge.

Davoudi, S. (1999) 'A Quantum Leap for Planners', *Town and Country Planning,* vol. 68(1), pp.20–24.

Davoudi, S. (1998) 'New Directions for Planning Systems and Planning Education', Paper presented at 12th AESOP Congress, Aviero (Portugal) 21–4 July.

Davoudi, S. (1997) 'Environmental Considerations in Minerals Planning, Theory versus Practice', in D. Borrie, A. Khakee, and C. Lacirignola (eds), *Evaluating Theory–Practice and Urban–Rural Interplay in Planning,* Dordrecht: Kluwer Academic Publisher.

Davoudi, S., Hull, A.D. and Healey, P. (1996) 'Environmental concerns and economic imperatives in strategic plan making', *Town Planning Review,* vol. 67 (4), pp.421–36.

Dear, M. (1995) 'Prolegomena to a post-modern urbanism', in P. Healey, S.J. Cameron, S. Davoudi, S. Graham and A. Madanipour (eds), *Managing Cities,* London: John Wiley.

Department of the Environment (DoE) (1997) *Planning Policy Guidance 1 (revised): General Policy and Principles,* London: HMSO.

Department of the Environment (1996a) *Regional Planning Guidance for the North West, RPG13,* London: HMSO.

Department of the Environment (1996b) *Speeding up the delivery of local plans and UDPs,* London: DoE.

Department of the Environment (1996c) *Planning Policy Guidance Note 6: Town Centres and Retail Development,* London: HMSO.

Department of the Environment (1996d) *Revision of PPG23 Planning and Pollution Control, Consultation Draft,* London: DoE.

Department of the Environment (1996e) *Household Growth: Where shall we live?* Cmnd 3471, London: The Stationery Office.

Department of the Environment (1995a) *Regional Planning Guidance for the West Midlands, RPG11,* London: HMSO.

Department of the Environment (1995b) *Making Waste Work: The UK Strategy for Sustainable Waste Management,* London: HMSO.

Department of the Environment (1995c) *Regional Planning Guidance Note 9a: The Thames Gateway Planning Framework,* London: HMSO.

Department of the Environment (1994a) *Regional Planning Guidance Note 9; Regional planning guidance for the South East,* London: HMSO.

Department of the Environment (1994b) *Planning Policy Guidance Note 23: Planning and Pollution Control,* London: HMSO.

Department of the Environment (1992a) *Planning Policy Guidance Note One: General Policy and Principles,* London: HMSO.

Department of the Environment (1992b) *Planning Policy Guidance 4: Industrial and Commercial Development and Small Firms,* London: HMSO.

Department of the Environment (1992c) *Planning Policy Guidance Note 3: Housing,* London: HMSO.

Department of the Environment (1992d) *Waste Management Paper No 1: A Review of Options,* London: HMSO.

Department of the Environment (1988a) *Planning Policy Guidance 1: General Policy and Principles,* London: HMSO.

Department of the Environment (1988b) *Planning Policy Guidance 4: Industrial and Commercial Development and Small Firms,* London: HMSO.

Department of the Environment (1988c) *Planning Policy Guidance 10: Strategic Guidance for the West Midlands* London: HMSO.

Department of the Environment (1986) *The Future of Development Plans*, London: HMSO.

Department of the Environment (1985) *Circular 14/85: Development and the Environment* London: HMSO.

Department of the Environment/Department of Transport (1994) *Planning Policy Guidance Note 13: Transport* (revised), London: HMSO.

Department of the Environment, Transport and the Regions (DETR) (1999a) 'Planning Policy Guidance Note 11: Regional Planning. Public Consultation Draft', London: DETR.

Department of the Environment, Transport and the Regions (1999b) *A better quality of life: a strategy for sustainable development for the UK*, London: The Stationery Office.

Department of the Environment, Transport and the Regions (1998a) *Modernising the Planning System,* London: HMSO.

Department of the Environment, Transport and the Regions (1998b) 'The Future of Regional Planning Guidance', Consultation Paper, London: DETR.

Department of the Environment, Transport and the Regions (1998c) *Transport: a new deal for everyone*, Cmnd 3950, London: HMSO.

Department of the Environment, Transport and the Regions (1998d) *Building Partnerships for prosperity*, Consultation Paper on Regional Development Agencies, London: HMSO.

Department of the Environment, Transport and the Regions (1998e) *Less Waste More Value, Consultation Paper on the Waste Strategy for England and Wales*, London: HMSO.

Department of the Environment, Transport and the Regions (1998f) *Draft Planning Policy Guidance Note 10: Waste Disposal and Management,* London: HMSO.

Department of the Environment, Transport and the Regions (1998g) *Digest of Environmental Statistics,* London: The Stationery Office.

Department of the Environment, Transport and the Regions (1998h) *Planning for the Communities of the Future*, Cmnd 3885, London: The Stationery Office.

Department of the Environment, Transport and the Regions (1998i) *Modern Local Government: in touch with people* London: HMSO.

Department of the Environment, Transport and the Regions (1998j) *Planning for Sustainable Development: Towards Better Practice*, London: The Stationery Office.

Department of the Environment, Transport and the Regions (1998k) *Breaking the logjam: The Government's consultation paper on fighting traffic congestion and pollution through road user and workplace parking charges,* London:HMSO.

Department of the Environment, Transport and the Regions (1998l) *Transport Statistics*, London: The Stationery Office.

Department of Transport (1989) *Roads for Prosperity*, London: HMSO.

Douglass, M. (1987) *How institutions think,* London: Routledge.

Douglass, M. and Friedmann, J. (eds) (1998) *Cities for Citizens,* London: John Wiley.

Drake, M., McLoughlin, J.B., Thompson, R. and Thornley, J. (1975) *Aspects of Structure Planning,* London: Centre for Environmental Studies.

Dunleavy, P. and O'Leary, B. (1987) *Theories of the State,* London: Macmillan.

Dyrberg, T.B. (1997) *The Circular Structure of Power,* London: Verso.

Edelman M. (1977) *Political language: words that succeed and politics that fail,* New York: Institute for the Study of Poverty.

Eden, C. (1996) 'The Stakeholder Collaborator Strategy Workshop' in C. Huxhan (ed.), *'Creating Collaborative Advantage,* London: Sage.

Edwards, J. (1997) 'Urban policy: the victory of form over substance', *Urban Studies,* vol. 34 (5), pp.825–43.

Elkin, S. (1974) *Politics and land use planning: the London experience,* Cambridge: Cambridge University Press.

Elson, M. (1986) *Green Belts: Conflict Mediation in the Urban Fringe,* London: Heinemann.

Esping-Anderson, G. (1990) *The three worlds of welfare capitalism,* Cambridge: Polity Press.

Evans, B. (1995) *Experts and Environmental Planning,* Aldershot: Avebury.

Fainstein, N. and Fainstein, S. (eds) (1986) *Restructuring the City,* New York: Longman.

Fairclough, N. (1995) *Critical Discourse Analysis: the critical study of language,* London: Longman.

Faludi, A. (1996) 'Framing with images', *Environment and Planning B: Planning and Design,* vol. 23, pp.93–108.

Faludi, A. and van der Walk, A. 1994, *Rule and Order,* Dordrecht: Kluwer Academic Publishing.

Feagin, J. (1988) *Free Enterprise City,* New Brunswick: Rutgers.

Flyvberg, B. (1998) *Rationality and Power,* Chicago: University of Chicago Press.

Forester J. (1993) *Critical theory, public policy and planning practice,* Albany: State University of New York Press.

Forester, J. (1989) *Planning in the Face of Power,* Berkeley, California: University of California Press.

Fothergill, S., Monk, S. and Perry, M. (1987) *Property and Industrial Development,* London:Hutchinson.

Friedmann, J. (1987) *Planning in the public domain,* Princeton: Princeton University Press.

Friend, J., Power, J. and Yewlett, C. (1974) *Public policy: the intercorporate dimension,* London: Tavistock.

Fukuyama, F. (1995) *Trust: The Social Virtues and the Creation of Prosperity,* New York: Free Press.

Gamble, A. (1988) *The Free Economy and the Strong State,* London: Macmillan.

Gandy, M. (1997) 'The making of a regulatory crisis: restructuring New York City's water supply', *Transactions of the Institute of British Geographers,* vol. 22, pp.338–58.

Gandy, M. (1994) *Recycling and the Politics of Urban Waste*, London: Earthscan.

Gatenby, I. and Williams, C. (1996) 'Interpreting planning law', in M. Tewdwr-Jones (ed.), *Planning Practice in Transition*, London: UCL Press.

Geertz C. (1983) *Local knowledge: further essays in interpretive anthropology*, New York: Basic Books.

Gibbs, D., Longhurst, J. and Braithwaite, C. (1996) 'Moving towards sustainable development? Integrating economic development and the environment in local authorities', *Journal of Planning and Environmental Management*, vol. 39 (3), pp.317–32.

Giddens, A. (1990) *The Consequences of Modernity*, Cambridge: Polity Press.

Giddens, A. (1984) *The Constitution of Society*, Cambridge: Polity Press.

Goldsmith, M. (ed.) (1986) *New Research in Central–Local Relations*, Aldershot: Gower.

Goodchild, B. (1992) 'Land Allocation for Housing: A Review of Practice and Possibilities in England', *Housing Studies*, vol. 7 (1), pp.45–55.

Goodwin, M. and Painter, J. (1997) 'Concrete research, urban regimes and regulation theory', in M. Lauria (ed.), *Reconstructing Urban Regime Theory*, Thousand Oaks, California: Sage.

Goodwin, M., Duncan, S. and Halford, S. (1993) 'Regulation theory, the local state and the transition of urban politics', *Environment and Planning D: Society and Space*, vol. 11, pp.67–88.

Goodwin, P. (1997) 'Solving congestion', Inaugral professorial lecture, University College London.

Goodwin, P. (1996) 'Road traffic growth and the dynamics of sustainable transport policies', in B. Cartledge (ed.), *Transport and the Environment*, Oxford: Oxford University Press.

Goodwin, P., Hallett, S., Kenny, F. and Stokes, G. (1991) 'Transport: The New Realism', Report to the Rees Jeffreys Road Fund, University of Oxford Transport Studies Unit, Oxford.

Government Office for the North West/Government Office for Merseyside (1995) *Draft Regional Planning Guidance for the North West Region*, London: HMSO.

Government Office for the South East (1996) *Regional Planning Guidance Note 9a: The Thames Gateway Planning Framework*, London: HMSO.

Government Office for the South East (1994) *RPG9: Regional Planning Guidance for the South East*, London: HMSO.

Government Office for the West Midlands (1995) *RPG11: Regional Planning Guidance for the West Midlands Region*, Birmingham: GOWM.

Government Office for the West Midlands (1994) *Draft Regional Planning Guidance: For the West Midlands*, Birmingham: GOWM.

Graham S.D.N. and Healey, P. (1999) 'Relational concepts of place and space: issues for planning theory and practice', *European Planning Studies*, vol. 7 (5), pp.623–646.

Graham, S.D.N. and Marvin, S. (1996) *Telecommunications and the City*, London: Routledge.

Granovetter, M. (1985) 'Economic action and social structure: the problem of embeddedness', *American Journal of Sociology*, vol. 91 (3), pp.481–510.

Grant, W. and McNamara, A. (1995) 'When policy communities intersect – the case of agriculture and banking', *Political Studies,* vol. 43 (3), pp.509–15.

Green Futures (1998) 'Do We Really Need Waste Incineration?', January/February, pp.19–21.

Greenhalgh, P. and Turner, E. (1997) 'A sustainable Strategy for Waste: the Latest Advice of SERPLAN', *Waste Planning,* vol. 23, June, pp.3–6.

Grove-White, R. (1991) 'Land, the Law and Environment', *Journal of Law and Society,* vol. 18 (1), pp.32–47.

Gualini, E. (1998) 'Perspectives on consensus-building in territorial policies: towards a research-and-action agenda', paper to Association of European Schools of Planning Congress, University of Aveiro, 22–5 July.

Hague, C. (1997) 'Town Planning into the 21st Century: diverse worlds and common themes', in A. Blowers and B. Evans (eds), *Town Planning into the 21st Century,* London: Routledge.

Hajer, M. (1995) *The politics of environmental discourse,* Oxford: Oxford University Press.

Hall, P. (1998) 'Planning in Limbo', *Town and Country Planning,* vol. 67 (3), pp.42–43.

Hall, P. (1997) 'The View from London Centre: Twenty-five years of planning at the DoE', in A. Blowers and B. Evans (eds), *Town Planning into the 21st Century,* London: Routledge.

Hall, P. (1988) *Cities of Tomorrow,* London: Blackwells.

Hall, P., Thomas, R., Gracey, H. and Drewett, R. (1973) *The Containment of Urban England,* London: Allen & Unwin.

Hall, P.A. and Taylor, R.C.R. (1996) 'Political science and the three new institutionalisms', *Political Studies,* vol. 44 (5) pp.937–57.

Hall, T. and Hubbard, P. (eds) (19980 *The Entrepreneurial City: Geographies of Politics, Regime and Representation,* London: John Wiley.

Hamer, M. (1987) *Wheels within wheels: a study of the road lobby,* London: Routledge.

Harding, A. (1997) 'Urban regimes in a Europe of the Cities', *European Urban and Regional Studies,* vol. 5 (4), pp.291–314.

Harding, A. (1995) 'Elite theory and growth machines', in D. Judge, G. Stoker and H. Wolman, (eds), *Theories in Urban Politics,* London: Sage.

Harper, T. and Stein, S. (1995) 'Out of the post-modern abyss: preserving the rationale for liberal planning', *Journal of Planning Education and Research,* vol. 14 (4), pp.233–44.

Harrison, C. and Burgess, J. (1994) 'Social construction of nature: a case study of conflicts over the development of Rainham Marshes', *Transactions of the Institute of British Geographers* , vol. 19, pp.291–310.

Harvey, D. (1996) *Justice, Nature and the Geography of Difference,* Blackwell: Oxford.

Harvey, D. (1989) 'From managerialism to entrepreneurialism: formation of urban governance in late capitalism', *Geografisker Annaler,* 71B, pp.3–17.

Harvey, D. (1985) *The Urbanisation of Capital,* Blackwell: Oxford.

Hassink, R. (1997) 'Localised industrial learning and innovation policies', *European Planning Studies,* vol. 5 (3), pp.279–82.

Hastings, A. (1996) 'Unravelling the process of "partnership" in urban regeneration policy', *Urban Studies*, vol. 33, pp.253–68.

Haughton, G., and Hunter, C. (1994) *Sustainable Cities*, London: Jessica Kingsley.

Healey, P. (1998a) 'Collaborative Planning in a Stakeholder Society', *Town Planning Review*, vol. 69 (1), pp.1–21.

Healey, P. (1998b) 'Collaborative approaches to urban planning and their contribution to institutional capacity building', *Environment and Planning A*, vol. 30, pp.1531–46.

Healey, P. (1998c) 'Regulating property development and the capacity of the development industry', *Journal of Property Research*, vol. 15 (3), pp.211–27.

Healey, P. (1998d) 'Reflections on Integration', paper to the Regional Studies Association Annual Conference, London, November.

Healey, P. (1997) *Collaborative Planning: Shaping Places in Fragmented Societies*, London: Macmillan.

Healey, P. (1994) 'Urban Policy and Property Development: the institutional relations of real-estate development in an old industrial region', *Environment and Planning A*, vol. 26, pp.177–198.

Healey, P. (1992) 'Development plans and markets', *Planning Practice and Research*, vol. 7 (2), pp.13–20.

Healey, P. 1988, 'The British Planning System and Managing the Urban Environment', *Town Planning Review*, vol. 59 (4), pp.397–417.

Healey, P. (1983) *Local Plans in British Land Use Planning*, Oxford: Pergamon Press.

Healey, P. and Barrett, S. (1990) 'Structure and agency in land and property development processes', *Urban Studies*, vol. 27 (1), pp.89–104.

Healey, P. and Shaw, T. (1994) 'Changing meanings of "environment" in the British Planning System', *Transactions of the Institute of British Geographers*, vol. 19 (4), pp.425–38.

Healey, P. and Underwood, J. (1979) 'Professional ideals and Planning Practice', *Progress in Planning*, vol. 9 (2).

Healey, P., McDougall, G. and Thomas, M. (eds) (1982) *Planning Theory: Prospects for the 1980s*, Oxford: Pergamon Press.

Healey, P., Purdue, M. and Ennis, F. (1995) *Negotiating Development*, London: E and FN Spon.

Healey, P., Hoch, C., Lauria, M. and Feldman, M. (1997a) 'Planning Theory, Political Economy and the Interpretive Turn: the debate continues!', *Planning Theory*, vol. 17, pp.7–85.

Healey, P., Khakee, A., Motte, A. and Needham, B. (1997b) *Making Strategic Spatial Plans; innovation in Europe*, London: UCL Press.

Healey, P., McNamara, P., Elson, M., and Doak, A. (1988) *Land Use Planning and the Mediation of Urban Change*, Cambridge: Cambridge University Press.

Healey, P., Cameron, S.J., Davoudi, S., Graham, S. and Madanipour, A. (eds) (1995) *Managing Cities*, London: John Wiley.

Heclo, H. and Wildavsky, A. (1974) *The private government of public money*, London: Macmillan.

Herbert-Young, N. (1995) 'Reflections on Section 54A and "Plan-led" Decision-making', *Journal of Planning and Environmental Law*, pp.292–305.

Hirst, P. (1994) *Associative democracy: new forms of economic and social governance*, Cambridge: Polity Press.

HMSO (1990) *This Common Inheritance: Britain's Environmental Strategy*, London: HMSO.

HMSO (1974) *War on Waste, A Policy for Reclamation*, Cmnd, 5727, London: HMSO.

Holliday, I. (1993) 'Organised Interests after Thatcher', in P. Dunleavy, A. Gamble, I. Holliday and G. Peele (eds), *Developments in British Politics 4*, Basingstoke: Macmillan.

House of Commons Environment Committee (1989) *Toxic Waste, 2nd Report (Session 1988–89, H.C.22)*, London: HMSO.

Hull, A.D. (1998a) 'The English Planning System: promoting the local democratic input?', paper to Association of European Schools of Planning Congress, University of Aveiro, 22–5 July.

Hull, A.D. (1998b) 'Regulation through the Development Plan: An evaluation', in D. Borri, A. Barbanente, A. Khakee, N. Lichfield and A. Prat, (eds), *Evaluation and Practice and Urban Interplay in Planning*, Dordrecht: Kluwer Academic Publishers.

Hull, A.D. (1997) 'Restructuring the Debate on Allocating Land for Housing Growth', *Housing Studies*, vol. 12 (3), pp.367–82.

Hull, A.D., and Vigar, G. (1998) 'The changing role of the development plan in managing spatial change', *Environment and Planning C: Government and Policy*, vol. 16, pp.379–94.

Hull, A.D., Healey, P. and Davoudi, S. (1996) 'Greening the Red Rose County: Working towards and integrated sub-regional strategy', Working Paper No. 54, Department of Town and County Planning, University of Newcastle.

Hutton, W. (1995) *The State We are In*, London: Virago.

Huxham, C. (ed.) (1996) *Creating Collaborative Advantage*, London: Sage.

Imrie R., and Raco, M. (1999) 'How new is the new local governance? Lessons from the United Kingdom', *Transactions*, vol. 24 (1), pp.45–63.

Innes, J. (1995) 'Planning theory's emerging paradigm: communicative action and interactive practice', *Journal of Planning Education and Research*, vol. 14 (3), pp.183–90.

Innes J. (1992) 'Group processes and the social construction of growth management: the cases of Florida, Vermont and New Jersey', *Journal of the American Planning Association*, vol. 58, pp.275–78.

Innes, J. (1990) *Knowledge and public policy: the search for meaningful indicators*, New Brunswick: Transaction Press.

Innes, J., Gruber, J., Neuman, M. and Thompson, R. (1994) 'Co-ordinating growth and environmental management through consensus building', California Policy Seminar Paper, University of California, Berkeley.

JAC, Waste Regulation Joint Advisory Committee for West Midlands (1995) *Landfill Capacity Availability and Utilisation within the West Midlands Region, Results of the 1995 Monitoring Survey*, Walsall: West Midlands Waste Regulation Planning Unit.

Jenks, M., Burton, E. and Williams, K. (1996) *The Compact City: a sustainable urban form*, London: E and FN Spon.

Jessop, B. (1994) 'Post-Fordism and the State', in A. Amin (ed.), *Post-Fordism: A Reader*, Oxford: Blackwell.

Jessop, B. (1991) 'The welfare state in the transition from Fordism to Post-Fordism', in B. Jessop, H. Kastendiek, K. Nielsen and I.K. Petersen (eds), *The Politics of Flexibility*, Aldershot: Edward Elgar.

Joint Unit for Research in the Urban Environment (JURUE) (1977) 'Planning and Land Availability', University of Aston, Birmingham.

Jones, A. (1996) 'Local planning policy – the Newbury approach', in M. Tewdwr-Jones (ed.), *Planning Practice in Transition*, London: UCL Press.

Jones, M.A. (1997) 'Spatial selectivity of the State? The regulationist enterprise and local struggles over economic governance', *Environment and Planning A*, vol. 29 (5), pp.831–864.

Judge, D., Stoker, G. and Wolman, H. (1995) 'Urban Politics and Theory: an Introduction', in D. Judge, G. Stoker and H. Wolman (eds), *Theories of Urban Politics*, London: Sage.

Judge, D. (1995) 'Pluralism', in D. Judge, G. Stoker and H. Wolman (eds), *Theories of Urban Politics*, London: Sage.

Keeble, L. (1952) *Principles and Practice of Town and Country Planning*, London: Estates Gazette.

Kelly, K. (1994) *Out of Control: the new biology of machines, social systems and the economic world*, Reading, Mass: Addison-Wesley.

Kent County Council (KCC) (1996) 'Invest in Kent – Kent Prospects Economic Strategy', Maidstone.

Kent County Council (1995) 'General Statement by County Planning Officer for Kent Waste Local Plan's Public Local Inquiry (WP2)', Maidstone: KCC.

Kent County Council (1994a) *Panel's Report on Kent Structure Plan's Examination in Public held on 12–29 April 1994*, vol. 1, Maidstone: KCC.

Kent County Council (1994b) *Kent Waste Local Plan, Deposit Draft*, Maidstone: KCC.

Kent County Council (1993a) *Kent Structure Plan, Third Review, Deposit Plan and Explanatory Memorandum*, Maidstone: KCC.

Kent County Council, 1993b, *Kent Waste Management Plan*, Maidstone: KCC

Kent County Council (1990) *The Planning Strategy for Kent: 1990 Approved Kent Structure Plan and Explanatory Memorandum*, Maidstone.

Kent County Council (1984) *The Kent County Structure Plan, Second Review*, Maidstone: KCC.

Kent Thames-side Partnership (1995) 'Looking to the Future', Stone Castle, 307 London Road, Greenhithe, Dartford, Kent.

Keogh, G. (1981) *Land use planning and the production of market information*, Discussion Papers in Urban and Regional Economics, University of Reading.

King, D. and Stoker, G. (1996) *Re-thinking Local Democracy*, London: Macmillan.

Kitchen, T. (1998) 'Time to rethink the system?', *Town and Country Planning*, vol. 67 (3), pp.98–9.

Kitchen, T. (1997) *People, Politics, Policies and Plans*, London: Paul Chapman.

Krabben, E. Von and Lambooy, J.G. (1993) 'A theoretical framework for the functioning of the Dutch property market', *Urban Studies*, vol. 30 (8), pp.1382–97.

Lambooy, J.G. and Moularet, F. (1996) 'The economic organisation of cities: an institutional perspective', *International Journal of Urban and Regional Research*, vol. 20 (2), pp.217–37.

Lancashire County Council (LCC) (1997a) *Green Audit II*, Preston: LCC.

Lancashire County Council (1997b) 'Greening the Red Rose County: Lancashire Structure Plan 1991–2006', adopted version, LCC, Preston.

Lancashire County Council (1997c) *Lancashire Minerals and Waste Local Plan, Deposit Draft*, January, Preston: LCC.

Lancashire County Council 1996, *Panel's Report on Lancashire Structure Plan's Examination in Public held in 1995*, Preston, LCC.

Lancashire County Council (1995) 'Getting the Balance Right', *Lancashire Minerals and Waste Local Plan, Consultation Draft*, October, Preston: LCC.

Lancashire County Council (1994a) 'Greening The Red Rose County: Lancashire Structure Plan', deposit edition, Lancashire County Council, Preston.

Lancashire County Council (1994b) *Reaction Report, Lancashire Structure Plan Consultation Draft*, Preston: LCC.

Lancashire County Council (1994c) *Report of Proceedings, Lancashire Minerals and Waste Local Plan, Preliminary Consultation Exercise*, November, Preston: LCC.

Lancashire County Council (1993) 'Greening The Red Rose County: Lancashire Structure Plan 1991–2006', Consultation Draft, Lancashire County Council, Preston.

Lancashire County Council (1991) *Green Audit*, Preston: LCC.

Lancashire County Council (1986) *Lancashire County Structure Plan*, Preston: LCC.

Lancashire County Council Planning Department (1995) *Lancashire Structure Plan 1991–2006 Report 21: Background to the Plan*, Lancashire County Council, Preston.

Lancashire Environment Forum (1993) *Lancashire Environmental Action Programme*, Lancashire Environment Forum, PO Box 160, Preston, PR1 3EX.

Lang, R.E. and Hornburg, S.P. (1998) 'What is Social Capital and Why is it Important to Public Policy?', *Housing Policy Debate*, vol. 9 (1), pp.1–16.

Latour, B. (1987) *Science in Action*, Cambridge, Mass: Harvard University Press.

Lauria, M. (1997a) 'Introduction: reconstructing urban regime theory', in M. Lauria (ed.), *Reconstructing Urban Regime Theory: regulating urban politics in a global economy*, Thousand Oaks: Sage.

Lauria, M. (ed.) (1997b) *Reconstructing Urban Regime Theory: regulating urban politics in a global economy*, Thousand Oaks: Sage.

Lauria, M. and Whelan, B. (1995) 'Planning theory and political economy: the need for reintegration', *Planning Theory*, vol. 14, pp.8–33.

Layder, D. (1987) 'Key issues in structuration theory: some critical remarks', *Current perspectives in social theory*, 8, pp.25–46.

Lefebvre, H. (1991) *The Production of Space* (tr. D. Nicholson-Smith), Oxford: Blackwell.

Le Gales, P. (1998) 'Regulation and governance in British Sites', *International Journal of Urban and Regional Research*, vol. 22 (3), pp.482–506.

Leo, C. (1997) 'City politics in an era of globalisation', in M. Lauria (ed.), *Reconstructing Urban Regime Theory: regulating urban politics in a global economy*, Thousand Oaks: Sage.

Lichfield, N. and Darin-Drabkin, D. (1980) *Land Policy in Planning*, London: George Allen & Unwin.

Lipietz, A. (1992) *Towards a new economic order. Postfordism, ecology and democracy*, New York: Oxford University Press.

Loftman, P. and Nevin, B. (1994) 'Prestige projects development: economic renaissance or economic myth? A case study of Birmingham', *Local Economy*, vol. 8 (4), pp.307–25.

Logan, J. and Molotch, H. (1987) *Urban Fortunes: the political economy of place*, Berkeley, California: University of California Press.

London Planning Advisory Committee (LPAC) (1997) *Supplementary Advice on Planning for Waste in London*, London: LPAC.

MacBryde, J.P. (1992) *Inspector's Report for the Birmingham Unitary Development Plan's Public Inquiry*, Volume 1:Main Report, Birmingham: Birmingham City Council.

McCormick, J. (1991) *British Politics and the Environment*, London: Earthscan.

MacLennan, D., Meen, G., Gibb, K. and Stephens, M. (1997) *Fixed commitments, uncertain incomes: sustainable owner-occupation and the economy*, York: Joseph Rowntree Foundation.

McLoughlin, B.J. (1969) *Urban and Regional Planning; a systems approach*, London: Faber.

Macnaghten, P., Grove-White, R., Jacobs, M. and Wynne, B. (1995) *Public perceptions and sustainability in Lancashire: indicators, institutions, participation*, Lancashire County Council, Preston.

Majone, G. (1989) *Evidence, argument and persuasion in the policy process*, New Haven, Conn.: Yale University Press.

Marsh, D. and Rhodes, R.A.W. (eds.) (1992) *Policy Networks in British Government*, Oxford: Oxford University Press.

Marshall,T. (1994) 'Dimensions of Sustainable Development and Scales of Policy Making', paper to ECPR Green Politics Standing Group, Crete, 21–3 October.

Mawson, J. and Spencer, K. (1997) 'The origins and operation of the government offices for the English regions', in J. Bradbury, and J. Mawson (eds), *British Regionalism and Devolution: the Challenges of State Reform and European Integration*, London: Jessica Kingsley.

May, A.D. (1995) 'Transport Policy: a call for clarity, consistency, and commitment', *Proceedings of the Institute of Civil Engineers Transport*, 111, pp.163–8.

Mayer, M. (1995) 'Urban governance in the post-Fordist city', in P. Healey, S.J. Cameron, S. Davoudi, S. Graham, and A. Madanipour (eds), *Managing Cities* London: John Wiley.

Mazza, L. and Rydin,Y. (1997) 'Urban sustainability: discourses, networks and policy tools', *Progress in Planning*, vol. 47 (1), pp.1–74.

Merrett,S. (1994) 'Ticks and Crosses: strategic assessment and the Kent structure plan', *Planning Practice and Research*, vol. 9, (2), pp.147–50.

Meyerson, M. and Banfield, E. (1955) *Politics, planning and the public interest*, New York: Free Press.

Ministry of Housing and Local Government (1970) *Strategic Plan for the South East*, prepared by South East Joint Planning Team, London: HMSO.

Motte, A. (1997) 'Building strategic urban planning in France: The Lyon urban area 1981–93 experiments', in P. Healey, A. Khakee, A. Motte and B. Needham (eds), *Making Strategic Spatial Plans: Innovation in Europe*, London: UCL Press.

Moulaert, F. (1996) 'Rediscovering spatial inequality in Europe: building blocks for an appropriate 'regulationist' analytical framework', *Environment and Planning D: Society and Space*, vol. 14, pp.155–79.

Mulgan, G. (1994) *Politics in an Antipolitical Age*, Cambridge: Polity Press.

Muller, P. and Surel, Y. (1998) *L'Analyse des Politiques Publiques* Paris: Montchrestien.

Murdoch, J. and Marsden, T. (1995) 'The spatialization of politics: local and national actor spaces in environmental conflict', *Transactions,* vol. 20, pp.368–80.

Murdoch, J., Abram, S. and Marsden, T. (1999) 'Technical expertise and public participation in planning for housing', in G. Stoker, (ed), *Power and Participation: the new politics of local governance*, London: Macmillan.

Myerson, G. and Rydin, Y. (1996) *The Language of Environment,* London: UCL Press.

Neuman, M. (1996) 'Images as institution builders: metropolitan planning in Madrid', *European Planning Studies,* vol. 4, (3) pp.293–312.

New Scientist (1998) 'Burn Me', 22 November, pp.31–4.

Newman, P. and Thornley, A. (1996) *Urban Planning in Europe,* London: Routledge.

Newson, J. (1992) *Cars versus communities: transport options in Birmingham,* Birmingham: Birmingham for the People.

North, D. (1990) *Institutions, institutional change and economic performance,* Cambridge: Cambridge University Press.

North West Regional Association (1997) *Waste Study of the Mersey Belt,* (produced by Coopers and Lybrand), August, NWRA, PO Box 36, Library Street, Wigan.

North West Regional Association (1995) *Greener Growth,* Regional Planning Guidance Sub Group, NWRA, PO Box 36, Library Street, Wigan.

North West Regional Association/North West Business Leadership Team (1993) *Regional Transport Strategy for North West England*, NWRA, PO Box 36, Wigan WN1 1YN.

Nuffield Foundation (1986) *Town and Country Planning,* report of a Committee of Inquiry appointed by the Nuffield Foundation, London: Nuffield Foundation.

Nussbaum, M. (1986) *The Fragility of Goodness,* Cambridge: Cambridge University Press.

Oatley, N, (ed.) (1998) *Cities, Economic Competition and Urban Policy,* London: Paul Chapman.

Oatley, N. (1995) 'Competitive urban policy and the regeneration game', *Town Planning Review,* vol. 66 (1), pp.1–14.

Office for National Statistics (1998) *Regional Trends 33,* London: The Stationery Office.

Owens, S. (1997) 'Giants in their path': Planning, sustainability and environmental values', *Town Planning Review,* vol. 68 (3), pp.293–304.

Owens, S. (1995) 'From "predict and provide" to "predict and prevent"? Pricing and planning in transport policy', *Transport Policy,* 2(1), pp.43–50.

Owens, S. (1994) 'Land, limits and sustainability: a conceptual framework and some dilemmas for the planning system', *Transactions of the Institute of British Geographers,* vol. 19 (4), pp.439–56.

Painter, J. (1997) 'Regulation, regime and practice in urban politics', in M. Lauria (ed.), *Reconstructing Urban Regime Theory,* Thousand Oaks, California: Sage.

Painter, J. (1995) 'Regulation theory, Post-Fordism and Urban Politics', in D. Judge, G. Stoker and H. Wolman (eds), *Theories of Urban Politics,* London: Sage.

Parsons, W. (1995) *Policy Analysis,* Cheltenham: Edward Elgar.

Peck, J. (1995) 'Moving and shaking: business elites, state localism and urban privatism', *Progress in Human Geography,* vol.19 (1), pp.16–46.

Peck, J. (1993) 'The Trouble with TECs ... a critique of the Training and Enterprise Councils initiative', *Policy and Politics,* vol. 21 (4), pp.289–306.

Peck, J. and Emmerich, M. (1994) 'Training and Enterprise Councils: Time for Change', *Local Economy,* vol. 8, pp.251–65.

Peizerat, C. (1997) 'An interpretation of Europe in Planning and Property Development based on Discourse Analysis: The example of business sites', *International Planning Studies,* vol. 2 (1), pp.27–44.

Pemberton, S., and Vigar, G. (1998) *Managing change in a fragmented institutional environment; the micro-politics of transport planning's "new realism" in Tyne and Wear,* Department of Town and Country Planning Working Paper Number 69, University of Newcastle.

Perrins, B. (1995) *Introduction to land law,* London: Cavendish Publishing.

Petts, J. (1995) 'Waste Management strategy Development, A case Study of Community Involvement and Consensus Building in Hampshire', *Journal of Environmental Planning and Management,* vol. 38(4), pp.519–36.

Pieda (1993) *Regional Economic Strategy for North West England,* Prepared for the North West Regional Association and the North West Business Leadership Team by Pieda, 5 The Parsonage, Manchester M3 2HS.

Plowden, S. (1972) *Towns against Traffic,* London: Deutsch.

Powell, W.W. and Dimaggio, P.J. (eds) (1991) *The new institutionalism in organisational analysis,* Chicago: University of Chicago Press.

Purdue, M. (1994) 'The Impact of Section 54A', *Journal of Planning and Environment Law,* pp.399–407

Putnam, R. (1993) *Making Democracy Work: Civic Traditions in Modern Italy,* Princeton: University of Princeton Press.

Quinn, M.J. (1996) 'Central government planning policy', in M. Tewdwr-Jones (ed.), *Planning Practice in Transition,* London: UCL Press.

Rabinow, P. (ed.) (1984) *The Foucault Reader,* London: Penguin.

Rhodes, R. (1997) *Understanding Governance,* Oxford: Oxford University Press.

Rhodes, R. (1996) 'The new governance: governing without government: order and change in British politics', *Policy Studies,* vol. 44, pp.652–67.

Rhodes, R. (1988) *Beyond Westminster and Whitehall,* London: Unwin Hyman.

Rhodes, R. (1986) '"Power dependence": theories of central–local relations: a critical assessment', in M. Goldsmith (ed.), *New Research in Central–Local Relations,* Aldershot: Gower.

Richardson, T. (1996) 'Foucauldian discourse: power and truth in urban and regional policy-making', *European Planning Studies,* vol. 4 (3), pp.279–92.

Richardson, T. and Heywood, R. (1996) 'Deconstructing transport planning; lessons from policy breakdown in the English Pennines', *Transport Policy,* 3 (1/2), pp.43–53.

Richardson, J.J. and Jordan, A.G. (1979) *Governing under Pressure: the policy process in a post-parliamentary democracy,* Oxford: Oxford University Press.

Roberts, T. (1998) 'The statutory system of Town Planning in the UK: a call for detailed reform', *Town Planning Review,* vol. 69 (1), pp.iii–vii.

Royal Commission for Environmental Protection (1988) *Best Practicable Environmental Options, 12th Report,* London: HSMO.

Rydin, Y. (1998) *Urban and Environmental Planning in the UK,* London: Macmillan.

Rydin, Y. (1993) *The British Planning System: an introduction,* London: Macmillan.

Rydin, Y. (1988) 'Joint Housing Studies: Housebuilders, Planners and the Availability of Land', *Local Government Studies,* vol. 14, (2), pp.69–80.

Sandercock, L. (1998) *Towards Cosmopolis,* London: Wiley.

Saunders, D. (1993) '*Regional Planning Guidance for the West Midlands Region: Report to the West Midlands Forum of Local Planning Authorities',* on conference held in Birmingham 8–19 February, WMRF, Birmingham.

Saunders, P. (1979) *Urban Politics: A Sociological Interpretation,* London: Hutchison.

Schneecloth, L. and Shibley, S.R. (1995) *Place-making: the art and practice of building communities,* New York: John Wiley.

Schon, D. (1983) *The reflective practitioner,* New York: Basic Books.

Schon, D. and Rein, M. (1994) *Frame Reflection,* New York: Basic Books.

Seidman, S. (1998) *Contested Knowledge: Social Theory in the Post-modern Era,* 2nd edn, Oxford: Blackwell.

Selman, P. (1998) 'Local Agenda 21: substance or spin?', *Journal of Environmental Planning and Management,* 41(5), pp.533–553.

Selman, P. (1996) *Local Sustainability,* London: Paul Chapman.

SERPLAN (1997) *Revised Waste Planning Advice: A sustainable waste planning strategy for the South East 1996–2010* (SERP 160), London: SERPLAN.

Shaw, K. and Robinson, F. (1998) 'Learning from experience: reflections on two decades of British urban policy', *Town Planning Review,* vol. 69 (1), pp.49–63.

Social Exclusion Unit (1998) *Bringing Britain Together: a national strategy for neighbourhood renewal,* London: The Stationery Office.

Standing Advisory Committee on Trunk Road Assessment (SACTRA) (1994) *Trunk Roads and the Generation of Traffic,* London: HMSO.

Stoker, G. (1999) *The New Management of British Local Governance,* London: Macmillan.

Stoker, G. (1995) 'Regime theory and urban politics', in D. Judge, G. Stoker and H. Wolman (eds), *Theories of Urban Politics,* London: Sage.

Stone, C. (1989) *Regime politics: governing Atlanta 1946–1988,* Lawrence: University of Kansas Press.

Storper, M. (1997) *The Regional World,* New York: Guildford Books.

Storper, M. and Scott, A. (eds) (1992) *Pathways to Industrialization and Regional Development,* London: Routledge.

Suh, S-T. (1998) 'Evaluating the capacity of plan-making in Seoul through institutionalist analysis: a case study of Seoul Metropolitan Plan', unpublished PhD thesis, University of Newcastle.

Susskind, L. and Cruikshank, J. (1987) *Breaking the Impasse: Consensual approaches to resolving public disputes,* New York: Basic Books.

Tarrow, S. (1994) *Power in Movement,* Cambridge: Cambridge University Press.

Taylor, D. (1994) 'Winning the economic war after the troops pull out', *Planning Week,* 1 September.

Tetlow, R. (1997) *An Overview of the Planning and Affordable Housing Debate,* York: Joseph Rowntree Foundation.

Tewdwr-Jones, M. (1997) 'Plans, policies and inter-governmental relations: assessing the role of national planning guidance in England and Wales', *Urban Studies,* vol. 34 (1), pp.141–62.

Tewdwr-Jones, M. (1996) 'Land use planning policy after Thatcher', in M. Tewdwr-Jones (ed.), *Planning Practice in Transition,* London: UCL Press.

Tewdwr-Jones M. (1995) 'Development control and the legitimacy of planning decisions', *Town Planning Review,* vol. 66, (2), pp.163–81.

Tewdwr-Jones, M. and Allmendinger, P. (1998) 'Deconstructing communicative rationality: a critique of Habermasian collaborative planning', *Environment and Planning A,* vol. 30, pp.1975–89.

Thomas, H. and Healey, P. (1991) *Dilemmas of Planning Practice,* Aldershot: Avebury.

Thornley, A. (1991) *Urban Planning under Thatcherism,* London: Routledge.

Truelove, P. (1994) 'The illusive transport package', *Planning Week,* 2 (49), pp.12–13.

Tsolacas, S. (1995) 'Industrial property development in the UK: a regional analysis of new orders', *Journal of Property Research,* vol. 12 (2), pp.95–125.

Underwood, J. (1980) *Town Planners in Search of a Role,* Occasional Paper No 6, School of Advanced Urban Studies, Bristol.

Urban Task Force Report (1999) *Urban Renaissance – Sharing the Vision*, London: DETR.

Vigar, G. (1999) 'Accessibility, mobility and equity in transport planning', in C. Greed (ed.), *Social Town Planning*, London: Routledge.

Vigar, G. (2000) 'Local "Barriers" to Sustainable Transport Planning', *Local Environment*, 5(1), pp. 21–34.

Vigar G., Steele, M., Healey, P., Nelson, J.D. and Wenban Smith, A. (2000) *Transport Planning and Metropolitan Governance*, London: Landor.

Wannop, U. (1995) *The regional imperative: regional planning in the UK, Europe and the United States*, London: Jessica Kingsley.

Wannop, U. (1985) 'The practice of rationality: the case of the Coventry-Solihull–Warwickshire Sub–regional Study', in M. Breheny and A. Hooper (eds), *Rationality in Planning*, London: Pion.

Ward, S. (1994) *Planning and Urban Change*, London: Paul Chapman.

Watson, G. (1992) 'The Recycling of derelict industrial land in the Black Country', unpublished PhD Thesis, Oxford Brookes University.

Waste Planning (1996) Waste Plans, vol. 19, pp.42–4.

Wenban Smith, A. (1994) 'The South Brimingham Study: reconciling local and strategic needs', PTRC-Proceedings of Seminar D, pp.61–73.

West Midlands Joint Committee (1995) 'Transport Package, West Midlands Joint Data Team', Solihull.

West Midlands Regional Forum (1996) 'Review of Housing Provision in the West Midlands Region', Report of Steering Group, WMRF, Stafford.

West Midlands Regional Forum (1993) 'Advice on Regional Planning Guidance for the West Midlands 1991–2011', WMRF, Stafford.

West Midlands Regional Forum (1992) 'The West Midlands: your region, your future, making the right choices', WMRF, Stafford.

West Midlands Regional Forum (1991) 'The West Midlands: your region, your future: asking the right questions?', WMRF, Stafford.

Williams, R. (1975) *The Country and the City*, London: PaladinBall.

Worpole, K. and Greenhalgh, L. (1999) 'The Richness of Cities: urban policy in a new landscape', Eco-Distribution, Woodhouse Eaves, Leicestershire.

Yanow, D. (1996) *How Does a Policy Mean?*, Washington, DC: Georgetown University Press.

Index

actor-network theory, 48, 50
'agency' perspective, 35–6, 37
arenas, policy, 51, 245, 250–2,
    258–60, 266
Ashford, 60, 80, 102, 133, 134
    housing, 103, 107

Beck, U., 283
Birmingham (City Council), 24, 65,
    138, 264
    transport policies, 163, 165–70, 182
    UDP, 86–7, 126–7, 165–6, 167,
        169, 194
Birmingham Chamber of Commerce
    and Industry (BCI), 72
Birmingham Integrated Transport
    Study (BITS), 165, 166, 167, 169
Black Country, 65
Blue Circle Industries (BCI), 67, 68,
    106, 199
Bluewater Retail Park, 68
Bourdieu, P., 48
brownfield sites, 121, 228, 230
Bryson, J., 251
business interests: and planning,
    34–5, 179, 260–1, 265
    in Kent, 67, 68, 146
    in Lancashire, 69, 142
    in West Midlands, 72, 138–9
    see also partnerships

CBI: in West Midlands, 139
Centro, 163
CEPOG (West Midlands), 100, 177,
    182, 258
Channel Tunnel, 134, 136
    Rail Link (CTRL), 59–60, 134,
        136, 171, 172, 179

Chorley, 109, 110, 114
City Challenge, 14
City Pride, 281
Commission for New Towns (CNT),
    109, 112, 132, 142, 143
communicative planning theory, 37,
    38, 45–6, 47
'communities of association', 248
'communities of reference', 248
competitiveness, economic, 119,
    231–3, 240–1, 283
Confederation of British Industry,
    139
conservation, see environment
Conservative governments, 14–15,
    17, 26–7, 92, 120, 155
Control of Pollution Act 1974, 186,
    188
corporatism, 35, 38, 151
    see also business interests;
        partnerships
'corridors', development/transport,
    177, 182–3, 235, 257–8
    in Lancashire, 82, 83, 109, 131,
        220
    in West Midlands, 85–6, 98, 164,
        220, 257–8
Council for Protection of Rural
    England (CPRE), 93, 94, 100,
        229, 253, 260
    in Kent, 66, 106
    in Lancashire, 70, 110, 111, 159
    and transport, 159, 178
Countryside Commission, 70, 178
Coventry, 65
CPOGs, 258–9
Crosby, B., 251
cultural capital, 48